CALIFORNIA DESERT TRAILS

BY
J. SMEATON CHASE

Introduction to this edition by Richard Dillon

Environmental Perspective and
Updated Plant List by Robert L. Moon

TIOGA PUBLISHING COMPANY
PALO ALTO, CALIFORNIA

Library of Congress Cataloging-in-Publication Data

Chase, J. Smeaton (Joseph Smeaton), b. 1864.
  California desert trails.

  Reprint. Originally published: Boston : Houghton
Mifflin, 1919.
    1. California—Description and travel—1869-1950.
2. Desert flora—California. 3. Deserts—California.
4. Trails—California.   4. Chase, J. Smeaton
(Joseph Smeaton), b. 1864— Journeys—California.
I. Title.
F866.C482   1987   917.94'8   87-40050
ISBN 0-935382-60-7

© 1987 Tioga Publishing Company
  P.O. Box 98
  Palo Alto, California 94302

Distributed by William Kaufmann, Inc.
  Box 50490
  Palo Alto, California 94303-9953

TO MY AUNT
IN THE LITTLE RED TOWN
AMONG THE RAINY CUMBERLAND MOUNTAINS
THIS UNCOMMONLY DRY VOLUME IS
AFFECTIONATELY INSCRIBED

I ACKNOWLEDGE a sense of mystical reverence when first I approach some illustrious feature of the globe, some coast line of ocean, some mighty river or dreary mountain-range, the ancient barrier of kingdoms. KINGLAKE: *Eothen*.

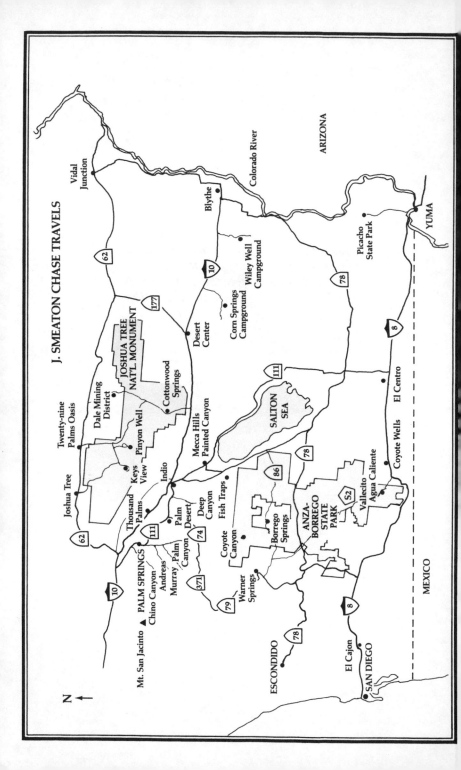

PREFACE

THAT appetite comes by eating I have found to be as true in the matter of geography as in the affairs of the table. After long wanderings among the incomparable forests and mountains and by the romantic shores of the most scenic and diversified of our States, I fell an easy prey to the beckonings of the other principal feature of California's topography, the dreamy, dreary desert. Long ago, on short expeditions into and across it at various points, I had fallen under its inexplicable charm; now I determined to know it more closely, by daily and nightly intercourse through months of travel in its sun-blasted solitudes: gaining the experience I desired at the price, certainly, of some discomfort, and, possibly, of a trifling degree of danger — merely enough for spice.

This volume, then, is the fruit of over two years' continuous camping and travelling on the desert. It might more exactly be named "Colorado Desert Trails" than "California Desert Trails," since there are within this State other expanses of desert (such as the Mojave, contiguous on the north to the region I describe) which are not touched upon in the book. But there seemed a danger of confusion in the other name, since, on a casual sight, the word "Colorado" in the title might give the impression that the subject-matter was some region in the State of that

PREFACE

name. The tract I deal with is, in truth, unfortunately named — though the misfortune is accidental, since, when it was labelled, in 1853, there was no State of Colorado — and out-and-out Coloradans might justly petition our common Uncle that the mere suspicion of harboring a desert should be lifted from them and the odium plainly fixed upon the rival tourist-claiming nephew, California.

The book might have been made of more instructive value, no doubt, had the writer been a man of science — naturalist, botanist, or geologist; for in all those fields, and others that are outside my range, the desert is full of matter. Yet it may not be unfair to say that the observer whose interest is trained upon a certain aspect of Nature may be to that extent incapacitated as regards the more general or purely scenic bearings of his surroundings. And so these discursive notes may possibly bring to the reader a truer, though in some ways less explicit, impression of the country described than would be the case if they came from the pen of one who was even a fractional *savant*.

For somewhat the same reason, little is here said of the really remarkable agricultural developments which in the past few years have come over considerable portions of this intractable-seeming region. I am no farmer, know little of potatoes or alfalfa, poultry, pigs, or cattle, until the stage when they issue in finished product from the kitchen. Thus I may seem to ignore what to the practical mind must appear the chief, or even the only, items of value. I do not forget those Imperialites and Coachellans who made hopeful suggestions — "I guess you'll boom up this section now, won't you, say? Finest land in the State" — and so on; nor their puzzled or pitying glances when I made the only possible reply, that I did not, could not, and would not boom; was, in fact, even averse to booms and boomers; and was more enthralled by desert sunsets than by desert dairies, astounding as these might be. In a word, it is the desert *as* desert — God's desert, not man's — that engaged my interest, and that, as I this moment call it up before my inward eye, seems to me the most memorable, in its totality of impressiveness, of all natural objects that I have met.

But I confess that the fascination of the untamed desert has proved to be of too subtle a quality for words of mine to render. That would necessarily be true, of course, of anybody's attempt in any field of Nature: but it would be tenfold true with respect to the desert, and I will be bold to say that it would be true without regard to the person in the case. Whether it be that the desert is too intrinsically alien to our psychology, or for some other reason, too baffling to trace, I believe it to be the fact that its genius is the rarest and the most elusive of all the elements that make up the wonder of this transcendent world. No "last word" on the desert will ever be written; no statement, I mean, that, to those who know the subject in any real degree, will not seem to fail of getting at the essence.

It is a pleasure to record botanical obligations to my friend Mr. S. B. Parish, of San Bernardino, California, whose thorough knowledge of the flora of

PREFACE

the desert, freely put at my disposal, was invaluable in revising the Appendix of Plants. I am indebted also to the United States Geological Survey for permission to reprint from one of their publications the "Hints on Desert Travelling" that appear in Appendix A.

In conclusion, it is most satisfactory to note that, since the following chapters were prepared, the United States Government has, by a small appropriation of funds, made at least a beginning towards bettering the conditions of desert travel by the marking of roads and water-holes.

J. S. C.

PALM SPRINGS, CALIFORNIA
November, 1918

NEW 1987 INTRODUCTION
by
RICHARD DILLON

Between the turn of the century and World War I, a remarkable group of writers emerged from California's awesome desert country. Best known today are John Van Dyke and, especially, Mary Austin. Van Dyke's *The Desert* led the way in 1901, followed by Austin's *Land of Little Rain* two years later. They are rightfully considered to be among the handful of genuine literary classics of the West, and not just in terms of their desert subject matter.

Only one other member of this talented desert group, which included George Wharton James and Charles F. Saunders, seriously rivaled Austin or Van Dyke as a literary stylist. He was Joseph Smeaton Chase, who approached greatness as a writer of California natural history and travel, even though he was English-born and a social worker by profession, a writer only by avocation.

Between 1911 and 1920, Chase wrote five books and coauthored another. His last book, *Our Araby* (1920), was on the surface simply a promotional tract for Palm Springs. But it makes a useful shelf companion to his *California Desert Trails* of 1919, not only because he sketched in the early history of the oasis, but also because he used it to propagandize for a desert national park centered on Palm Springs's Palm Canyon.

J. Smeaton Chase is perhaps California's most neglected and underrated writer. At his best, he rivaled not only Van Dyke and Austin, but the Sierra's John Muir and the coast's Richard Henry Dana as well. Although Lawrence Clark Powell insisted that Chase lacked "genius" and was, therefore, only a minor writer, he nonetheless included Chase as one of only 31 authors in his survey, *California Classics*. He felt that *California Coast Trails* had a fine sense of form, but that the complexity of the desert dispersed the thrust of *California Desert Trails*.

I see the flaw in *Desert Trails* to be the decision, perhaps the publisher's, to make the book all things to all men. It is weakened by sandwiching the author's highly personal and intriguing travel narrative between a preliminary description of trees, cacti, and wildflowers and two appendixes. The first is a descriptive listing of plants. The second, a cautionary document (not even in the author's words) on the dangers of desert travel in the dawn of California's auto age, further dilutes the book's effectiveness.

The reason for the undervaluation of Chase's writing in general, as opposed to the weakness of form in his desert book, is the fact that American academics usually stereotype "literature" to mean fiction and poetry. Nonfiction is, ipso facto, nonliterature. With a weaker essay tradition than Great Britain's, America tends to dismiss all natural history and travel books as literary artifacts.

I first encountered Chase's poetic prose in his coast book. An early affection for the Sierra brought me to his Yosemite volume, and teaching at UCLA's summer session in 1964 reconfirmed for me the value of *California Desert Trails*.

Kevin Starr in *Americans and the California Dream* echoed Powell in calling *California Coast Trails* Chase's best book. But their assessment of it applies to all of Chase's writing. Powell pointed out that its charm and quality, as well as the winning personality of the writer, continue to be visible between every line.

The late dean of desert bibliographers, E. I. Edwards, considered *California Desert Trails* to be indispensable, not only because of its information, but also because it was beautifully written. He ranked Chase as among the best of all those who wrote about the Colorado Desert. Still, he described C. W. James's encyclopedic *Wonders of the Colorado Desert* as the definitive account of the desert, so complete that little was left to be said by others. Chase would have none of this nonsense, however. "No 'last word' on the desert," he wrote, "will ever be written."

When *California Desert Trails* appeared, the *Book Review Digest* of 1919 cited six major reviews, all of them favorable. The *Review of Reviews* was content to call the book "a readable, humorous account." *Dial* magazine even grumbled that it lacked the full "tone range" of its subject before admitting that it was so well written and unpretentious that reading only a chapter would stir a longing for wide-open spaces. A long extract from the *American Library Association Booklist* stressed that the author was neither scientific nor practical in approaching the desert as a target for agricultural reclamation. Chase was interested in the *untamed* desert, "God's desert—not man's." Although no misanthrope, and genuinely interested in desert people, whether Indians, Mexicans or hermitic "Anglos," he was enthralled by the chromatic explosions of desert sunsets, not by the prosperity of desert dairies and date palm groves.

Chase protested that no one, including himself, could successfully capture in mere words the subtle, baffling magic of the desert. He wrote that "Its genius is the rarest and the most elusive of all the elements that make up the wonder of this transcendent world . . . The magic of the desert is a riddle. Not only does it defy putting into words, but I have never found the person who felt that he could even shape it vaguely to himself in thought." Still, the *Booklist* concluded that "From a literary point of view, the book is tinged with this elusive charm of the desert which, for those who have once fallen under its spell, is deeper and more endearing than is the charm of forest, or sea, or mountain." The *Wisconsin Library Bulletin* reviewer described Chase's volume as "an unusual travel book which gives one the impression of the silence, the vastness, the beauty, the terror, and the lure of the desert."

Born in London in 1864, Chase did not come to California until 1890. He was 55 when his desert opus appeared, but he was a born writer with that peculiarly British gift for the poetic travel essay. He came from a bookish family; his father was a publisher, his brother a bookseller. In order to eat, Chase worked in social welfare as a "settlement resident" for Bethlehem Institutional Church in Los Angeles. He later clerked in a camera store to polish his skills as a photographer, and he illustrated the first edition of his major books with half-tones from his own photos.

In his three pilgrimages, Chase wandered on horseback over more of California than any writer except, perhaps, geologist William H. Brewer. But his heart was mainly in the desert he had seen when he first crossed into the state from Yuma. It was in Palm Springs that he made his home and was married, where he died in 1923 and was buried.

Because he wrote with humor and honesty, with strong personal feeling as well as with lucidity and a restrained elegance, Chase has become one of the best interpreters of the California landscape. His major books were elegiac farewells to a simpler age of a rural, pastoral, and wilderness-filled California. He savored the state's still unspoiled sierra, coast, and desert, and he preserved their images in his poetic prose before the forces of so-called progress could trample them in the dust. He did so without pessimism, hopeful that they could be salvaged, at least in part, as healthful, redemptive counterbalances to progressive, i.e., runaway modernity in California.

If Chase did not get in the last word on the desert, his words remain among the very best about the incongruous sublimity of a barren region of heat and thirst whose hostility toward man is symbolized by sharp-edged geology and sparse and shadeless, spiny botany. He faithfully interpreted the desert, sometimes with lyrical eloquence. His book is undeniably literature and, in part, prose poetry. There is no lack of realism in his work, but more important are his gifts of imagination, insight, and intuition. All these made possible his perception of the indefinable lure of the desert country, a magic that is much more than the sum total of its parts—its light and color and the line, form, mass, texture, and patterning of its botanical and geological scenery.

Richard Dillon is the author of many historical books, including Fool's Gold *and* Meriwether Lewis, *and is the retired director of San Francisco's Sutro Library.*

A 1987 ENVIRONMENTAL PERSPECTIVE
by
ROBERT L. MOON

Like other explorers of California's diverse ecosystems, Smeaton Chase saved the desert for last. He used the "village" of Palm Springs as a base camp for excursions into the surrounding desert. Palm Springs is no longer a sleepy village; however, most of the desert's *natural* wonders that Chase found so attractive can still be found. The fact that this book is not outdated attests to the truth in Chase's own words. "Here Time and all things of Time seem to have ended or not yet begun."

The reprinting of this work, based on its literary merits alone, is well justified. Concomitant, however, is its value as a modern guide to the desert with a unique and compelling historical perspective. Many of the places and phenomena eloquently described by Chase still exist. Lush palm oases, spectacular mountains, painted canyons, Indian and explorers' trails, prospectors' mines and wells, many having picturesque names like Thousand Palms, Coxcomb Mountains, Taquatiz Canyon, Anza Trail, Virginia Dale Mine, and Pinyon Well still remain and are readily accessible to the modern explorer. And the elements Chase found most compelling — sunrises, ephemeral wildflowers, dark star-filled skies, and solitude — can still be experienced. The desert remains a place where "the traveller seems to himself the last life on the planet."

The contemporary reader embarks on an armchair adventure across the Colorado Desert, often in the hazardous heat of summer with its everpresent uncertainty about the next drink of water. For those with a desire to go into the desert itself and to relive Chase's experiences, note the new map showing his sites in relation to today's roads and parks.

Two private nonprofit organizations provide significant contributions to desert preservation through education. The Palm Springs Desert Museum offers a diversity of displays as well as public programs and research to further understanding of the desert's natural and cultural histories. The Living Desert in Palm Desert is a wild animal park and botanical garden dedicated to conservation, education, and research. For those who want to see the Colorado Desert's plants and animals conveniently, both institutions provide excellent experiences.

Chase felt so strongly about the significance of the many arid wonders he saw that he proposed the creation of a national park to protect them. While this has not taken place, a credit to Chase's insight is the fact that, with few exceptions, the areas he felt were of special significance have been protected for future generations by a variety of organizations and government agencies. The following are examples of areas Chase visited that are now protected for public enjoyment.

National Park Service — Joshua Tree
National Monument
  Pinyon Well   Squaw Tank
  Twentynine Palms Oasis   Cottonwood Oasis
Bureau of Land Management
  Corn Springs   Wiley Well
Anza Borrego State Park
  Seventeen Palms   Coyote Canyon
County Parks
  Agua Caliente   Mecca Hills/
  Vallecito   Painted Canyon
                    Salton Sea Fish Traps
University of California Natural Lands and Water
Reserve System
  Deep Canyon
The Nature Conservancy
  Thousand Palms Oasis
Agua Caliente Indian Tribal Lands
  Palm Canyon   Andreas Canyon
  Murray Canyon

While some unique areas have been set aside, this is not to say that the desert looks as it did during Chase's explorations. Southern California's rampant growth has had a profound effect. The desert's sometimes harsh and barren appearance makes it difficult for people to realize how fragile these systems actually are. Land development, offroad vehicles, and illegal plant collecting have taken tremendous tolls on the desert's fragile plant and animal populations. An area known for its unique cactus flora, the Devil's Garden at the west end of the Coachella Valley was described by Chase to be so densely covered with cacti that it was impossible to ride a horse safely through it. The barrel cactus display in this area was once one of the finest in California. Illegal collectors have reduced these specimens to a fraction of their original distribution and diversity.

We hope that in some way Chase's eloquent descriptions of the desert's treasures will provide modern explorers the heightened awareness and understanding that begets love and concern. Look. Listen. Allow the desert to work its spell.

"Yet I believe that its hold upon those who have fallen under its spell is deeper and more enduring than is the charm of the forest or sea or mountain."

Appendix A, Hints on Desert Travelling, has been reprinted to preserve the historical integrity of the original printing. However, be aware that while most recommendations for safe travel are still relevant, some represent practices that have since been proven erroneous. For example, the advice to "drink heartily in the morning and at night and as little as possible during the day" should be instead to drink heartily throughout the day as heat and thirst dictate. Those who plan to travel in out-of-the-way areas are advised to check with local agency information offices to receive information on safe travel.

Appendix B, Noticeable Plants of the Desert, also has been reprinted in its original form. Although Chase was not a professional botanist, his descriptions of desert plants could be little improved by a modern revision. It was not his intent to create a comprehensive desert flora, but instead to offer simple descriptions of common plants. A new list of revised terms and of a few common-name references to botanical names has been included on page 380 after Chase's plant list.

Robert L. Moon is the Chief Biologist at Joshua Tree National Monument.

CONTENTS

*New Introduction and an Environmental
Perspective follow Preface
Updated Plant List precedes Index*

CALIFORNIA DESERT TRAILS

CALIFORNIA DESERT TRAILS

CHAPTER I

INTRODUCTORY

The Desert a riddle — Its charm a contradiction — Attraction of the unattractive — The desert fringe a contrast — Supremacy in color — "Opal" the word — Sand as a reflector — Sunset — Rock-color — Mountain contours — Bleached ranges — Color on levels — Rock-mosaic — Austerity of the open desert — Color-flood of spring — Sky-color — Morning and evening hues — Battles in the skies — The "wistful" quality — London *versus* the Colorado — Solitude our native air — The awe of silence — The desert as antidote.

THAT stony mystery the Sphinx, fixed in eternal reverie amid the immemorial sands of Egypt, might well stand as a symbol of the desert itself; not that desert only, but deserts everywhere. One point out of many that make up the analogy is the baffling nature of the spell that people find in the famous monument. One will say it is due to a sense of its immense age; another, that the features bear a supernatural expression, or hold some secret meaning; another feels its awe to lie in the riddle of its purpose; and another, in some supposed significance of its proportions. Similarly, the magic of the desert is a riddle. Not only does it defy putting into words, but I have never found the person who felt that he could even shape it vaguely to himself in thought.

For one thing, it is in its essence a contradiction.

The desert is the opposite of all that we naturally find pleasing. Yet I believe that its hold upon those who have once fallen under its spell is deeper and more enduring than is the charm of forest or sea or mountain. This must seem a strange statement to make, but I make it with consideration and in the light of others' experience besides my own. The beauty of great woodlands, the mystical solemnity of the sea, the power and glory of mountains — right well we love all these: yet somehow, that pale, grave face of the desert, if once you look long upon it, takes you more subtly captive and keeps you enchained by a stronger bond. It is as if you were bemused by the gaze of a sorceress: or had listened over long to some witching, monotonous strain: or had pondered too deeply on old legends of weirdry or parchments from tombs of strange, forgotten lands. Certainly it is not love, in any degree, that one feels for the desert, nor could any other single term convey the sentiment. But whatever it is, there is something of haunting in it, and it is a haunting that lasts for life.

The explanation of this puzzling allurement may lie partly in the fact that the mind of man is not steadfast in its attitude toward Nature: it seems to change in reverse, as it were, to the spirit of the time. As usual, it is the opposite that attracts. The gentler features of the earth, its flowers, meadows, quiet hills, have always met response, and most so when the times were most troublous. But the vast and the wild raised no thrills but those of dislike and fear so long as life was, in a manner, similar; that is, while civilization was unborn or young. True, mountaineers have of old loved their mountains, but that was due, we may guess, more to appreciation of the protection they gave from foes, in times of chronic war and foray, than to any sense of their beauty and sublimity.

But now the pendulum tends to the other extreme. After centuries of home, security, satisfaction of want, we come to a revulsion. Ease and tame ways of living having reached, for most of us, the present far stage, there has arisen a zest for things rugged and wild. Hardship looks attractive, scarcity becomes desirable, starkness turns an unexpected side of beauty. If the sun that has pleased me with warmth has power to blast as well, *Homo sum*, let him try it on. If Mother Earth has rooms from which she would bar me with threats, let her make the threats good if she can. If the eye loves verdure and low, cool tones of color, let it take a Spartan course of whitest light and fiercest color-wave. These things also are part of our estate, and we cannot afford to leave them out of the accounts. Thus, the desolate, gaunt, and dreadful in Nature at last have their day: the risk is, indeed, that they may run to over-valuation. (Perhaps even the pranks of those funny fellows the "futurists," "cubists," and "vorticists," in poetry, music, and art, might be explained by this clue: civilization has got on their nerves, and they simply have to scream.)

As scenery merely, the desert is the last field that could take the fancy. The forest, even if gloomy, gives a sense of companionship, and is filled with life and the means of life — food, fire, and shelter. The ocean, impersonal and insincere as it is, has motion and color, play of ripple and breathing grandeur of tide. The mountains give pleasant boundary to our little lives, shutting in friends and kin, shutting out strange humanity and alien climes, and vaguely gratifying the sentiment for home. But the desert yields no point of sympathy, and meets every need of man with a cold, repelling No.

There are, it is true, about the fringes of the desert, spots of sylvan beauty. Cañons break down from these sterile walls, where, following a cascading brook, cottonwoods and sycamores come trooping in verdant file, and palms hold broad fans aloft against opaque screen of rock and deep transparency of sky. In spring, mating birds find these places out, and live in transient busy colonies while they raise their broods. Flowers, under unbroken days of sun, crowd into sudden bloom, the frail annuals growing quickly and hurrying to mature blossom and seed before the last moisture is drained from air and soil. The hardier plants here keep up a lively show, noticeably strong in the primary colors, well into summer, though short will have been their shrift on the open desert. Even ferns contrive to live within perhaps a quarter-mile of the boundary of strict aridity.

But these are only local conditions, quite the reverse of typical. One feature of loveliness the desert has, however, that is essential: in one field of beauty it is supreme. That is the field of color. Professor John C. Van Dyke, who has made that fine study of the desert which takes the rank of a classic, gives to a companion volume on the ocean the title of "The Opal Sea." A better term than "opal" could scarcely be found for describing in a word the color of the desert itself. The marvellous air, wholly free from the vapors and impurities of coast and valley places, while it sharpens detail and reduces difference of plane, at the same time throws over every object in far or middle distance a veil of lilac atmosphere wonderfully thin and transparent. Owing, perhaps, to the high power of these color-waves, the eye is hardly interfered with in penetrating shadows. As a result, one receives the full effect of every tone of color, whether in light or shade: while all come to the eye softened but enriched, and with that indefinable opaline quality that gives magic and fascination to the most poetic of gems.

The geological simplicity of sand and rock does not result, as might be expected, in poverty of color. Sand, particularly, might seem to be capable of little change of hue. But, on the contrary, its reflecting power gives it special value as a color agent, a means of taking on varying effects from the ever-changing sky. In the northwestern arm of the Colorado Desert are two great masses of sand. Flattened domes in shape, the higher one rises, I should guess, to five hundred feet above the surrounding levels. The sand probably overlies a rocky abutment of the adjacent foothills, and has been heaped there by that scarifying wind, the terror of railway employés whose lines are cast in the division which includes the San Gorgonio Pass. For months these sand-hills were in my daily view, and to describe the shades of color I have noted on them would make tedious paragraphs. From almost snow-white they have taken, often in rapid turn, all the hues of gray, of blue, of rose, of chrome, of brown, and purple, reaching even, under gloom of storm, an approach to absolute black. Sand is actually as responsive as a chameleon, and I could never tire of the vagaries of those dunes.

But most they charmed me at sunset — that hour when the soul itself is suffused with changing hues, and comes to its best perception. Then none but warm and gentle shades are seen, and the mind, like a tranquil lake, receives them and renders them into something clearer and deeper than thought. (Is it not at evening that we most naturally and truly *reflect?*) Words quite fail to disclose the felicity of those spiritual moments of color. Like music, they speak the unearthly tongue, and it is only into music that they could be translated. I mean, of course, the real accents of the Heavenly Maid, not the new, loud, German noise which goes with the rattling of the sabre and aptly illustrates *Kultur*. Far from that, my sand-hills at evening are an *Abendlied*, a child's ethereal dream, a reverie, a sigh.

Rock, contrary to sand, gives back its own color; but here it is pure and vivid color, untinged with overlying hues of vegetation that elsewhere come in to perplex the eye. The prevailing surface hue of desert rock is a dark rust-red. I should name it Egyptian red, for in my mental picturings of the land of the Nile this same dull but powerful note rules like absolute Pharaoh. The color, however, is not inherent in the stone, which is mainly granite of the common gray. But in course of ages this material, lying usually in huge slabs, has taken on a surface sheen and coloring due to weathering and baking by the sun. It is spoken of as "desert glaze," and is really something like the artificial glaze of pottery. Even when the rocks take boulder form they are generally great, house-like cubes or rhomboids, offering flat surfaces which sun and weather have painted in the same broad, strong hue. Only where cañons choked with more freshly shattered rock score the mountain walls does one catch the native tint of the granite, making a startling contrast. From these cañon mouths wide, fan-like sheets of similar débris sweep down to the level. Up these the eye ranges, higher and higher, into gloomy galleries and chasms until the thread is lost in a maze of braided folds of mountain, these overlooked often by some far, high crest, in winter white with snow, in summer gray with iron crag and precipice of granite, but always softly clouded with humanizing pines.

The characteristic contour form of the desert mountain ranges is another element in the beauty of desert color. Like geological models set on a table, they stand up sharply defined from the general level, arresting the glance with new, conspicuous effects. No gently modelled approaches prepare the eye for the change of plane. From gray or drab expanse of sand they rear up wall-like profiles of red or ochre. Perspective is dwarfed by the clearness of air, increasing the sense of verticality. Instead of rising from the desert, these mountains stand upon it, explicit, bald, almost artificial.

Whatever form of geological action may explain the peculiarities of these mountain shapes, it has resulted in a great irregularity of surface: but this irregularity is worked in small scale. The long, almost isolated spur of the San Jacinto that lies before me can only be likened to one of those vast surges one sees in mid-ocean, driven into infinite complexity by hurricane or tornado. In a mile or less of mountain-side I count ten or a dozen well-defined main cañons. They have one general trend, and score the barren, red-brown flank sharply from almost the crest down to the sudden dead level. Interwoven with these principal cleavages, meeting and crossing them at every angle, are hundreds of lesser depressions, miniature passes and divides. The result is a positive cross-hatching of intricate contours, resembling in midday light a choppy sea, giving at evening and morning a chequer of delicious color, molten gold in light, amethyst in shade; or, under sunset or sunrise warmth, like the glow of red-hot iron flecked with touches of purple more than Tyrian. I think the coldest-blooded of men would stand and gaze while that pageant was passing. For others, the experience, which can never be made stale by custom, is more than æsthetic or emotional: it is moral, I would almost say religious.

But the remark that rock gives back its own color must be qualified, for rock also responds to circumstances. The eastward extension of San Bernardino Mountain, lying beyond the sand-hills to which I referred above, gives a good example of the possibilities of this stubborn material. In actual hue the range is the usual deep reddish-brown; but under diffused sunlight I have seen it pale down to milky white, a tone that one would never suppose could come within its scope. Breaking of light-rays by vegetation is not the cause, as it might be elsewhere; for plant-life is here at its lowest volume, a joke, almost a myth, like a Chinaman's beard. It impresses one oddly, this wholesale bleaching away of essential color. Withered, ghastly, monstrously old, the mountains seem like geologic wraiths, such mountains as the ghosts of moon-men may wander among in the ashy lunar world.

The great stretches of level desert also show some diversity of color, arising partly from absence or presence (and kind) of vegetation, and partly from difference of surface material. But it is only when seen in great extent, from a good elevation, that atmosphere and grouping of shades lend enchantment. In near view, seen from slightly above the level, a vast drab, tinged usually with olive, is the general hue. The olive comes from an infinite stipple of low shrubs, so uniform in spacing — for each plant jealously guards its little territory — as to show no cloudings of heavier and sparser growth. The effect is about as lively and original as fifty square miles of tweed in "pepper-and-salt mixture." But though not themselves in the least degree stimulating to fancy, these dull plains have value as foil and foreground to the color display of ever-present hills and mountains. And when, as often may be the case, the close foreground is laid in blocks of that deep, powerful red, the landscape, though bare of any recognized elements of beauty, yet is perfect, in its way incomparable.

In places the drab gives way to other tones. There are large extents of unmixed sand, boulders, gravel, or of pavement-like rock-mosaic in yellow, red, lava-black. On these the vegetation is so sparse as to yield no element of color. This is the desert entire and austere, the realm of geology alone among the sciences. Here Time and all things of Time seem to have ended or not to have begun. The sun rises, flames through the sky, and sets; the moon and stars look coldly down; the traveller seems to himself the last life on the planet. Awe that is close on terror grasps him: he feels himself alone in the universe — he, and God. His footsteps cease: why should he go on? and whither? for there is no whither. Nothing moves, nor can move, but the elemental wind, vacantly roaming the empty earth (and those great airs, what a sense they bring of age, of eternal solitude, of cold, sidereal space!). The life of towns, of farms, all that signifies humanity, seems totally unreal: the Great Question confronts, closes one in, and must, but cannot, be answered. At such moments, reader, you may find foothold in thoughts perhaps long unthought or cast aside — "I believe in God the Father Almighty, Maker of heaven and earth": and so on to the end. They will not now seem contemptible, I assure you.

There comes in spring, on all but these barrenest spaces, a startling interlude, a sudden wave of color. Even in the desert, Nature, though here least humane, most indifferent, longs for change, and softens for a time at the entreaty of her most winsome child, virginal, petal-eyed Flora. It is only a transient flush, rising, culminating, and fading quickly, almost as fleeting as sunset on cloud or mountain; but it is enough: Draco does relent, Colonel Absolute has been seen playing horsey on the hearthrug. It proves the desert livable and possibly lovable: and for all the rest of the year one bears in mind that brief touch of graciousness.

In speaking of the color of the desert there remains the great field of the sky. Let not the reader stay, as I did too long, under the conventional notion of an ever-cloudless blue. Clear skies, of course, predominate, but even in summer no long time passes without grateful show of vapor — glorious white or yet more glorious gray. Nearness to the Pacific and the Gulf of California gives the sky of the Colorado Desert a degree of cloudiness far greater than that, for instance, of the Sahara, though the rainfall on our desert is as scanty as there. In both summer and winter the sun may rise, make his march, and set, day after day for weeks, in undimmed power; but at any season there will not be many mornings or evenings together without some skeiny film of rose, some shimmering bar of madder, purple, or coppery gold, though for months the sky through all the middle hours of the day may be a hard and uniform cobalt.

There is in fact a constant battle in these skies, often to be seen by interested mortals below, like the scrimmages of *pro* and *anti* deities that went on above the plains of Troy. From the spot where I

make these notes I have often looked for hours while
the struggle remained in deadlock. Over the pass
between San Jacinto and Santa Rosa battalions of
cloud come rolling, stream out far to the east, and
threaten the kingdom of the sun. But that old
tyrant seldom sleeps, or, after the manner of tyrants,
sleeps with an eye open, and it is hard to catch him
unaware. His intrenchments are all but impregnable.
Leagues of radiant air form invisible ramparts from
which the invaders are continually thrown back, and
ever from the heated desert new ranks of warriors
come rushing up to maintain the fight. Now one
side gains, now the other. Some hero of the gray
leads a charge, and a tongue of vapor leaps out far
in the advance, may even fling down a slant of rain
or snow on the anxious pines of Santa Rosa. But
before the Grays can establish themselves the Blues
are at them and press them back. "A Pluvius! A
Pluvius!" "Phœbus! Phœbus to the rescue!" And
so it wages, to and fro, strangely and ominously like
the battles of men; ominously, lest it prove that
these are no farther from coming to a final end.

With all the glory of desert evening skies, I miss
one accustomed element of sunset: I mean that
spiritual touch, impossible to put into words, but
which we know so well. Perhaps the word "wistfulness" states it best, and the desert (so you might
think until you know it) is not wistful. But yet it is:
to be old, weary, and wise is wistful, as much as are
the young, asking eyes of a child. But wistfulness is
hard to define. Why in music, for instance, should
a chord, a turn of rhythm, even an interval, start

sometimes a wave that reaches boundless shores, or, sinking like a burning ruby into depths we never guessed were there, show us ourselves "as gods, knowing good and evil"? How does it come that the leaf of an autumn bramble expresses a hero's soul better than epic verses ever can? And what magic is there about sunset and the West that has always drawn men's longing (so that, indeed, for wistfulness one might fancifully say westfulness)? Is it that we feel the sun's daily going as so great a loss that we must follow him with our pensive hopes? Not so with us all, certainly. To me, for one, the sun has always seemed an enemy, the ally of tedium, a huge Evaporator sucking the spirit and leaving naught but the plodding clay. "The gaudy, babbling, and remorseless day" — well said, Shakespeare! But this is verging on metaphysics: the point is, that somehow there is not in desert sunset hues that deepest, most sensitive note. They are fairyland, a sheer marvel, the quintessence of beauty in color; but they have not the ineffable quality that goes, perhaps, with murkier, less all-revealing skies. It may be that, being mysterious to ourselves, anything less than mystery in Nature must fall short. "*Abyssus abyssum invocat.*"

As a fact, I have seen more of that moving glory in sunset skies from the top of a London 'bus than anywhere else, even Sierra crest or open vastness of the Colorado. Perhaps it is the presence of six million human souls (I do not mean bodies) that gives the needed atmosphere, the spiritual haze.

But the metaphysical must be reckoned with,

after all, to explain the strange attraction of the desert. Space, solitude, quiet — our minds at their best are tuned to these, and when they find them they expand like the anemone welcoming its native tide. The merely objective things of the desert are another and transitory matter: I am speaking of its underlying, undying charm. It is a somewhat awful attribute, with more of subjugation in it than of charm. It disembodies us, takes away what hides us from ourselves. The aged earth speaks now in solemn tone to its child, and he must listen. No friendly tree or buoyancy of wave meets the daunted eye with encouragement or excuse for levity. Here justice is the word, not mercy. The universe seems listening for your word, and appraising you by your silence. If there comes a sound it is so momentary as only to startle, swallowed up instantly in the waiting void — the thin, single note of the cactus wren, one of the lonesomest of sounds, more lost and eerie than the midnight bleat of sheep on Cumberland fells.

Is there attraction in this, then? To most people, No: to a few, Yes: and Yes to an increasing number, I think and hope, as the loud roar grows louder; the times more complex and out of joint; the strife of tongues more clever and useless; simplicity, the touchstone of good, more than ever reverend yet less than ever revered.

CHAPTER II

THE PALM OASES AND CAÑONS

THOUGH the palm is certainly not the most beautiful, it is perhaps the most poetic of trees. In symmetry of tapering shaft, fountain-like burst of crown, and play of glossy frond, it is the ideal of gracefulness in plant life. Incidentally, there is the charm of its "atmosphere" of literary allusion, of which it probably has more than any other tree can claim. To dwellers in cold or temperate climates it brings also alluring thoughts of tropic warmth, skies normally sunny, and a life emancipated from winter flannels.

Spreading up from Northern Mexico, a number of groups of the fan-palm, *Washingtonia filifera*, are found in the cañons and oases of the Colorado Desert. They are known to but few, and those are mainly prospectors and such stray characters, whose business or hobby makes them wanderers in that harsh region. Such human life as the desert has — that is, the actual desert, the unconquered and unconquerable wastes of burning sand and mountain — drifts and circles about these spots: necessarily so, since the presence of palms means the presence also of that rarest, strictest necessity, water. The Arabs' axiom regarding the date-palm, that its foot must be in water and its head in open sun, is true of its relative the fan-palm. Thus, in the talk of desert men the palm figures constantly. You hear of Dos Palmas, Thousand Palms, Palm Springs, Twenty-nine Palms, Seventeen Palms, Two-Bunch Palms, and so on; and the names mean to the traveller not only water, but shade, with the chance of grass for his animals, and the relief of verdure for his sorely harassed eyes.

Some of the groups occur about the boundary of the sea that anciently filled the great depression which is now partly occupied by the Salton Sea, and whose beach-mark is to-day startlingly plain at the base of the encircling hills. Such groups, probably, represent the indigenous growths. A number more are found at higher altitudes, but of these many are known to have been planted by the present or former Indian inhabitants of the region.

The westerly limit of growth is a rocky defile on the south side of Snow Creek Cañon, which is a rift of San Jacinto Mountain, about opposite Whitewater Station on the Southern Pacific Railway. This group marks the nearest approach made by the wild palm to coastal conditions of climate, for the spot is within a few miles of the crest of the San Gorgonio Pass, which here forms the dividing line between California barren and California fertile. A thread of tepid water moistens the roots of the trees, while not a mile away rushes the icy brook that gives its name to the cañon.

I camped, at various times, in most of the considerable cañons of the upper part of the desert. Each has its special charm, while those that come down from the high mountains that shut off desert from coast possess a dual beauty — the characteristics of a true mountain cañon, such as trees, cascading streams, and the varied life that goes with them, together with the features of a land made savage by torturing sun, unblessed by the mercy of rain. The mingling of the two elements gives often a fascinating result.

It was still winter, the end of January, when I pitched my little six-by-three-foot tent in Chino Cañon. This is a great rift opening on the northwestern arm of the desert directly under the peak of San Jacinto Mountain. It gets its name from old Chino, a former chief of the Agua Caliente Indians, whose *rancheria* adjoins the little village of Palm Springs, a few miles to the south of the cañon. I had visited the spot years before, and kept an affectionate memory of a warm spring that breaks out near the head of the great apron of talus that sweeps down from the neck of the cañon to the level desert. It was toilsome work navigating my burro, Mesquit, through these miles of boulders, with a rise from five hundred feet to two thousand feet of altitude, and there was neither mood nor leisure for scenery until we reached the little clump of palms that marked our destination.

But when camp was pitched and serenity returned I found a high coign among the rocks and took my satisfaction. I was at about the limit of growth of the water-loving trees that accompanied the creek as far as they dared — sycamores, alders, cottonwoods, and willows. Here they stopped short abruptly, and from here desertward only the starveling vegetation of drought held the ground. The pale shrubs seemed to have copied the look of the gray boulders, as if hoping by subterfuge to escape the notice of the sun. Each bush of encelia or burroweed grew rounded and compact, and in twilight or moonlight would not be distinguished from the rocks, except where they grew among the rust-brown slabs of the cañon walls, when one would swear he saw a flock of grazing sheep, every one distinct to the eye.

Straight in front the cañon opened in steep, smooth descent, bounded by high and barren walls, the western already dark in shadow, the other in full sun and glowing with volcanic intensity of red. At three miles' distance these ran out into the level like capes extending far to sea — a sea of lifeless gray that broke southward in one huge crest of sand that was like a tidal wave stopped and held in full career. In sharp relief against the neutral hue of the sand stood the dark, gleaming fans of palms. The distance was closed by a level rampart of mountains in faint ethereal tones of rose, chrome, and amethyst.

I had not many such evening prospects during the two weeks I camped in Chino Cañon. It was a wet winter, and I was not far from being perpendicularly below the ten-thousand-and-odd-foot peak of the mountain, which was engaged in perpetual storm. After days of rain I would determine to move, at the first cessation, down to the valley, which I could often see stewing in sunshine while I shivered over an unwilling camp-fire in the rain (I don't know why it did n't occur to me to get into the warm spring and wait until the clouds had rained themselves out). But when a change came my mind changed with it and I stayed. At last there came a drop in temperature, and after three days and nights of torrential downpour I awoke one morning to find the sun shining and the mountains sheeted with snow down to a few hundred feet above camp. Then it was high luxury to lie in my thermal pool and get a startling effect of shining green palm-fronds with background of solid snow.

The Indians hereabouts have a legend that Tahquitz, *alias* Chowk, their evil spirit, lives in San Jacinto Mountain, and attribute to his operations the peculiar noises, rumblings, and so forth, that are sometimes heard proceeding from his haunts. Several times, while in this cañon, when lying on the ground at night, I heard the sounds plainly. There was no tremor of earthquake, but it is possible that the heavy rains caused a movement of the rocks on the mountain-side. The sounds, whatever made them, were easily transmitted to me, since my ear was practically in contact with the earth. Who knows but it was "the fellow in the cellarage," old Truepenny himself?

Some miles to the south is Andreas Cañon, another of the gateways of the same mountain. It also is named after an Indian, old Captain Andreas, the remains of whose adobe hut and orchard of vines and figs are yet in evidence. Here the following winter I camped for nearly three months, gratifying aboriginal instincts by a return to cave life. The cavern which served for dining-room, study, and kitchen had been the home of Indians, and was adorned with their picture-writings, while a sort of upper story was quite a museum of age-dimmed records in red and black. One upright stone was worn into grooves like knuckles, where arrow-shafts had been smoothed; another showed evidence of having been used for polishing the obsidian points. The great table-like rock where I kept a store of hay for my horse Ka- weah (Mesquit and I had had a difference and parted) was bored in a dozen places with circular holes where acorn and mesquit meal had been ground by gene- rations of diligent squaws, whose deer-horn awls and ornaments of shell and clay I occasionally unearthed: as I did also bones in remarkable numbers and of questionable shapes.

Of Andreas, now long gathered to his fathers, the word goes that he was given to the distilling of *aguardiente* from his grapes, breaking thereby the law of the land. However, considering that the art had been learned from the whites, that he had no voice in making the law, and that the land in question had been taken from him and his people, there seems not much logic in blaming him. Peace to your ashes, Andreas! I can certify that your fig trees still do bud, and yield better fruit perhaps than some of us.

The same striking conjunction of desert and coast vegetation rules here as in Chino Cañon. Down to the very neck, a bare hundred yards from where open desert comes in view, trees grow in full verdure, curtained in wild-grape vines that make an arbor of summer green or autumn chrome and sienna over the darkling pools of the creek. At the point where they cease they are met by a colony of palms, and these give place to the low-toned herbage of the desert. The cañon is notable for a fine rank of "palisade" cliffs, which with their massive sculpturing and dark Egyptian hue make a wonderful foil for the beauty of the palms. Some of these stand statue-like in vertical alcoves of the wall: others bend in tropic grace above crystalline pools, or spring in rocket-like curve from thickets of mesquit or arrowweed.

One cluster, arranged in the form of a great hall, especially took my fancy. The palms that compose it have kept all their dead foliage, which, hanging in straw-yellow masses about the stems, gives them impressive girth and solidity. While wind is stirring the fronded capitals, these massive pillars, standing in unbroken stillness, seem like the immemorial columns of Babylon. My nights in that strange place, worked up into mystery by glimmer of star or trickle of wandering moonbeam through the tracery of the roof, were the sort of experience one loves to repeat in memory.

In a narrow gateway of the upper cañon stands a single stately palm, framed by tall cliffs of Egyptian red. Its solitariness, spiry grace, and statuesque pose give it special individuality, and sentimentally I allowed myself to name it "La Reina del Cañon."

Evenings by the camp-fire in the cave were enlivened by visitors, kangaroo-mice, skunks, and tarantulas, who adopted me without reserve into the ancient order of cave-dwellers. The mice were charming companions, eating beans and hardtack with me off our common plate, and only occasionally needing an admonitory rap with the spoon. By day, quail were frequent callers, aligning themselves on a shelving rock overhead to criticise my housekeeping: and once a lynx halted bashfully when ten yards from the breakfast-table. Bighorn tracks were often fresh on the cactus mesa beyond the creek, and my regular morning alarum was the practising of chromatic scales by a cañon-wren midway up the cliff.

Andreas Cañon had become endeared to me by these and other social ties when, about noon one Saturday, a gentle but persistent rain began — one of the occasions one recognizes as meant for the cooking of beans. I charged my biggest pot and passed the afternoon in holding the fire at that scientific minimum that the "free-holy"[1] justly de-

---

[1] The red or pink Mexican bean, *frijol* in Spanish, pronounced free-hole' or, affectionately, as above.

mands and wondrously repays. The rain continued, taking on the industrious look that Californians know and love as forecasting a successful season in real estate. At intervals I brought in fuel, storing it in dry crannies of the cave.

Kaweah, protected by his heavy blanket, was tied close to the creek, under a tree against which I had built his manger. Darkness came early, and the rain increased to a heavy downpour. I ate supper in dusk, fed and watered the horse, covered the hay with a tarpaulin, and turned into the blankets on my camp-cot to smoke a pipe. This proved more than usually cheering. A tent with sousing rain were revealed as the ideal conditions for the combustion of Virginia Long-Cut. This discovery I had opportunity to confirm in the days that ensued.

Before turning in finally I lighted the lantern and took a look at the creek. It had risen a few inches, as was natural in a cañon stream, but the tent was six or eight feet above it and a rod back from the bank. Nothing to worry about, so I went to bed, and, lulled by the roar of rain on the canvas, was soon fast asleep.

This placidity was ill-judged. Some suffocating object, something heavy and wet and cold, came down and embraced me with what I felt to be undue familiarity. For a few moments I was puzzled, then realized — the tent: it had sagged with weight of water and the pegs had pulled from the softened ground. I noticed, too, that the sound of rushing water was oddly close. Pushing away the wet canvas I put out a foot. Instead of the expected boot it encountered a cold swirl of water that came half to the knee. Next my groping hand took note of the abnormal position of the tent-pole, which leaned almost horizontal under the ruin of the canvas. I saw what had happened: the creek was over its banks, had undermined the pole and brought down the tent, and was making a clean breach through my quarters.

My thoughts flew to Kaweah. He was some twenty-five yards downstream from me and on lower ground. Struggling under the water-logged canvas I hurriedly got into my soaking clothes and somehow got clear of the tent. It was pitch-dark, raining like fury, and the water was now knee-high and running like a sluice. I stumbled down to Kaweah, who neighed shrilly when he saw me. He had taken the highest spot his rope allowed him, but the water was almost to his belly, and we were both in some danger of being swept away. Cutting the rope I scrambled with him up the bank and tied him on high ground near the cave.

Then for an hour I slopped to and fro rescuing what remained of my effects and storing them in dry corners of the cave. Not a few articles had been carried away, but most were caught under the collapsed tent, which itself was anchored by a rock against which it had stranded. It was wet work, but warming, and I soon worked up a first-rate Turkish bath.

The next need was fire. By now the cave was a poor refuge, though it might have looked enjoyable to a naiad. Rain dripped everywhere from the shelving rocks that formed at best a nominal roof, and cascades ran picturesquely down the walls. The floor was a mere bog. Only a space about three feet square was free from overhead drip, and on this islet I built a tiny fire over which I crouched in partial shelter. I supposed it was near daybreak, but on looking at my watch found it was eleven o'clock.

I cherished that fire as few things are cherished on this planet. When gusts blew the rain in upon it, I covered it with my hat. When it sulked and sputtered because the bog encroached, I fed it with splinters from my tripod. When the wind scattered the cupful of embers, I scraped them up reverently like a Parsee. At last I got a good blaze, made a billy of coffee, and settled to the night's work of drying myself, blankets, gun, camera, and "et cæteras."

The storm maintained a headlong deluge which did not moderate for a moment. The creek had risen higher, and was making wild uproar as huge boulders began to come down from the upper cañon, thundering and bumping along like barrels tumbling down a stairway. With the boulders went the trees. The one to which Kaweah had been tied (a full-grown sycamore) had disappeared soon after I moved him. Only by a few minutes had he escaped going with it. Now I watched tree after tree succumb. First their tops, which showed dimly against the sky, would begin to shiver as the water tore away the earth like a terrier at a rat-hole: then as roots broke from their grip the victim stooped lower and lower, until water and granite between them gave the *coup-de-grâce*, and the unlucky alder or sycamore toppled over and was whirled off to make camp-fires for fortunate prospectors.

Daylight came, and with it the end of my fuel. By now the cave was worthless: water poured in steady streams from roof and walls, and the floor had become a pool. Among my salvaged traps was a little three-by-six-foot tent of light waterproof stuff which I carry on winter horseback trips. This I pitched on the highest spot available, first laying a thick stratum of arrowweed over the sodden ground. Inside I spread half a bale of dry hay: then crept in and sat tight.

This was Sunday. It passed; also Monday, Tuesday, and Wednesday, and not for a moment did the storm hold off. I read, smoked, ate, slept, and dashed out when necessary to attend to Kaweah or drive the tent-stakes deeper into the spongy earth. When I awoke on Thursday a yellow glow was brightening my tentlet. It was the sun, shining in the old, whole-hearted, California way, and I hurried out to renew acquaintance. Looking up the cañon there was little that I recognized. The place where the other tent had stood could be known by a scrap of canvas projecting above a new creek-bed of dazzling, freshly scoured granite, while Kaweah's former quarters were submerged in mid-stream.

In the afternoon came Pablo, Marcos, and Miguel, to round up their remaining cattle and mourn the six or eight head that had vanished in the storm together with all their possibilities of *pesos*, *carne*, and *cuero*. Finding me in the act of replenishing the bean-pot they expressed slight Indian surprise, and mentioned that, certain of my belongings having been picked up some miles away where the flood had carried them, it had been supposed that I was drowned. By way of congratulation they stayed to help with the beans. It was fifty years, they said, since so heavy a storm had visited the desert, and news that came later of broken dams and loss of life in the adjoining coast region made this seem likely to be true.

Just to the south of Palm Springs there is an imposing gash in the mountain wall which goes by the name of Tahquitz Cañon. The stream which debouches here rises on Tahquitz Peak, a subsidiary summit of San Jacinto Mountain and whispered to be the private eyry of Tahquitz himself. The cañon is remarkable for magnificent cliffs, forming at the mouth a cirque with walls rising sheer for hundreds of feet. This titanic Colosseum makes a superb effect by morning light, when the vast, crater-like shadow is outlined by grim though sunlit rock-bolts that guard the towering gateway. It would be a worthy portal to Avernus, and when Tahquitz has his waterfall in full blast a quite infernal uproar reigns in the confined place, while the great southern cliff, acting as sounding-board, projects a full-mouthed roar upon the ears of the villagers of Palm Springs.

Twelve miles to the southeast is Magnesia Spring Cañon (or, to give it the old Indian name, Pahwah'-te, signifying, "the drinker"), where I made camp for a couple of weeks in early spring. It is different from the cañons already described, being a long, winding gallery instead of the usual wide-mouthed triangle narrowing suddenly to a gorge, and is typical of strictly desert conditions. Here no "Cataracts blow their trumpets from the steep." One finds no growth of water-loving trees, for the cañon does not lead down, as do the others, from rain-compelling peaks, and only the slenderest thread of water trickles in it, for the most part underground. This was enough, however, to maintain one lovely rock-bound pool in which, by skinning one's knees, a miniature swim could be achieved. High falcon-haunted cliffs partly encircled the pool, and a couple of palms growing in a niche fifty feet above gave a tropic touch of luxury.

On arriving at the pool I found fresh tracks of mountain lion in the damp sand. My main object in this cañon was the chance of photographing bighorn, which are rather plentiful hereabouts, but there would be small prospect of these so long as lions were in the neighborhood. It would be some compensation, I thought, to add a cougar pelt to my coyote-skin mattress, so I built a brush blind twenty yards from the spring, made an early supper, and took my station, shot-gun with full charge of buckshot across my knees, seven-shooter and hunting-knife in reserve. There was a half-moon, and on the open space of sand around the spring even a small object could be plainly seen. But my warlike preparations went for naught. For five hours I crouched at *qui vive*, but no such dark shape as I looked for came pacing across the moonlit sand. A fox trotted by, stopped with paw upraised, and trotted on: and later I made out a group of shadowy

forms sixty yards away that certainly were bighorn,
the first I had met in their own haunts. My nerves
tingled: suppose the cougar were stalking the band!
But the moon sank behind the cliff, and when I
could no longer see my gun-sights I concluded that
the coyote-skins would do very well alone, and
turned in. The next two nights I again sat on watch,
and not unprofitably, though with no result of
cougars. It is in the purity and stillness of such hours,
in tranquil fall of moonbeam on rock and shrub,
and in such sense of awful but calming solitude, that
one learns, by the sacredness of Nature, the beauty
of God.

The face of the cliff near the spring showed a
number of likely crannies, which I searched for
Indian relics. Most of them were packed with bits
of stick or cactus, the *caches* of those punctilious
thieves the trade-rats. In a side cañon, however, I
found a handsome *olla* (or ka'-wo-mal, to give it the
Indian name). It had been hidden in a breakneck
place, fifty feet up a precipitous cliff, where I
glimpsed it by chance. It stood upright on a bed of
earth that must have been carried up from below,
and was protected by slabs of rock with padding of
palm-fibre. Probably it had held water, perhaps
stored in case of siege, but that had long vanished,
and it contained nothing but a deposit of dust almost intangibly fine, like dust of mummies or of
Time itself, which had somehow gathered in spite
of the neck being closed with a flat fragment of rock.
I suppose this mysterious dust would distil, in course
of ages, from the upper ether itself, some product of

cosmic disintegration. How many years the *olla* had stood there is matter for free guessing — perhaps fifty, perhaps five hundred. Its circumference was over fifty inches, and its capacity about eight gallons. A furious wind was blowing that threatened to throw me from the cliff and gave me trying moments, but hugging *olla* with one arm and cliff with the other I got my prize safely down.

Next I moved some miles farther south to Deep Cañon (To'-ho of the Indians, commemorating some "hunter-who-never-gets-his-game"). This is a cañon of Santa Rosa Mountain, opening just west of the long, rocky point that runs out on the desert at Indian Wells. It is notable for its vast apron of débris, through which Mesquit and I struggled for endless hours, being forced at last to make a dry camp when nightfall overtook us in a jungle of cholla. In the morning we soon reached water, and also the ocotillos, the view of which in flower was my special object here. Since first meeting the plant the previous year I had looked forward to camping among them when in full blossom, as these now were (it was the middle of March), and so entering them in my lasting book of remembrance.

I have described this remarkable plant of the Western deserts in another chapter. Here I pitched my tent in a thicket of them, enjoying their splendor of color by day and their weird shadow-play on my moonlit canvas at night. The dead canes and stumps made an excellent camp-fire, burning with a white flame, as of wax, that justified the plant's alternative name of "candle-wood." Near by were specimens of the agave, or wild century-plant, some just beginning to send up their giant flowering-stalks. Measuring the rate of growth of one of these I found that it gained five inches in twenty-four hours.

Tracks of bighorn were plentiful about camp every day, and their deeply worn trails marked the cañon walls in all directions. Often at night the rattle of falling stones told of their movements on the cliff-side above. Wild-cat and coyote also left their footprints in my absence. I met here a flock of the interesting piñon-jays, which long puzzled me by their unjay-like traits, as they flew swiftly along the face of the mountain, uttering a wild, sweet, plaintive cry. Who ever heard of a plaintive jay! Eagles, too, I often saw, and ravens croaked from unscalable crags. Friendlier birds were the acrobatic flycatchers and phainopeplas that performed from the tops of the agaves, and a pair of rose-breasted linnets that regularly came to breakfast and made me long confidences in happy *cavatina*. The cactus wrens gained my respect by the nonchalance with which they treated the formidable chollas. Since the nightingale prefers to lean her breast against a thorn, it seems a pity she cannot try the effect of a cholla.

A tramp at dawn up the higher cañon was full of pleasure. At the point where it narrows to the main ravine the stream became a series of cascades linked by many a circling pool so fishable in look that there was pathos in the thought that they must be forever troutless. As the cañon doubled and twisted, the walls became ever higher and more precipitous.

When the sun came up, the western cliff became the battlements of some castle in the realm of faëry. I often halted in wonder as some reach opened before me, filled with mystical light. The conjunction of extreme beauty of color with savagery of giant walls and thundering water gave a strange effect of unreality.

A few isolated groups of palms were set high up on the walls. They seemed to have a conscious air, as if they had been waiting until now for first recognition. Mountain-sheep make these lonely groves their shelter in summer heat and winter storm; but human foot, unless perhaps some Indian hunter's, may never have been set in them.

On little benches here and there I came upon delightful beds of flowers, usually of one kind. Here I first met the exquisite malvastrum, in delicacy and fragility more like some hothouse product than the child of desert sand and sun. Those who know the globe-tulip of our coast mountains may picture this as a blossom of the same ethereal character, but palest lilac instead of white, and stained at the base of each petal with a spot of carmine. A plant with half a dozen of the lamp-like flowers is as fairy-like a thing as a child could dream. Another new acquaintance was the fagonia, a low-growing relative of the creosote, having starry blossoms of pale magenta. Dwarf lupines occupied stretches of pure sand, and eschscholtzias, with pale yellow flowerets comically small, showed the effect of drought upon the magnificent *copa de oro* of the coast. On the driest places, exposed to the sun's full blast, the lovely little eremiastrum, or desert-star, looked up, winsome as daisies on an English lawn.

Upon returning to camp I found the first rattle-snake of the season had arrived and was enjoying my blankets in the tent. He seemed firm but calm, as if open to any reasonable offer. While I sought a tripod he vanished. In the night I felt something creeping over my chest under the blankets, and with panic remembered my visitor, who might have come to claim a share of the accommodation. I made a really brilliant jump, struck a match, and met the reproachful gaze of a large, stout, comatose lizard that was searching affectionately for the nice warm bedfellow who had suddenly turned unkind.

Crossing to the east side of the desert, here not many miles wide, a wonderful spectacle is seen in the crowding groves of Thousand Palm Cañon. In this wide gallery, opening from the foothills of the San Bernardino at near sea-level, the palm seems most thoroughly at home, growing in companies of hundreds that make what might almost be termed a forest. One has a sense of strangeness in threading these pillared aisles. One's steps rattle harshly on a pavement of dry yellow leaves whose mahogany-brown stems, long, tough, and thorny, impose care in walking, while the mind does not easily ignore the thought of snakes, tarantulas, and scorpions that find the deep dry cover highly agreeable to their constitutions. The summer temperature here is of the hottest, for weeks ranging daily over 100° in the shade, and often over 110°, with not infre-quent excursions into the hundred-and-twenties.

A few miles out on the plain another group shows a distinctive feature of chance arrangement. Twelve palms stand approximately in line, and the number has given them the name, "The Twelve Apostles." Local fancy takes pleasure in pointing out that one of them is headless and dead, the result of lightning-stroke. This, of course, is Judas, and verily there is something infamous in the mean, misbegotten shape. Nothing in the vegetable world is so hideous as a headless palm. Other trees when killed or decayed have at least the touch of the grotesque or pictorial. The palm that loses its head loses all: there remains merely a hateful stick, not even pathetic, only sinister.

Out on the wind-swept plain to the east of Palm Springs lies the oasis of Seven Palms. The name does not now describe the group, though no doubt it once did so. Placed here and there in picturesque mode, singly or in twos, threes, and one larger cluster, a score or so of *Washingtonias* inhabit a space of a few acres, surrounding a pool of alkaline water. Years ago a settler made a homestead here, and his flat-roofed, unpainted dwelling, weathered into drab conformity of hue, merges with gray thickets of arrowweed. The charm of the place, apart from its palms, is in the grandeur of its mountain prospect, dominated to the south by colossal San Jacinto, whose two-mile height soars close at hand, undwarfed by intervening foothills. San Gorgonio rises somewhat more distant, but not less superb, a little to the west. The spot has a special drawback too — the pestilent wind which blows down the pass for days and weeks, or, for aught I know, months and years, together, making the daylight hours a misery, the nights a howling nightmare. Relief could generally be found, however, by the margin of the pool, and always enjoyment in noting the quaint, humorous ways of the bird and animal life that resorted there.

Four miles farther north, near the foothills of the San Bernardino, are twin colonies, which have given the place the name of "Two-Bunch Palms." Growing at the edge of a little bluff they are finely placed; and from among them one gets again vistas of those two great peaks, always claiming the gaze, whether serene under cloudless blue, hallowed with snow, or darkly freighted with storm. Such things are unique in American landscape, and send one's thoughts wandering for comparisons to Ararat, Ruwenzori, or famed Kashmir.

I shall not soon forget one spring night when, beneath these palms, I was for once near the intoxication point of moonlight. For hours I lay unable to sleep, while I was showered with moon arrows, "passionately bright," that streamed from the polished fronds as they thrashed and undulated in a screaming wind. It was the Valkyries' ride translated into moonlight, but outdoing Wagner, almost beating the incoherencies of Strauss.

The village of Palm Springs, ten miles to the south, has some fame as a winter health resort. It also offers the tourist, by comfortable accommodations, the means of exploring with ease a few of the palm communities. In the village there is a valuable medicinal spring, which rises, with a temperature of 103°, beneath a flourishing cluster of palms. The spring is on the Reservation of the Agua Caliente Indians, and the bath-house is operated for their financial benefit. It is a new, crude affair, and I confess I enjoyed more the quite primitive contrivances of a few years ago, when to the weird sensation produced by the gulpings and gurglings of the spring, which is a kind of quicksand in consistency, was added the excitement of guessing whether the rickety little hut would fall to pieces while you were taking your bath or would spare you and collapse over the next comer. This zest of adventure has now been lost, as has also the healthful exercise of pursuing the key all over the Reservation to its lair in the capacious pocket of old Maria's wrapper of antique, well-washed blue.

The arm of desert that reaches southward from the village ends in a long, winding ravine known as "Palm Cañon." Hundreds of palms grow here along the course of a romantic stream, bending in dreamy beauty over glassy reach and pool, or disposed in natively artistic attitudes on the lower slopes of the cañon walls. The combination of arrowy brook, wild ravine, and tropic multitude of palms makes the spot an enchanting one, and it never fails to draw a tribute of surprised approval from even the callous globe-trotter. In winter and spring a feature of contrast is added when one may catch from some high viewpoint the gleam of San Jacinto's snow. Then it is a scene over which artists rave, the note of white giving the last touch to a landscape already crowded with powerful colors.

Naturally, those nuisances the motion-picture people have seized on Palm Cañon for their antics, with the result of setting fire to some of the finest of the palms. But why repine? Rather let us rejoice that Nature is thus honored in serving Art. Hardly less picturesque than Palm Cañon is the adjacent Murray Cañon. Here again clusters and files of palms give brightness to a ravine sombre with high-piled rocks. Not far away are Eagle and Andreas Cañons, similarly beautified with these graceful trees.

It is much to be desired that some square miles of this locality, with Palm Cañon as a centre, should be set aside as a National Park. Scenically the place is more than remarkable; it is strictly unique for this country, as well as strangely beautiful: while for its botanical rarity alone it should be preserved in the public interest. As facilities for reaching it improve, ever larger numbers of people will come to view this bit of pure Arabia that has somehow fallen within our territory. As it is, I am expecting shortly to find installed at the strategic point a notice-board, a fence with little gate, and a cool highwayman collecting dollars, halves, or quarters — "whatever the traffic will bear."

CHAPTER III

TREES AND TREE-LIKE GROWTHS

Flora's gifts to the desert — The palm — The two mesquits — Nature's great benefaction — Deep-rooted mesquits — Cicadas — A mesquit-clump camp — The Gambel quail — Beans for all — The tree that bears screws — The palo verde, green but leafless — Laburnum of the desert — A desert Goliath — The smoke-tree — A transformation — Complaint of a layman — The desert willow — The ironwood: a desert forest — The affectionate cat-claw — Desert mistletoe — A vegetable pirate, the Joshua tree — The ocotillo, epitome of the desert — A miracle of blossoming — The saguaro, giant of the cacti — An elf-owl hotel — Sunset and the saguaro

CONTRARY to the general notion, the desert is far from being neglected by Flora. Even in the matter of trees, she has denied to a few valuable and interesting kinds the territory they would have preferred, and has bestowed them on these unkind regions, where they are a first-class boon to the scanty animal life that shares their hardships. There is a good assortment of shrubs too; and of the smaller growths a surprisingly large number, though it is only in spring that most of these show themselves. For the rest of the year they exist only in embryo as seeds, or as a final minimum of brittle stems and shrivelled leafage, making no contrast in the universal drab, yet the hope and support of the forlorn cattle that stray "with melancholy steps and slow" about the parched and starving ranges.

Among the trees, the palm *Washingtonia filifera* claims first place (though I always feel that the name of tree hardly applies to those columnar shapes, so opposite to our thought of out-reaching branch, shady gallery, and spreading contour). But I have spoken of the palm at length in another chapter. And, after all, it is rather an incident of the desert than a characteristic, appearing only sporadically and as a rule about the margins of the territory, limited always to the rare spots that yield the needful conditions of moisture.

The principal desert tree is the mesquit. Of this there are two species, differing in size, mode of growth, and some other details, the most noticeable of which is the seeding. The larger, *Prosopis glandulosa*, bears a typical bean, the other, *Prosopis pubescens*, a unique seed-vessel exactly like a rather large screw. From this feature the latter tree takes the name of "screwbean," or *tornillo*, the Spanish word for screw.

The larger mesquit is the one great benefaction of Nature to her desert-dwellers. Were it only in the matter of shade, what songs should be raised to it by man, bird, and beast; and indeed are raised by sparrow, wren, linnet, and, to the best of his ability, by that arch black sprite, phainopepla, who thinks the topmost spray of a mesquit the cap of the universe! Reptile and insect revel in it too, for, as I write these pages under the shade of a mesquit (driven from my tent by a mid-morning March temperature of 108°), I am buzzed and bitten by gnats and flies of all degrees, cobwebbed by spiders, explored by serious beetles, and adopted by caterpillars as a happy idea: while nimble lizards scamper about sniping my tormentors. Every mesquit is a green caravanserai, and one that is patronized to the full.

These islands of shade are naturally the preferred spots for camping-places by desert travellers, and that they have been so from of old may be known by the presence near them of unusual quantities of the broken pottery that everywhere amazes one by tokens of the large populations that the desert once supported. In places, mesquit thickets may still be found that extend for miles, though near the railway great stretches have been cleared for cultivation, and the wood, which makes excellent fuel, is regularly sold in the towns and cities of the coast. The aboriginal passion for rabbit would itself render these thickets the pick of desert real estate to the Indian, for they are always alive with bouncing bunnies, easy targets for his arrows or throwing-clubs.

The mesquit is also evidence of water, though not necessarily of water near the surface, as in the case of the palm. Far down below the burning surface sands the great cable-like roots of the mesquit go searching for the beds of water-bearing gravel, and the plant that shows only a five-foot tangle of thorny scrub aboveground may have roots running to ten times that depth. As the sand is constantly heaped higher about the mesquit by the wind, the plant struggles to keep its head above the drift, and in places, as at Seven Palms, mile-long dunes have formed that show a mere fuzz of twigs aboveground while your feet may be tripped by the great cylindrical roots, as thick as your leg and almost as hard and rigid as iron, from which the sand has been blown away. In examining a small one of these roots, with a thickness of about two inches and looking like a smooth brown rope stretched taut, I noted that in a distance of twenty feet it showed no variation of diameter.

Besides its boons of game, fuel, shade, and possibly water, the mesquit yields food for man and beast and insect. The vivid young green of late February becomes tinged in March with clouds of fragrant yellow catkins. This is the bonanza of the thrifty desert bees: now or never they must re-stock those rows of empty golden honey-pots in the rocky cranny of the hillside, and they go to the work with all the proverbial ardor, plus the stimulus of needful haste. Later the mesquits form the great harborage for those most objectionable creatures the cicadas. All day the thickets ring with their nerveracking pipings, like the whizz of steam escaping under high pressure. I frankly hate these insects for their way of dashing out and squirting at one a spray of some vile secretion. I was puzzled to account for these disgusting anointings, which fell upon me even at night, until, camping under a big mesquit near Indio, I tracked the offenders down.

That camp, by the by, deserves description as illustrating the possibilities of growth of the mesquit. Other wayfarers, probably Indians or Mexicans, had used the place before me, and had spent no little labor on making it convenient. From the outside it was a dome-shaped, isolated clump, a hundred yards or so in circumference and perhaps fifteen feet in height. A sort of tunnel had been cut leading to the centre, which when reached revealed the fact that the whole clump was one enormous tree. The short butt, a yard or so in diameter, broke into several big recumbent branches which went rambling about on hands and knees, all crooks and elbows, and threw out a young forest of twigs and branchlets cantankerously thorny. Near the main stem there was ample space and head-room for camp quarters, and the friend who left his comfortable Pasadena bungalow to visit me there had no fault to find with the accommodation, though he had now and then with the temperature. It was pleasant at odd hours to listen to the conversations of a family of Gambel quail that shared our mesquit with us, pater's loud clear call, or quieter admonishment of Mrs. G., answered by absent-minded twitterings or headlong scamperings of the youngsters.

At this camp Kaweah had to be picketed outside, but in a similar mesquit clump, that furnished me quarters for a week a few miles farther on my way, a stable had been installed by some predecessor, with manger and room for two or three horses. There was ample space here also for an average family's camp requirements.

The mesquit yields excellent food for both man and beast. One authority says that the bean, of which husk and all are used, contains over fifty per cent of practicable food elements. The Indians nowadays do not call on it to the extent they did formerly, when the meal ground by the squaws from the beans of this plant was the staple of their diet, though they still use it freely: but horses and, needless to say, the omnivorous burros and the desert cattle rejoice at sight of a bean-hung mesquit. Many times, during expeditions that took us far out of range of orthodox fodder, the situation has been saved for Kaweah by our finding a mesquit or two, the twigs pendent with plump clusters and the ground whitened with the fallen fruit. I sometimes feared that dislocation of the neck would be his portion as I watched his giraffe-like manœuvres over the capture of some coy, high-hung *bonne bouche*. Nature did a kind turn to her deserving poor when she reserved the mesquit for the desert.

The screwbean is a more spindling tree, sparser of foliage, and content with poorer alkaline soils where the other mesquit seldom cares to dwell. It is equally good, perhaps even better, as a source of food, but has little to offer in the way of shade — a mere thin grayness that scarcely breaks the stroke of the sun. In the diary of that fine Borrovian character, Fray Francisco Hermenegildo Garcés, who was roaming these deserts, with the enthusiasm of an explorer as well as of a missionary, in the years just about the birthtime of this nation on the other side of the continent, one easily identifies the tornillo when he writes that he has found a tree that bears screws. Flora had one of her quaintest fancies when she fashioned these odd seed-vessels, which one finds sprinkled in tousled clusters all over the tree.

Next in size to claim attention is the palo verde, *Cercidium torreyanum*. To give the Spanish a literal translation, it would be the "green stick," or, more suavely, the "greenwood tree." It has no recognized

English name, and to speak of it as the greenwood tree raises a most incongruous association of ideas. Shades of Arden, what a difference! Yet the Spanish name, taken literally, is apt enough, for green the tree certainly is, vivid green and green all over: only one must banish all thought of whispering forest and woodsy lawn.

An odd thing is that this very green tree is a tree almost without leaves; at least, the leaves are so small, and so short-lived as well, as to cut little figure in the general effect. It is the skeleton of the tree — trunk, branches, branchlets, and twigs — that is green, a green vivid and smooth, though the butt of a very old palo verde may be roughened and blackened by age. Such scanty foliage as the tree puts forth in spring, in response to some old vernal urge still strong after ages of forced adaptation to desert conditions, falls by early summer, and leaves the airy, broom-like branches bare against the china blue of the sky. Often the branches are hung with great globes of the desert mistletoe (*Phoradendron*) so dense as to look like bee-swarms, adding to the remarkable appearance of the tree.

The palo verde, however, is a miracle for bloom. In mid-March it takes a tinge of yellow, and soon each twig becomes a jewelled chain, petals of whimsical gold set with chips of ruby for anthers. Its other Spanish name, *lluvia de oro*, shower of gold, then fits it well. For charm and profusion of bloom it is the desert's premier tree, and reminds me often of that glory of England's spring, the laburnum. Ah, those Thames-side gardens, spilling their over-

flow of lilac and laburnum over old rosy brick walls!
Those sea-washed Devon villages, each cottage
plot a bower of floral gold! Those steep lakeland
streets which I used to climb with you, lady of my
dedication, to the dark-firred Beacon, each garden
raining yellow largess upon its neighbor next below!
Excuse the lapse, good reader, and in return I will
wish that you may never know the sharpness of exile.

On the side of usefulness the palo verde has its
virtues as well. Its beans are grist for the pestle and
mortar of the Indian squaw; and though usually a
small tree, it is capable of growth to a size that
would furnish lodgment to man. There is a palo
verde near the mouth of Deep Cañon that I take to
be the Goliath of its tribe. The trunk at its narrow-
est aboveground is eight and a quarter feet in girth,
the largest limb five feet around, and the space covered by the tree has a circumference of seventy
yards. For the desert, that is a triumph of tree
growth. I do not know of another palo verde that
comes to half its size.

The smoke-tree, *Parosela spinosa*, may hardly be
called a tree, though sometimes tree-like in size of
stem. More common than the palo verde, it is always a strange and noticeable object. It, too, is
leafless, but it is wholly pale gray, a mass of prickly
interlaced twigs that at a distance has much the
look of a cloud of smoke. It is the characteristic
plant of the desert "washes" or water-courses. I
have often found the beds of these fugitive streams
filled for miles with this ghostly semblance of a river.
To see this phantom river come winding out, snake-

like, upon the plain from some red, mysterious
cañon brings nightmare thoughts of the grim genii,
Thirst and Famine, that might here have their
abode.

In early summer one may see this torrent turn
suddenly from gray to liveliest color. The smoke-
tree, like the palo verde, makes up for absence of
foliage by a huge burst of blossom. In this case it is
blue, the purest ultramarine, each tree a cloud of
small, pea-like flowers that as they shrivel and fall
collect in windrows like drifts of azure snow. (Another name for the tree is indigo bush, though the
true hue of the blossom is not indigo: yet another is
desert cedar, which is totally without point.) Some
day a painter will chance upon this sight, and at
danger of death by thirst will refuse to move from
the spot until he has fixed upon canvas the desert
at its highest color power. He had better, though, be
a painter unusually reckless of his reputation, for all
the world will swear he lies.

The smoke-tree gives me occasion to voice an old
grudge that I have long held against the botanical
tribe. Harmless, even kindly, as botanists in general
appear, how is it that they take delight in embitter-
ing the lives of laymen by their eternal juggling
with the names of genera and species? If they really
wish to discourage us poor "popular" chaps, all
right; let them say so and we can turn to something
lighter, say eugenics, or those frivolous things, conic
sections. For many a year the smoke-tree and its
relatives were known to all the world as of the
genus *Dalea*. To-day the puzzled amateur finds that

name tacked to a quite different class of plants, and only by chance recognizes his old acquaintance under the title of *Parosela*. And this is but one case in a long and grievous list. When I hear of convocations of botanists I smile and say, "This is no innocent convention. What are they up to now?"

Often found near the smoke-tree in the gravelly washes is the desert willow, *Chilopsis linearis*. It is not really a willow, and only slightly resembles that tree in its leafage and irregular shape. In size, however, this often becomes a genuine tree, and I have found specimens with trunks two feet thick and an area of thirty yards diameter or more. The notable feature of this tree also is its flower, which is a large, fragile, orchid-like blossom, white relieved with lavender and yellow, and very delicately scented. There is something childlike about it, a hint of dainty pinafores in the crinkled edges of the petals: altogether a rare, undesert-like bloom. In the withering summer heat of a torrent bed there is refreshment in meeting these airy blossoms with their fresh, cool look and gentle fragrance — a thought of violets and primroses in mossy woodland ways.

The desert willow blooms profusely and remains long in flower. The fruit is a long, narrow bean, which, on shedding its seeds, leaves the tree hung with silky gray pods that flutter in the wind like pennons on the lances of Indian warriors.

One true tree remains, the ironwood, *Olneya tesota*, called *arbol de fierro*, or *palo fierro* (alternative *hierro*) in Spanish, meaning iron-tree or ironwood. This is a sturdy, trim, well-branched growth reminding one of a well-shaped apple tree. The foliage is abundant, yielding welcome shade, and the wood is exceedingly hard and makes excellent fuel. Its dull-blue flowers are not specially attractive, and it bears beans that, so far as I know, are not eaten by man or beast, though I have seen my horse nibble the young leaves with a resigned air when sugary mesquit, humdrum galleta grass, and even that furniture-polish sort of stuff, burro-weed, have all left us in the lurch.

The ironwood has not a wide range, and one might travel the desert for a long time without meeting it. In the northeastern part of the Colorado Desert, not far from the river, there is a little-visited range of hills called the Ironwood Mountains, or sometimes the McCoys. On their southern outskirts I rode for hours through what, for the desert, might be called a forest of these trees, some of which had trunks more than two feet in diameter.

There is a widely distributed, straggling bush that at a cursory glance looks rather like an unthrifty mesquit. It is the cat-claw, *Acacia greggii*, an affectionate creature that grapples you to its soul with hooks of steel and loves to keep you there, taking a double hold for every claw you gently disengage. The leaf is mesquit-like, but smaller and finer, the blossom also similar, a fuzzy catkin, and the fruit a curious curly bean that dries into gouty-looking contortions. You will not go far on the desert without meeting the cat-claw, nor will you part without cursing it.

A feature of all desert trees, except the palm, is

the great quantity of mistletoe, *Phoradendron californicum*, they often carry. It is a common thing to see mesquits in which one half of the bulk of the tree is made up of dense masses of this parasite. It has no leaves, but in spring carries berries of a pretty coral color. Though classed by botanists as a "false" mistletoe, it has, I know, played the good old Christmas part with entire success.

In speaking of the ironwood as the last true tree of the desert, I must not overlook three other plants that in size may deserve the name — the tree-yucca or Joshua tree, the ocotillo or candlewood, and that giant of the cacti the saguaro. They are hardly to be thought of as trees, however, but rather as growths allied to trees, but wanting in almost all tree-like features.

The first is *Yucca arborescens*, of the tribe of that "Spanish bayonet" which is so common about the foothills of Southern California and so noticeable for its gigantic spike of cream-colored flowers. The Joshua tree (so named, it is said, by Mormon immigrants who, meeting these eccentric growths as they neared the end of their long march, hailed them as heralds of the promised land) is more typical of the Mojave than of the Colorado Desert, but it extends southward into the mountain ranges that divide the twin desolations.

It is a weird, menacing object, more like some conception of Poe's or Doré's than any work of wholesome Mother Nature. One can scarcely find a term of ugliness that is not apt for this plant. A misshapen pirate with belt, boots, hands, and teeth stuck full of daggers is as near as I can come to a human analogy. The wood is a harsh, rasping fibre; knife-blades, long, hard, and keen, fill the place of leaves; the flower is greenish white and ill-smelling; and the fruit a cluster of nubbly pods, bitter and useless. A landscape filled with Joshua trees has a nightmare effect even in broad daylight: at the witching hour it can be almost infernal.

The ocotillo, *Fouquieria splendens* (commonly but wrongly taken for a cactus), is to me the most striking and characteristic of the desert plants. In it are expressed the desert's intrinsic qualities, its haggardness and gray sterility, its cruelty of thorn and claw, its fierce, hot beauty. In a landscape crowded with these lean, sinuous shapes, as one finds them filling great tracts of the barrenest desert of the Colorado, one feels an added wildness and fascination. Of the cacti, a few are really beautiful, many interesting or quaint, others ugly but grotesque. The beauty of the ocotillo is the beauty of Cleopatra or Carmen, fierce and fatal. The scarlet streamer that comes in spring at the tip of every stem is like a darting dragon's tongue. A company of ocotillos writhing in a hurricane makes as eerie a sight as anything I know in the vegetable realm.

In shape the ocotillo is a sheaf of thin, whip-like canes from six or eight to twenty feet long, spreading more or less widely from a main stump near the ground. The canes are closely armed with curving thorns, which give the plant a cactus-like appearance. For nine or ten months of the year it stands gaunt, leafless, seemingly lifeless, and one strange feature is the suddenness with which, on the coming of the rains, it changes from dead, dry gray to living green. Small leaves appear as if by magic and feather the canes with vivid green. The canes themselves become a delicate lavender; even the thorns put on a half-inviting look and entice the unwary to closer acquaintance. Then a flower-spike starts from the tip of each cane, and bursts into a flame-like tongue a foot or so long, made up of scores of tubular scarlet and yellow blossoms.

I have been told that the flowers of the ocotillo are used as food by some of the desert Indians. I tried them once, but failed to find them attractive. But I had no recipe: perhaps they should be served with a tarantula sauce, or stewed with lizards' tails.

The giant cactus, *Cereus giganteus* (Spanish *saguaro*), is a common object of the Arizona deserts, but in California is only represented to the extent of a few individuals, probably not many over a hundred all told, that have gained a footing on the western bank of the Colorado. It, too, is an abnormal plant, but not an ugly one. Indeed, it is beautiful in an outlandish kind of way, but so far is it removed from all the shapes that we think of as trees that it might be a type of vegetation belonging to Mars or the moon.

Ordinarily the saguaro, for ten or fifteen feet of its height, is a single dark-green column, regularly ridged or fluted, and set with rosettes of spines. Then it sends out arms, one or very few, which stand up parallel with the main stem; or it may divide into a number of equal branchings, taking the form of a candelabrum. A mature saguaro may be fifty feet high or more, but the tallest specimen I found on the California side of the river was not over forty feet. It was an odd-shaped, untypical growth, with a few stumpy arms that looked as if they had been amputated.

In nearly every saguaro one finds a number of neat round holes, the entrances, originally, to woodpeckers' nests, but often used rent free by that quaint little goblin the elf owl, *Micropallas whitneyi*, the Tom Thumb of his tribe, hardly six inches high when full grown. My tallest saguaro must have had a score of these holes, a veritable hotel or skyscraper of owls. I was disappointed that I could not make camp beside it, but I think I can warrant any other traveller who may do so some pretty weird music for his lullaby.

The plant bears large waxy blossoms that grow directly on the stem and branches, and the fruit is a first-class luxury to the Indians.

When the red flood of sunset comes on those great plains and hill slopes, where no other object breaks the far expanse, while the ancient river moves silently on to the lonely gulf and the mysterious sea, and the traveller's steps halt under that old spell of evening, then the dark, upward-pointing finger of the saguaro gives an added solemnity to that impression of the vast, unchanging, and elemental which is the eternal note of the desert.

CHAPTER IV

THE SMALLER CACTI, SHRUBS, AND FLOWERS

The cacti, children of the desert — The *biznaga* or "nigger-head" — An emergency water-supply — The villainous cholla — A cactus that jumps — The Devil's Garden — A torturing imp — Deer-horn cactus and the cactus wren — Gorgeous blossoms — Beware of *basilaris* — Fish-hook cactus or *chilito* — The ubiquitous creosote-bush — Solitude and monotony — Arrowweed thickets — Protective shapes — Desert holly — The self-defensive agave — Indian confectionery — Baking mescal — A floral surprise, the desert lily — The encelia or incense-plant — Billows of bloom — An ambiguous color — The desert verbena — Rose-purple acres — A memorable spring flower show.

THE desert is the kingdom of the cacti, for the cacti are the special offspring of the desert. With ingenious pains Nature has wrought out this unique family, fitted to endure the very reverse of ordinary plant conditions. Their part is to hold the frontier that meets the Empire of Drought, and they are shaped and armed for the task. Since leaves yield too much to evaporation, spines and thorns are adopted. Rainfall being a matter of doubt, the cactus models itself on the canteen, and fills up to the limit when it gets the chance. And since a canteen is a temptation to thirsty tramps such as jack-rabbit and coyote, the spines are hooked, barbed, clawed, and made as generally troublesome as possible. Yet, it seems as if when the matter of blossoms came up, Nature's heart relented: she could not bring herself to fashion a forbidding flower.

After the giant saguaro, described in the previous

chapter, the barrel cactus, *Echinocactus cylindraceus* (*biznaga* or *viznaga* of the Mexicans) is the one that first claims notice. Here and there about the rocky hillsides and mesas stand these odd shapes, upright cylinders from two to six feet high. The surface is beautifully fluted and covered with a close network of spines three or four inches long, hard as ivory and sharp as needles, real works of art. On the top of the cylinder there comes in spring a circle of papery, rose-like, lemon-yellow flowers. They sprout directly from the cylinder, making a dainty pale gold coronet that seems strangely out of place on that preposterous tousled "nigger-head" (as the plant is sometimes called).

This portly vegetable is, as I suggested, really a reservoir of water. The interior is a sponge of water-holding tissue, protected from evaporation by the leathery skin. Desert men, of course, know all about this convenient arrangement, and draw upon it at need: and many a life forfeited to the thirst-demon would have escaped out of his hand if the doomed wretch had but known the secret. He is an unwise man, indeed, who dares that demon without the key to many of the desert's problems.

The process of tapping this source of water is simple enough. The top of the "barrel" is cut off; a depression is scooped in the pulp; the surrounding tissue is crushed by pounding with axe-helve or anything that will serve as a pestle; and then a clear liquid, rather flat in taste but quite drinkable, will gradually exude into the hollow that has been made in the pulp. Like Samson's conundrum, "Out of the eater came forth meat," one may say of the *biznaga*, "Out of the drinker came forth water."

Next, if not first in obtrusiveness, is the cholla (pronounced choy'a), *Opuntia bigelovii*. First it certainly is in villainous traits and in the ill-regard of every desert traveller. It is an ugly object three or four feet high, with stubby arms standing out like amputated stumps. The older parts are usually black with decay, the rest of a sickly greenish white, and the whole thing is covered with horrible barbed spines, uncountable in quantity and detestable in every regard. It has, moreover, a very vile habit of shedding its joints, and these roll by instinct into the places where they can most easily achieve their purpose, which is to stab the feet of horses and spike pedestrians through their boots, as they readily can do. Every one who has travelled with horses on the desert has had the job of ridding his animals of these devils, which in many places grow so thickly that to dodge them is out of the question. The Indians say that they jump at you: this sounds like an exaggeration, but upon my word I don't know. Often when I have felt sure that I passed clear of a certain cholla I found he had me after all.

I remember some years ago crossing the Devil's Garden, a great cactus thicket between the Whitewater Wash and Seven Palms. My companion and his Arizona cow-pony were both old desert habitués and past-masters in cactus, while my mount also hailed from the Arizona ranges, where cactus is "the daily round, the common task." Yet our combined sagacity came far short of keeping us out of trouble.

First one and then the other of us had to stop, kneel in the roasting sand (with the sun at somewhere about 140° Fahrenheit), and pull out one by one the long, barbed thorns from the feet and knees of the wincing animals. In these minor surgical operations we gradually lost sight of each other, and it was not until long after dark that we met again at our designated camp at Whitewater.

The cholla is the general enemy. In autumn, when the range is at its poorest, I have often seen cattle in horrible distress from a great lump of this fiendish plant that had got hooked on to their muzzles as they searched for browse. At every attempt to feed, the tormenting imp of course took a stronger hold. As one cannot come near these half-wild cattle of the ranges except by lassoing them, many an unlucky steer has died of starvation from sheer inability to pick up feed.

I could willingly devote a chapter to abusing the cholla. Enough, however, to add that the blossom is of a pale, unwholesome green, hardly noticeable; and that if the plant bears any helpful or even innocent part in the scheme of things on this planet, I should be glad to hear of it. I do, indeed, remember to have seen hornets in search of building-sites inspecting the cholla with evident approval, but that hardly counts for a virtue.

Prominent almost everywhere in the view is another cactus, often called, from its branching, antler-like habit, the deer-horn cactus (*Opuntia echinocarpa*). Unobservant people are apt to confuse this species with the last-named, and call it cholla. If one should do so, it would be proper to apologize. Without being a saint, one may object to being taken for a murderer. The deer-horn grows in spreading shape to a height of six feet or more, a maze of bristling ramifications that form the favorite nesting-place for one of the desert birds. Here the cactus wren builds and broods, as secure from snakes and other enemies as if she were housed in the interior of a hedgehog. I have once seen the nest of this bird in a true cholla; probably the device of some super-careful mother who had had unfortunate experience in speaking with the enemy at the gate.

The deer-horn bears a rather pretty flower of an uncommon brownish green or bronze hue, seen, I think, in this plant alone.

Less frequently met is a species much like *Echinocarpa*, but with stems and joints much thinner, and thorns fewer though not less aggressive. This is *Opuntia ramosissima*. It bears a small brown flower, a hue that Flora does not greatly love. But though she is no Quaker, variety is her breath of life, so even brown is adopted as a novelty.

The handsomest of all the cactus blossoms, to my mind, is that of *Cereus engelmanni*, which grows usually in company with the two foregoing species. The plant looks like a colony of a dozen or so spiny cucumbers, set up on end, generally under the shade of a creosote bush or in the lee of a boulder. I have no grudge against this fellow, who bites only if you strike him. The blossom is a most charming one, a sheeny, rose-like cup of superb purple or wine color, crowded with golden-anthered stamens and with a pistil breaking into soft green plumes that curl as daintily as a moth's antennæ. One who is on the desert in spring should on no account miss the sight of this exquisite flower.

Almost as handsome is the blossom of another common desert cactus, *Opuntia basilaris*. This is one of the flat-lobed or "pancake" species, and is similar in general habit to the common tuna, prickly pear, or Indian fig. The flower-buds sprout in a row from the edges of the lobes, and make a fine show with their cups of silky cerise. This plant, like the tuna, is valuable to the Indians, who achieve a special delicacy by cooking the young buds in a pit heated with hot stones.

But let the unwary beware; there is more in the *basilaris* than meets the eye. The lobes have a downy, innocent look, spines apparently absent. "Trust her not, she is fooling thee." The velvety surface is covered with myriads of infinitely fine prickles that come off at the lightest touch and form a sort of plush on the rash person's skin, almost invisible but most aggravating to the touch. The removing of them, though a fine exercise in patience, is one of the most melancholy occupations that I know.

All the foregoing bear cup-shaped, papery blooms of what may be called the usual cactus character. There is a quaint little cactus, not very common, *Mamillaria tetrancistrus*, usually only two or three inches high, that has an entirely different flower. It is claret-color, fleshy, and vase-shaped, and bears for fruit a bright coral-red vessel like a tiny *chile*,

from which it gets its Mexican name of *chilito*.
I have heard it called "strawberry" cactus, a puzzling misnomer. "Fish-hook" is another and better
name, arising from the inch-long thorns, curving
sharply at the tip; and "pin-cushion" has an evident bearing on the little green cushion stuck full of
shining prickles. But as is so often the case, the
Spanish word is the most apt. Do the Mexicans love
flowers more than we? Perhaps they understand
them better, if only because they look at them with
more simplicity.

There is another species of *Mamillaria*, almost
identical in appearance with the foregoing except
that its flowers are white, rather like the tube-
rose.

Leaving now the thorny subject of the cacti, the
ruling plant and the one of widest distribution over
our southern deserts is the creosote bush, *Larrea
glandulosa*. It is a handsome bush, often eight or ten
feet high, airy and spreading, with small leaves of
brilliant varnished green which give it a pleasing
effect in the general scheme of gray. From the tarry
feeling and smell of the foliage it gets its common
name of "greasewood," or among the Mexicans and
Indians, *hediondía*, meaning "bad-smelling," though
the peculiar odor is not to me disagreeable. In spring
the plant is set profusely with starry yellow flowers,
which mature into little woolly globes as pretty as
the blossoms. Over wide tracts of desert the creosote is the sole object that breaks the cheerless
expanse, and I often felt that the sense of solitude,
vastness, and monotony, was deepened by the

presence of this plant, growing for league on league almost identical in size and spacing, now stirred to a momentary sigh by the fitful wind, then, in a moment, motionless as death in the trance-like stillness of the heat.

A noticeable plant about water-holes and oases is the arrowweed, *Pluchea sericea*. It wears the desert's regular livery of gray, and forms dense thickets, six or eight feet high, through which it is not easy to push one's way. The cane-like stems grow straight and stiff from the ground, needing only smoothing, by rubbing on a grooved rock, to make excellent shafts for the light Indian arrows. The feathery leaves have an acrid smell, always associated in my mind with the thought of jaded arrivals at long-expected camping-places, and eager draughts of tepid, unsatisfying water. The blossom is a fuzzy, dingy, pink affair, appropriate to the unwholesome alkaline soils which the plant seems to prefer.

The general grayness of desert vegetation is largely due to one class of plants, the genus *Atriplex*, which with its many species makes up a large proportion of the total growth. Wide areas of low-lying desert are dotted with great hummocks of quail bush, *A. lentiformis*, curious in their perfect, dome-like form and easily mistaken at a little distance for drifts of sand. This shape, typical of the desert growths, no doubt represents an effort at self-protection from the general persecutor the sun. The canny tortoise seems to have set the model with his make-what-you-can-of-that contour; and there really is not much to be made of it, either by wind, sun, or sand-storm. I often wished that I had been cast in a similar mould.

Another *Atriplex*, of the species *canescens*, is noticeable for the bright-green tassels of its seed-vessels, of a papery texture and peculiar shape for which it has been given the common name of "shadscale." Since it fruits in the late summer, when the desert is doubly deserted, its unique feature is not generally known.

One more relation of the quail bush that is worth noting is the little prickly leafed *A. hymenelytra*. The young foliage, of palest gray with rose or lilac shell tints, whitens under the summer sun to almost a look of ivory. At Christmastide it is sold in the coast cities as "desert holly," sometimes with red berries of other plants artfully attached to make it better fill the part. The leaves are really holly-like in shape, but after all a poor substitute for the royal green ilex without which Christmas is only half a festival.

Often found growing with the ocotillo, which was described in the previous chapter, is the *Agave deserti*. This is a relative of the century plant of parks and gardens, and is almost identical with the indispensable *maguey* of Mexico. Again we have the desert's eternal note of gray, in the huge bayonet-pointed leaves, from the midst of which, when the plant is from twelve to twenty years old, a single straight flowering-stalk shoots up to a height of eight or ten feet, breaking into crowded blossoms of honey-dripping yellow. Once having bloomed, the plant dies.

Like the ocotillo, the agave makes a striking figure in many a desert landscape. On scarred, sun-smitten hillsides and down league-long stony *bajadas*, the earth bristles with their blue-white daggers in impenetrable *chevaux-de-frise*, stuck here and there with leaning poles, relics of former years' flowering. Flora is again on the defensive, for without those pikes and lances she could never hold her own against the cattle, bighorn, and deer that covet the succulent flower-stems, and whose tracks you find in spring all about these forbidden preserves.

From time immemorial the agave has supplied the desert Indians with one of their few luxuries, one, moreover, that is both food and confectionery. Now that every country store offers easy satisfaction to stomach and sweet tooth, this old source of supply has fallen into neglect; but now and then the Indian, answering the call of the wild, still goes afield to bake mescal. One recent spring I was able to join a friendly Volcan Indian who was bound on this time-honored function. Briefly, this is the manner of it:

Arrived at the mescal ground, which was on the southern desert overlooking the Borego Valley region, our first work was to search for plants with flower-stalks in the right stage of growth. The deer and wild-sheep had been before us, and it took an hour or two to secure a dozen young and tender shoots that Antonio pronounced *bueno*. With his axe he cut deep into the core of the plant, at the base of the great asparagus-like stalk. The shoot was cut out, its top struck off, and the leaves trimmed away, leaving a clean butt fifteen inches or so long, eight or ten thick, and weighing several pounds.

Next a pit was dug, two or three feet deep and somewhat more in diameter. This was lined, bottom and sides, with flat slabs of rock, and a loose coping was laid also about the edge. On this coping the agave butts were laid. A good bonfire was built over the pit, and allowed to burn for twenty minutes or so, the embers falling into the pit and covering the bottom thickly. Then the butts, already charred by the fire, were tumbled into the pit, and with them the heated coping stones and all the still-glowing embers. Earth was banked up over all, and the pit was left for the day. The next afternoon we resurrected our booty after some thirty hours' baking. The charred lumps had much the appearance of elephants' feet. Cutting away the blackened skin we arrived at a golden brown mass, as sweet as molasses and with a flavor that I first found peculiar, then interesting, finally seductive.

In a cranny of the rocks, Antonio's quick eyes had sighted a relic of mescal-bakings of old — a long, straight pole of the heavy wood of the mountain mahogany, one end shaped to a chisel-like edge. It was, Antonio said, a *peh-wee'*, the tool used for cutting out *a-moosh'* (mescal) by his people of bygone days, before the white man and his wonderful things of iron and steel had come within their ken. It had an uncouth look that suggested the weapons of cave-dwellers, and I wondered whether the formidable old tool might not have seen wilder service in its day than just the peaceable reaping of agaves.

I early learned that the desert is full of floral surprises, but I was not prepared to find among them a snowy, virginal lily. Down on the sun-seared flats about the upper end of the Salton Sea I came upon the wonderful *Hesperocallis undulatus*, a flower that might be looked for in some carefully warmed and watered greenhouse, but never in these arid spaces of sand. It was mid-April, near the end of the plant's flowering season, and only a few of them were left in bloom. I was told that a week earlier they had stood in thousands all over the gray levels that stretch from the edge of the bitter sea back to the ochre mountains. Tall and slender, they carried their delicate large bells, three or four to a cluster, knee-high above the mat of wavy, ribbon-like leaves. One rubs one's eyes at meeting these Easter-lily-like flowers in this "dry and thirsty land where no water is."

In the same region, but scattered over a wider territory, is found another choice flower, one of the *Mentzelias*. Its blossom is creamy white, of the most satiny sheen of any flower I know, each petal closely pencilled with vermilion in very fine parallel lines. The foliage, however, is harsh and scaly, rather a drawback to the beauty of the plant, whereas the lily is wholly gentle and Madonna-like.

I must pay tribute also to the great white evening primrose, *Œnothera trichocalyx*, which on moonlight nights throws the glamour of fairydom over the dry, commonplace sands. The huge four-inch blossoms shine up like little moons; but beware how you stoop to handle them, for the plants are a favorite harborage for the sidewinder, that wicked little horned rattlesnake that goes sideways and bites without "ringing the bell."

I have not yet spoken of the plant that makes the greatest show of all about the borders of the desert, where it covers dark cañon walls and the lower slopes of mountains with a stipple of gray that changes in spring to gold. This is *Encelia farinosa*, a stiff bush up to two feet high, growing in the favorite hemispherical shape of desert shrubs, with pale gray leaves and brittle twigs that exude a yellow resin. This resin, it is said, has been used, under necessity, in place of orthodox incense, so that Mexicans and Indians call the plant "*yerba de incienso.*" The flowers are yellow stars, profuse and beautiful, and are borne on long slender stems that project evenly several inches beyond the outline of the bush, which then is like a big gray pincushion stuck full of yellow floral hatpins. The plant is very prolific, and, whether in flower or not, is a noticeable feature in any landscape in which it finds a place. Another species, *E. californica*, with dark-green leaves, is found oftener on the levels than on hillsides.

The mention of the encelias brings to mind spring days a year or two ago that I spent in Deep Cañon, one of the principal cañons of the northwestern part of the desert. The winter had been one of unusually heavy rains, and every desert plant was doing honor to the rare event. It is hopeless to attempt to give the reader any true impression of the floral outpouring that year as it was revealed to me in Deep Cañon. To put it in one weak figure of speech, it was a torrent of floral color, billows of red, yellow, and blue, that filled the long cañon from side to side; the enclosing walls, for hundreds of feet up, all painted to one hue of yellow by uncountable myriads of encelia blossoms. To name all the plants that entered into the spring show would be impossible, but the three plants that were most overpowering in volume were the encelia, the beloperone, and the phacelia, yellow, red, and blue respectively. The cañon was a jungle of these plants, the bushes of beloperone especially wonderful, many of them six feet high and eight or ten feet long, wholly covered with the crimson blossoms. Humming-birds were whirring about, nonplussed like myself at the sight (the plant is known as *flor de chuparosa*, humming-bird flower, in Mexico, I am told), and honey-loving insects of every degree joined in keeping the air in a conglomerate hum.

The other plant I named, the phacelia, or so-called wild heliotrope, grew in loose tangles all about the sturdier encelias and beloperones, climbing as high as their support allowed and encircling their yellow or crimson in wreaths of delicate blue.

I must not overlook, either, that glory of desert cañons in late spring, the flame-colored wild hollyhock, *Sphœralcea ambigua*. I call it flame-colored, but it is not that, and everybody whom I have asked to name the color has either named it differently or politely declined to try. Along the base of rocky walls you find bushes of the plant, with pale gray-green leaves and superb sprays of blossom which you may call pale vermilion, or apricot, or brick red, or flame, without being correct in any of the terms.

In the neighborhood of Palm Springs and in Deep Cañon I have seen it at its best, but every one who sees it in a good season will agree that it is a splendid, strange, and wonderful flower.

One other notable flower must be mentioned, the so-called desert verbena, *Abronia aurita*. This, like all desert plants, varies greatly in its show of blossom according to rainfall and other conditions; but when the season is propitious the verbenas make a never-to-be-forgotten impression. The rosettes of blossom, of a color between pink and purple, are crowded together in solid acres, almost miles, of bloom, so closely as to be crushed at every step. The gentian meadows of the Sierra and the golden poppy carpets of our few yet unploughed foothills are matched and outdone by these rosy purple verbena plains of the desert. My little sleeping-tent, six feet by three, pitched where the ground was freest of blossoms, enclosed scores of the clusters, and the scent within was like that of an orchid house.

It would be impossible to give here even a brief reference to all the desert growths that are interesting for their uses, strange in their characteristics, or beautiful in their flowering: for instance, the odd sandpaper plant, *Petalonyx thurberi*, whose name indicates its peculiarity to the touch; the dye weed, *Parosela emoryi*, that announces itself too late by a deep yellow stain on your hands or clothing; and a great number that the Indians value for medicinal or other purposes. My notebook shows over a hundred plants that I found remarkable. Some of them will be spoken of in the chapter on Indian lore.

From the bladder-pod of February to the lowly but lovely navarretia that in midsummer tints wide spaces with its delicate harebell blue, there is an unbroken flow of color. Any one who may find himself on the desert in spring, especially if it be a spring following a winter of good rainfall (as rainfall goes on the desert) may count on an experience of wild flowers that, if he is a stranger, will yield him a memorable and surprising impression.[1]

[1] In an Appendix are given brief descriptions of other desert plants, by which many, at least, of them may be identified.

CHAPTER V

SOME DESERT INDIAN LORE

Doubtfulness of Indian lore — The Tahquitz demon: his haunt —
The Pleiades legend — *Toluache* and its properties — The raven
again ill-omened — Indian word-building — Cahuilla fire-makers
— A desert Indian views the sea — Uses of sundry plants — Coyote
tobacco — Bows, arrows, throwing-clubs, baskets — Ever-useful
cacti and yuccas — Mesquit and *chia* — The hunter's instinct —
Fruits, wild and cultivated — Indian baskets and pottery, passing
arts — Medicines and other things — All necessities supplied.

IN this chapter I pass on to the reader some items
of information that I have gathered, in some instances directly, in others at second-hand, of the
beliefs and practices of the desert Indians, especially
with regard to the uses of certain plants. The topic
is a large one, and cannot here be more than touched
upon. Even so, much of what follows cannot be
taken as trustworthy. Every one who has attempted
to delve into affairs ethnological, even if he be fitted
for the task by study and training, knows the hopelessness of efforts to clear up the doubts and contra-
dictions that arise at every step. Hence these scraps
of supposed fact or belief are offered more for the
passing interest or amusement of the reader than as
reliable fragments of knowledge. The only items
not subject to this qualification are those referring
to the medical qualities of plants, in so far as they
may have been proved and accepted by authorities.

Of Tahquitz, or Tahkoosh, the bad spirit of the
Cahuillas, an Indian friend tells me that his visible
manifestation is as a meteor: not, however, any

ordinary shooting-star, but such as carry a train of sparks. If an explosion is heard (the sound of the meteor striking), it is said that Tahquitz has caught a victim: otherwise he is supposed to have failed in his attempt. The Tahquitz meteor seen in daytime is called Tahm-ya-su'-wet. It also tries to catch the spirits of men. There is a certain rock on Palomar Mountain, many miles to the south of San Jacinto Mountain (where Tahquitz has his home), to which this methodical demon is said to carry his prey, there to pound the flesh and prepare it for his maw. (My criticism that spirits have no flesh was thought irrelevant. "I tell you what *we* say," was the take-it-or-leave-it reply.) The Diegueño Indians — that is, those formerly tributary to the Mission of San Diego — recognize the same evil spirit, having his haunt on the same mountain at a spot they call Awik' Kai-yai', but they name him Chowk.[1] The curious rumblings sometimes heard to proceed from this mountain, and which I have noticed myself, are, of course, attributed to Tahquitz's operations.

A Diegueño Indian with whom I camped, pointing one night to the Pleiades, said, "We call them *Siete Cabrillas*" (seven buzzards). He went on to explain that when the First People — that is, the original inhabitants of the earth — were seeking to escape from death, they were taken up into the sky and became the stars. There were seven sisters, with one of whom Coyote (who figures largely in Western

[1] It is seldom one finds anything like agreement on any point of belief between the various tribes, or even between villages of the same tribe. The remarkable diversities of language that occur among these little tribal divisions make another source of confusion.

Indian mythology) was in love. The sisters climbed
up by a rope, and the love-lorn Coyote, catching the
end of the rope, was drawn up after them. But the
sisters, once safe, cut the rope behind them and he
fell; but not back to earth, for, "See," said Antonio,
pointing to Aldebaran, "there he go. All the time he
try catch that girl, but he never catch her yet."

The creosote bush, *Larrea glandulosa* (*at-a-qual-
sa'-na*), produces scantily a red, scale-like gum which
is considered very valuable. It is used for repairing
ollas, attaching arrow-heads to shafts, and also as a
medicine for the throat. Of this gum the barrel was
made in which the semi-divine hero of the Pápagos
(a southern desert tribe) was saved from death in
the great flood. The creosote bush itself is used
medicinally, a strong decoction of the twigs and
leaves, taken internally, being thought excellent for
maladies of the throat and chest and of the stomach.

The virtues and vices of the datura, a common,
rank plant very similar to the well-known jimson-
weed, with large trumpet-shaped, white or lilac-
tinted, sickly-sweet flowers which open at night, are
well known to the Indian. They call the plant *tolu-
ache* (to-loo-ah'-che) and put its narcotic properties
to use in connection with certain of their social and
religious ceremonies. It is believed to confer clair-
voyance, so that by its use one may recover lost
articles; though it is capable of more difficult feats.
For instance, it was reported to me of a certain blind
Indian of my acquaintance, who was formerly a
noted gambler, that he had lost his sight through
too frequent use of *toluache*, by means of which he

used to read the faces of his opponent's cards. The pounded leaves, applied hot as a poultice, are said to be effective for relieving pain, however acute, "but you must not eat hard" (that is, heavy or indigestible) "food soon before, or it will kill you," said Lugardio. As a remedy for saddle-galls it is reputed to be sovereign, as is also a powder of the mistletoe of the desert juniper, or of the root of the common wild gourd, or *calabazilla*, mixed with sugar.

The raven, or carrion-crow, eminent for sagacity since Noah's day, and made half supernatural by Poe, is a bird of omen to the Indian also. A certain part of Santa Rosa Mountain (Wa-hut-now'-ha) is known, in Spanish, as *Casa de Cuerva*, raven's house, or in Indian, *Ahl-wah-tem-hem'-ke*, house of many ravens, and is held in superstitious regard. Rock-crystals are believed to be missiles which the raven has cast at men with evil intent. I have noticed that any piece of glittering rock is apt to be considered "bad medicine," and such are always part of the stock in trade of the *pohl* or medicine-man (Spanish, *hechicero*).

It is natural that the two great contiguous mountains, San Gorgonio and San Jacinto, should be thought to be brothers. Their names are Kwaid'-a-kaich and Ai'-ya-kaich, respectively, the former being looked upon as the elder.

It is a pretty idea that is embodied in the use of the Spanish word *ojo*, meaning eye, for a pool or spring of water (with *ojito* for diminutive). The Cahuillas have the same poetic thought in their word *pal-he'-push*, for a pool. In the word or phrase applied to their ancient wells, now non-existent, to which one descended by steps cut in the earth, we have an example of natural language-building. The Cahuilla word for a water-jar (Spanish, *olla*) is *ka'-wo-mal*, and that for earth or ground, *te'-mal*. Hence the well was *te'-ma-ka'-wo-mal*, or earth-*olla*, neatly enough.

Making fire by friction of dry sticks is an art not often practised in these days, but two Palm Springs Indians with whom I once camped were experts at the game. Two pieces of dry palm-fruit stem were the tools, one an inch or so broad, length immaterial, the other less than half as thick, about a foot long, and perfectly straight. A few dead leaves were placed in a little heap: the larger stick was laid beside them and held in place by one of the men, a hollow having first been made in the surface of the wood, with a little groove leading from it to the leaves. Then the smaller stick, trimmed to a blunt point, was put to the hollow, and rapidly revolved by rolling between the open hands of the other Indian. His hands moved down as he rolled, returning again and again to the top. The friction sent a fine stream of wood powder down the groove upon the leaves. In less than two minutes smoke showed at the point of friction, then sparks began to fall on the tinder, and finally a flame was started by blowing. Less than three minutes sufficed for the operation. It was hard work while it lasted, for the fire was endangered by the perspiration caused in kindling it.

An Indian woman, one whose industry, dignity, and general high character I admire, when on her first trip "inside," was taken by friends of hers and mine to see the ocean. The place chosen was a seaside resort near Los Angeles, one that aspires, I believe, to the proud title of the Coney Island of California. On coming in view of the sea she was deeply excited, though self-possessed. The car was stopped so that she might gaze her fill. Her childlike wonder and murmured words of awe were a study in natural emotion. Approaching the water's edge she was a little reluctant at the boom and wash of the surf. Then she stood quiet and intent, as if striving to grasp the hitherto unimaginable fact of such an infinity of water. Her companions made no unwise attempt to overwhelm her with statements of the real vastness of the ocean. When at length they turned to leave the beach she still stood enthralled: then knelt by the margin and tasted the water, beckoning to it, and speaking to herself, or to it, in the Indian tongue. It was hard for her to turn away. Again and again she stopped to gaze; and when they came among the side-shows and switchbacks she had no eyes for these irrelevancies, but at every opportunity she turned afresh to the great simple marvel of the sea. It was to that, not to Fat Ladies or Pink-Eyed Cannibals, that the "uncultured" Indian nature reacted.

The leaves of the quail-bush, *Atriplex lentiformis*, whose hemispherical gray hummocks are almost the sole feature of the monotonous silt flats, are used for soap, and the seeds are boiled for food. The twigs and leaves of the *Suæda*, which inhabits the same localities, besides being boiled and eaten, yield a black stain that is used for dyeing the material for baskets. A more sophisticated use for the plant is that of a hair-dye, for which purpose it is mixed with wet clay and plastered on the head, where it is left until dry.

The common *Isocoma acradenia* (*mah'-cha-wal*) is a standard remedy for cold and sore throat, and is used by pouring boiling water on the bruised leaves and inhaling the steam. The leaves after being so used may be applied as a poultice on the forehead. It may be noted that the genus *Isocoma* is closely akin to another, namely, *Solidago*, whose etymology tells the curative properties of the genus.

An odd-looking, not uncommon plant, in appearance like a mass of stiff green straws, is *Ephedra californica*, or desert tea. A decoction of the twigs is of well-recognized benefit in stomach and kidney complaints. Indians, Mexicans, and whites alike are firm believers in its efficacy. It is occasionally found in drug-stores.

For tobacco the desert Indians had *Nicotiana attenuata*. It is a true member of the tobacco family, though prospectors, jealous for the honor of Navy plug or Black-Jack, name it "coyote tobacco" in contempt. It was used both for smoking and chewing. The dried juice of a milkweed, and the gum of one species of oak and of the incense-bush, *Encelia farinosa*, supplied the primitive chewing gum. Thus it may be proudly claimed that the great American habit is truly national, even aboriginal. It was thought *comme il faut* to chew flowers of the poppy (*Eschscholtzia*) with one's gum, a touch of senti-

ment not more misplaced than some that the world
of fashion can show. Tobacco pipes were made of
clay, but were usually stemless, which suggests that
the smoker took his whiff lying down — perhaps
an excuse for enhancing the luxury.

Bows were made of the screwbean mesquit, *Prosopis pubescens*, or of willow, and light hunting arrows of arrowweed, *Pluchea sericea*, or of carrizo,
Phragmites communis, with points of mesquit hardened by fire. The carrizo also supplied a fibre for
bow-strings. War-arrows, of course, were more formidable, armed with barbed points of bone or obsidian that were of excellent craftsmanship. I have
seen such arrow-points several inches long and as
finely wrought as a piece of jewellery. For clubs
used in hunting rabbits or birds the wood of the
mountain chamiso, *Adenostoma sparsifolia*, was preferred.

The large storage baskets for holding the family
stock of acorns, piñon-nuts, and so forth, are usually
made of willow withes (sometimes of a species of
arrowweed), often in ingenious shapes. They are
called *may'-a-nut-em* (the syllable *em* is the mark of
the plural).

The cacti, from tiny *Mamillaria* to giant saguaro,
almost all yield food to the Indian, and many of
them serve other purposes as well. Water in quantity sufficient to sustain life may be taken from the
great barrel cactus or "nigger-head," *Echinocactus
cylindraceus*, and the saguaro, *Cereus giganteus*. The
former, hollowed out, has been known to be used
as a cooking-vessel, by means of dropping heated

stones into the food which has been placed in it. The fruit of another kind serves as a hair-brush. My fire-making friends brought a new vegetable to my notice, in the shape of the flower-buds of the barrel cactus (*ko'-pash-em*, they called them). They grow in a circle at the top of the plant, and we had no difficulty in gathering enough for a meal. When boiled they taste midway between Brussels sprouts and chestnuts, a very satisfactory dish.

In another chapter I spoke of the agave. All its relatives, the yuccas, are plants of many uses to the Indians. One still finds old men and women wearing sandals of yucca-fibre, and excellent saddle-blankets are made from it. The root of one species, *Yucca mohavensis*, makes very fair soap, and its seeds are roasted for food. Of another species, *Y. whipplei* (the well-known "Spanish bayonet," or *quijote*), both fruit and flowers are eaten. So also are the scarlet blossoms of the ocotillo, and the yellow flowers of the agave; the latter, probably, for the sake of their honey, which is very plentiful, but somewhat bitter. The ocotillo, by the by, when not in sap, makes a capital torch, burning with a white, steady light as if there were some waxy ingredient.

For food purposes, the two kinds of mesquit and the *chia* sages, *Salvia columbariæ* and *S. carduacea*, were the great stand-by of the desert Indians, together with acorns and piñon-nuts from the surrounding mountains. Comparatively little use is made nowadays of these wild resources, but one may still chance to see some old housewifely crone seated on the ground and embracing with outstretched legs the wooden mortar in which she pounds out the family flour; or creeping about among the brush, beating with bat of palm-fibre the *chia* seeds into her bowl-basket: a basket that she wove, perhaps, threescore years ago, while her Hiawatha was stalking antelope or wild-sheep, and into which she may have woven more of legend and romance than wise men of the Smithsonian would easily unravel.

The hunter's instinct is strong in the men still. The other day I met old Tolomeo, patriarch of his *rancheria*, ambling homewards on his wall-eyed pony with rifle and half-a-dozen jack-rabbits at his pommel. Tolomeo is old, very old, but the jack that gives the slip to the old *capitan* must be endowed with more than the supernatural speed of most jacks, and Lugardio, just home from prosaic prune-picking in the mountain orchards, finding that my plans did not admit of an autumn hunting trip, remarked with a sigh, "Then I guess I don't get a buck this year again. Two years now I don't get me a deer. '*Sta muy malo*."

The nourishing properties of *chia* seed should be better known. It is said that a handful or two of them, roasted and ground, will sustain a man through a day of hard exertion, such as continuous running. Mixed with flour it becomes the famous *pinole* of the Mexicans, the staff of life of the common people. It is believed to have stomachic as well as nutritive value. The mesquit bean is a good second: analysis of the meal has shown it to contain over fifty per cent of food elements, largely sugar.

The beans of the palo verde, and even of the cat-claw, though not so good, were formerly pressed into service.

The curious martynia, with its great curved seed-vessels and claws like spring steel, was not over-looked. A use was found for it in basket-making, and it also served for riveting broken pottery. Holes were bored in the pieces to be joined, and the tough hooks, inserted in them, gripped the parts together. The seeds were chewed by Indian boys, who relished their sweet taste.

Many uses were found for the palm. Its fibres were woven into baskets, though these were not of the finest grade, and brushes were also made from them. The broad fronds were excellent as thatch for houses, and strips from them made material for plaiting where close texture was not needed. The leaf-stems were handy flails for threshing seeds, and the fruit, which is small and hard, but with sweet, date-like flavor, when ground entered into the com-position of the all-embracing *atole*.

The sweet tooth is well developed among our des-ert Indians, and Nature has provided for it by fur-nishing many of the cacti with fruits that are sweet and healthful. The flat-lobed *Opuntias* yield the prickly-pear, or tuna, sometimes called Indian fig. The little *Mamillaria* bears a small, red, pleasant-tasting fruit: even the hateful cholla has a fruit that is said to be agreeable, though I refuse to believe it. The saguaro is held in highest regard by the tribes that inhabit its range, for the lusciousness of its fruit and for its many other uses, included in these being the furnishing of an intoxicating drink little less atrocious than the mescal from across the line. According to Mr. Lumholtz, the Pápagos date their year from the commencement of the saguaro harvest, which occurs about the middle of our year.

In many desert cañons the so-called wild apricot, *Prunus eriogyna*, is plentiful and bears good crops of small sweet berries. Prime luxury of all, however, is *a-moosh'* (a Diegueño word), which is secured by baking the heart of the agave, as I have described in another chapter. But these natural dainties are coming to be little prized now that sweets of greater charm, because *americano*, are offered in paper bags or lace-frilled boxes at the store.

On the Reservation at Palm Springs there are a number of magnificent fig trees, descendants of the old historic figs of San Gabriel Mission. One that I measured showed a circumference of over nine feet. These furnish an abundance of delicious fruit, the surplus of which the Indians are not slow at turning into money, finding a demand for it in Los Angeles, where it brings high prices, as it comes early into market. Old Marcos is the proud owner also of a few fine date-palms, real Deglet Nur aristocrats imported many years ago from Algeria and planted here by the Department of Agriculture to test their adaptability to our climate. No wonder if the tunas from his great cactus hedge, full twelve feet high, are less prized than of old.

The Indian who panted for cooling drinks "when heated in the chase" was not condemned to water alone. A handful of crushed beans of the mesquit, or the berries of the sumac, *Rhus ovata*, or, when obtainable, those of the manzanita (*Arctostaphylos*) of the upper cañons, added to the water in the *olla*, gave it a refreshing flavor. For society occasions a "pink tea" effect could be obtained by serving a decoction of ocotillo flowers.

The vogue for Indian baskets that has arisen in late years, quite justified by their beauty of shape and design and their admirable workmanship, will help to keep alive for a time this ancient and honorable craft. Many of the older women are wonderfully adept, but it is rare to find a young one who has learned the art; and there is, besides, a tendency towards discarding the old traditional designs in favor of wall-paper patterns or crude attempts at realism. The woman whose introduction to the ocean I described above is one of the best basket-makers I know, and I was pleased lately to find her giving her little niece, eight or ten years old, a first lesson in basketry. In even a small basket of fine weave there may be ten thousand or more "stitches," so it was not surprising that little Conchita was not enthusiastic. It was remarkable to meet recently an Indian woman of certainly over eighty years who had taught herself the craft in the last few years, and whose baskets are marvels in design, color, and texture.

Pottery-making is now seldom practised among these desert Indians. With the necessity for hand-made utensils the art has almost ceased. I found pottery still being made recently at San Ysidro, a mountain village of the Cahuillas, and at Rincon, a

Luiseño *ranchería*. The shapes were good, but the workmanship clumsy or careless. In graceful outline and delicate construction, the older specimens one finds are admirable. The old *ollas* were sometimes decorated, though seldom elaborately. In view of the fragility of the vessels it is not to be expected that great pains should have been spent over ornament. The ground about the sites of old villages is littered with an astonishing amount of pottery débris, and the traveller reflects with awe upon the centuries of spanking to which these countless tokens of youthful misadventure solemnly bear witness.

Of medicines that were resorted to by the Indians in olden days there were too many to be more than briefly touched upon here. Some have already been noticed. To name a few others that were most in vogue:

The gum of the incense-bush, *Encelia farinosa*, was heated and applied for pain in the chest, whence the plant was known as *yerba del vaso*. The twigs of the chamiso of the desert mountains, *Adenostoma sparsifolia* (*yerba del pasmo*), furnished an emetic. A famous remedy, almost a cure-all, was the *yerba santa* (*Eriodictyon*). The wild buckwheat, *Eriogonum fasciculatum*, yielded an eye-wash and alleviated pain in head or stomach; and an infusion of the leaves of the sumac, *Rhus ovata*, gave relief in case of colds. Another herb of renown was the *yerba mansa* (*Anemopsis californica*), found in damp places and thought excellent in sundry complaints. The herbal remedies were supplemented by the curative virtues of the thermal springs and by the very effective *temescal* or sweat-house, prototype of our Turkish bath.

Cord for fish-lines, snares, slings, and nets was procured from several plants. The agave and yucca were the principal sources, but a superior fibre was taken from one of the milkweeds, *Asclepias eriocarpa*. Brushes came from the ever-useful agave. Glue was at hand on the mesquit, or was ingeniously prepared from other plants. A sort of coffee was made from the roasted nuts of the *Simmondsia*. Paints of various colors were taken from the earth, and splendid dyes were obtained from sundry herbs. In short, there were few, if any, needs of a natural life in a mild climate that these people — whom the early whites, in conscious superiority of whiskey and six-shooter, named "Diggers" in contempt — had not found the means of supplying. Many more pages could be filled with the list of their discoveries and appliances, for those I have named are but examples drawn at random from an astonishing number.

CHAPTER VI

A DESERT RIDE: PALM SPRINGS TO SEVEN PALMS

A circuit of the desert begun — My burro Mesquit — And horse Kaweah — Nonchalant orioles — Rebellion of Mesquit — Hot engagements, a parting, and a new start — Engulfed in gray — Last flowers — Enchanted sand-dunes — San Gorgonio Pass: a blow-pipe and sand-blast — Wind-trained shrubs — The sand-chisel — Lilac the desert's color — Railroad flotsam — Nature's hydraulics — Seven Palms oasis — A desert homestead — Effects of alkaline water — An inhuman wind — Coyotes oblige.

AFTER some months spent about the northwestern part of the desert, with headquarters at the village of Palm Springs, I made ready to launch out on a complete circuit, with variations, of the Colorado Desert. It was within a few days of the end of May, a much later date than I should have wished for the start, for the sun had settled down to his summer's work, and came up each morning at full blaze in a merciless sky, with that baleful mien which always throws me into anticipatory perspiration, and which still brings to mind the morning burst of my old dominie into the classroom, menacing, bloodshot of eye, and gnawing on his fingers like a famishing ogre.

Delay had been caused partly by a long course of unsettled weather, partly by fly-sores on the neatly striped legs of my burro, Mesquit. I had purchased her at Banning, the desert-portal town lying in the neck of the San Gorgonio Pass, where the railroad had dropped me in January. We had had bickerings, such as are bound to occur when similar constitu-

tions are thrown together: but on the whole the connection had been pleasant and I think profitable on
both sides. In many a cañon "we twa had pu'd the
gowans fine," and in friendly tandem we had "wandered monie a weary fit" of unprofitable sand and
cactus; and for my part I had no thought but that
our fortunes would keep one trail for many a mile
yet untrod. I meant, moreover, to get Mesquit a
comrade when we reached the settlements down the
valley, for though her load for the long journey was
no more than her accustomed one, I wished to make
the best arrangements so as to ensure reasonably
fast travel. Also, I hoped thus to have the means
of carrying water in excess of the capacity of my
two canteens, one of gallon, the other of half-gallon
size.

For my mount I had bought from an Indian acquaintance a small, tough horse. Born and bred on
the desert, he promised (or Francisco promised for
him) to be excellent for my purpose. His Indian
name of Po'say (meaning "little") did not quite
please me, with its inapt suggestion of flowery
meads, and I rechristened him Kaweah, partly in
allusion to the name of the tribe to which his old
master, and therefore he, belonged, namely, the
Cahuilla (of which *Kaweah* is a phonetic variant),
but more out of compliment to the memory of the
loyal companion to whose virtues Clarence King
does honor in a book which I am never tired of
praising, "Mountaineering in the Sierra Nevada."
Let me say at once that in many a hard day's march,
and sometimes, under necessity, night's to follow at

a stretch, Kaweah *secundus* did full honor to his name.

On the morning of starting I had been up since four o'clock, and we got on the move while Palm Springs was yet rubbing its eyes. As we passed the Reservation there came the chatter of orioles breakfasting with nonchalance on old Rosa's early figs at forty cents a pound. The racket, checked while the thieves listened with bored amusement to the rattle of her warning bell, — a kerosene can with horseshoe clapper, hung high among the branches of the patriarchal tree, and operated by Rosa's foot, so as not to interfere with the fashioning of baskets or *tortillas*, — went on again the moment the tattoo was ended. Not so, I guessed, the slumbers of her neighbors.

Turning northward I struck toward the western point of the great sand-hills that rise conspicuously across the valley. I had long been tantalized by their artificial shape, their mysterious changes of color, and the secret of what lay behind them, whether palmy cañon, wind-swept mesa, or characteristic characterless plain. I meant now to find a way in their rear, more interesting than the regular road down the valley, already familiar to the point of tediousness.

Before we were a mile on the way, certain doubts that I had had as to Mesquit's good-will toward the expedition hardened into certainty of trouble. Of all the crimes that are latent in these complicated beasts, the most terrifying is that of lying down under the pack. In my dealings with Mesquit hitherto, when I had either led her by halter-rope or marched alongside or behind, this had occurred once or twice, but, laying it to some momentary qualm, I had passed it by. Now, whether it were some sudden access of those traits for which the tribe is notorious, awakened by a suspicion that we were bound on a long hard voyage, or mere spite at seeing me for the first time riding while she was left to walk, I cannot guess. Anyhow, of a sudden I felt a check on the rope by which I was leading her, tow-line fashion, and, looking quickly round, saw her deliberately gather her feet, kneel down, and compose herself in an attitude of luxury. I dismounted and pulled; she was uninterested: I shouted and feinted blows; she seemed coldly to smile: rope-ended, she put her head to the ground and tried to roll, and though the pack balked the attempt, I knew by disastrous sounds that ruin was rife among the contents. In the last resort I hit on a goad. Prodded lightly, she grunted in contempt: prodded urgently, she kicked, but shivered: prodded ruthlessly, *usque ad sanguinem* (reader, the case was extreme, and the temperature a good hundred and forty in the sun) — triumph! she scrambled to her feet and stood quaking and defeated — for the time.

Another quarter-mile, and the whole business was enacted again: a furlong, and yet once more: and, in brief, within the space of six miles, which brought me to my first intended stop, eight several battles were fought — I cannot say, *and won*, for the strife was but intermitted, never closed. And on three occasions the load had all to be thrown off and repacked.

This settles it, my fine girl, I said at the second repacking. Kaweah and I can manage without your help, since this is an instance of it; and the last of your disastrous tribe shall perish from the earth before ever I put faith in burro again.

To dispose of Mesquit finally from these pages I may say that the next day I took her back to Palm Springs (with no trouble whatever, now that she was not outward bound). There I left her, and with no such relentings as Stevenson noticed in himself on parting from the classic Modestine. I sorted over my baggage, cutting down to the barest needs and to the point where they could be contained in two pairs of saddle-bags. One of these fitted at the horn and one at the cantle of my McClellan saddle, with two light blankets strapped behind the rear pair. The two canteens were necessities, and I carried also a light hatchet, a picket-pin, and a single-barrel 20-gauge shot-gun (though this, useful as it was, I later discarded for saving of weight). My camera, of course, was indispensable. Thus equipped I made a second start.

The circumstances of the former attempt had not conduced to enjoyment of the scenery or other natural incidents of the way. Now, with "peace of mind, dearer than all," I had leisure and mood for observation. I was riding northward to the oasis of Seven Palms. Almost before the last stunted pepper-tree outpost of Palm Springs was passed, I was engulfed in the gray waste, gray not alone of sand and boulder, but also, in the main, of vegetable and animal life. Isolated bushes of creosote rose here and there above the level, enough of them merely to accent the general hue by momentary relief of glossy olive. Encelia and burro-weed made up the bulk of the plants, but by now the yellow stars of the former had burned to ashes; the latter makes little show of bloom and wears a perennial garb of gray. These dense-growing, round-topped shrubs afford the minimum relief of shade to the eye. The light is thrown back unbroken from their hemispherical surfaces, and all there is of shadow is kept for their own needs as if under a close-held umbrella. Of animal life little was to be seen but scurrying lizards, themselves mostly gray, but some of ivory white. These are bony little goblins with sharp tails and a leer in the eye that comes near being devilish.

A few late flowers were out, principally the ethereal sky-blue navarretia, with which one slowly but surely falls in love. Large white evening primroses were still blooming under the creosotes, and here and there the daisy-like desert-star (*Eremiastrum*) showed like floral Pleiades. A desert willow in a dry water-course kept a few of its frail, orchid-like blossoms, and the indigo sparks of the dye-weed were plentiful, but almost lost in the wide sea of gray. A month earlier a page would hardly have held the list of the flowery multitude: now, by late May, floral autumn had come on the desert, and this in spite of its being a season of unusually late rains.

But desert color does not lie in vegetation alone. A few miles north of Palm Springs there rises a great dome of sand that for color effects I can only compare to a vast opal. I have seen it pass in a few hours from milky white, through pale chrome, gold, ochre, rose, madder, royal purple, indigo, and duskier purple, to almost black: such enchantment does this desert atmosphere work, even at no distant range. As I now passed near it the magic was as totally gone as that of Hamlet's dull firmament; it was "a foul and pestilent congregation" of sand atoms, weary to foot, weary to eye, most of all weary to thought, the embodiment of drought, hopelessness, infinity of number, infinitude of Time.

This strip of desert, lying at the eastern approach to the San Gorgonio Pass, is a veritable blow-pipe and sand-blast. The heated air rising under this fierce sun acts as a suction-pump, drawing from the coast a compensating volume, and this pass forms the main channel for the daily interchange of sea and land air that gives the Southern California climate its peculiar quality. It is by means of this regular wind-current that the great sand-hill has come into being. On most days, especially of spring and summer, to cross this tract is a highly unpleasant job. The force of the wind is phenomenal, and the steady, concentrated action results in launching volumes of sand with hurricane power against any object in its path.

As an instance of the violence of this wind, I recall an average day of a former spring, when a party of whom I was one stopped hereabouts for a meal. A sheltered spot was chosen and a canvas sheet rigged against the wagon-wheels for extra protection: yet a cup of coffee set on the ground would be instantly blown over unless weighted down with a sizable stone, and no amount of dodging availed to prevent every mouthful getting liberally sanded in transit. The conversation was lively, yet it was not a cheerful meal.

On the present occasion, for a miracle, only a harmless breeze was blowing. It was instructive to note the effect of these sand-laden winds upon vegetation, and even rock. Wherever a fair-sized stone or boulder stood in the windway, some thrifty shrub, usually creosote or dalea, crouched in its shelter, growing to leeward in a long streamer, like a quickset hedge. Some of these bushes were from ten to fifteen feet long, with height and width strictly regulated by the size of their rock protector. Any attempt to extend by so much as an inch beyond shelter was rendered hopeless by that deadly sandscour.

In other cases, where some hardy, low-growing shrub kept a foothold, a long dune had formed in the rear where the check to the wind allowed the sand to settle. Both hedges and dunes ran invariably to eastward, following the course of the wind. For variety, here and there were creosotes with a grotesque look of being on stilts, the soil having been gouged away from the roots by the wind to the depth of two feet or more. Many are the quaint comparisons suggested by the postures of these wind-thrawn plants.

A yet more impressive token of the power of the sand-blast is seen in the scarred and corrugated faces of boulders. The rocks hereabouts are all of the igneous kinds, but often differentiated, as geologists say; that is, not homogeneous, but made up of strata of varying degrees of hardness. Many of these bear deep-etched testimony to the sand-storms of ages, the softer parts being chiselled away and the harder left in bold relief. They might have been antiques carved from fragments of the bones of Chronos.

The same thing happens, of course, and in very brief time, to softer structures. The telegraph poles along the railroad used to need renewal constantly, being soon cut through, a few feet above the ground, by the beat of hail-like gravel and the fret-saw of the sand. Now they are sheathed with iron. Fragments of clear glass quickly take on the appearance of ground glass or dull metal. Upon everything, living or dead, the flying sand stamps its seal.

Another noticeable thing, by the by, about glass that is exposed to the desert sun is that it quickly takes a hue of amethyst or lilac. This tint, expressive of light at its highest actinic power, may almost be called the characteristic color of the desert. I have often been forced to admire the beauty of the shadow tones cast by rock or tree — a thin, pure, violet hue: nay, I have even been charmed with my own image, drawn in this ethereal air-color by my enemy the sun.

Half buried in sand I noticed some weather-worn timbers. They proved to be railway ties, with twisted rails still spiked to them. This was the mark of another destroyer, one that comes seldom to the desert, but is apt then to come in fury. It was water that had tossed this scrap of railroad miles from where it had been laboriously placed: either some rare, long-continued winter storm, or, more likely, a sudden summer flood. A glance at the surrounding mountains makes the matter plain. Figure the certain effect of a heavy fall of water on those two-mile-high walls of almost barren rock. Like raging giants the floods come leaping down, torrent reënforcing torrent, and burst roaring from the cañon gateways. What work of man's hands could withstand that assault, even when the shock is weakened by miles of distance? In the path of these desert floods a railroad might as well be a bit of fish-line. Here, at any rate, as I said to Kaweah, who stood with pricked ears, pondering at the sight, the age of horseflesh is not yet gone by.

Partly hidden among dunes of sand bristling with a scrub of mesquit, there is an oasis and a pleasant group of palms. Its name, dating from bygone decades, is Seven Palms, but there are now a score or so of the trees scattered about the place. A cowboy acquaintance of mine years ago "homesteaded" the spot, captured by the charms of a patch of dingy salt-grass, a pool of barely drinkable water, and unlimited quail, rabbits, snipe, and duck. Perhaps he had also an eye for a landscape which might move the toughest of "punchers" to admiration. His cabin, sheds, and corral, almost lost in the jungle of arrowweed, made up the picture of a typical desert home, and three slender palms, in shadow cameo upon an amethystine sunset, gave the touch of perfection which is seldom far from the commonplace.

I made camp under a cluster of palms that grew

in a hollow where a spring of alkaline water breaks out and spreads a white, unwholesome efflorescence among the arrowweed. It is one of the drawbacks of desert travel that the water, scarce at best, is generally charged with substances that not only impair the thirst-quenching quality, but may have ill results on the health. One of the minor effects of alkalinity (which is an almost universal fault of desert waters) is a swelling and cracking of the lips, and I have known hardy cowboys, inured for years to desert life, to be disfigured, hardly able to speak, and positively refusing cigars, after a week or two of water unusually "tough." I came near serious illness myself, from this cause, when I camped here for some weeks earlier in the year: yet this is comparatively good water, as desert water goes.

There is another black mark against Seven Palms — the inhuman wind that constantly blows here all through spring and summer. After half a dozen visits to the place I fail to recall one day uncursed by that harrying wind. Ordinary wind I can stand; a breeze is often refreshing; but this sort of thing is frankly beastly. It seems a sort of horseplay, aggravating, useless, simply silly.

On this occasion, though the day had been decently quiet, toward evening the old nonsense began. The palms took up the regulation scream and rattle that had blasted so many a night's sleep for me, and by sundown you would have thought the Valkyries were in full career. I picketed Kaweah on the most sheltered patch of salt-grass I could find, and passed the evening in my cowboy's cabin with a phonograph that screeched its best, yet failed to drown the racket that reigned outside.

The locality is prolific in coyotes, and in fact has supplied me with the trio of skins on which I spread my blankets when Mother Earth's ribs are my bed-stead. It must have been the songs of some of these vocalists that put me and kept me asleep, for in spite of the uproar I slept calmly in my palm bivouac till Kaweah's shrill neigh called me at daybreak.

CHAPTER VII

A DESERT RIDE: SEVEN PALMS TO THOUSAND PALM CAÑON

An oasis aviary — Desert farmers and the *non possumus* — Poor man, poor land — Two-Bunch Palms — A plucky woman-settler — Thirsty poultry — "Desert rat" and poet — Pottery fragments — San Jacinto and San Bernardino Mountains — Desert light-houses and sunset — A morning of heat — Storm brewing — Hospitable settlers and a phonograph — A thunder-storm on San Jacinto — Abruptness of desert contours — Roof-like slopes — Lilac lights and shadows — Questionable landmarks — Thousand Palm Cañon — Drought-mountains — Night visitors.

MY plan on starting had been to make the first day's march a few miles longer, and to camp at the next water beyond Seven Palms. This spot, known, somewhat uncouthly, as Two-Bunch Palms, now became an easy objective for the second day: for one's marches in desert country are figured from water to water, be the distance little or great. The wind had somewhat lessened by morning, gathering breath for the next attack, so I lay at middling ease for an hour, interested in the morning business of the birds that made the grove a literal aviary. The matted heads of the palms, with their dead hanging fans, made the snuggest of roosts and was as full of small sleepers as a boarding-school dormitory. These now came bursting out in twos and threes, linnets, sparrows, finches, buntings, totalling scores, with an enthusiasm for breakfast that I soon found infectious. They had the weather gauge of me there, however, for even in the best-sheltered corner it was hard to keep fire enough together to boil my billy of tea.

A few swallows were racing about, like little incarnations of joy. A prospector who is a frequent camper here had told me that they built their nests against the smooth boles of the palms, and I looked, but without success, for this example of the skill of the jolly little masons.

Kaweah showed more than his usual alacrity when I led him in to be saddled, and we took our way again northward. There was no trail, but none was needed, for after a mile or two we came in sight of the two palm groups, conspicuous objects against the light ochre of the foothills. In recent years a few land-hungry settlers have come into this region and are engaged in what seem, to my judgment, pathetic attempts at farming. Lack of water is, of course, the first obstacle, and almost certainly a fatal one. Surface water, sufficient for household use, is easily got in most parts, but this may be counted a misfortune, since it merely makes possible a losing fight. Next stands the poor quality of the soil, which, with the exception of a patch here and there, is much too light to produce crops, except of one of two kinds that could only succeed by means of copious irrigation. It is possible that wells sunk to sufficient depth would yield a good supply, but there the checkmate comes in: it is the poor man who clutches at poor land, better being beyond his means (a truism that has special point in this State of booms and fantastic valuations): while, *per contra*, the sole chance of productiveness with such land lies in a heavy initial outlay for securing water. It is the tribe of Scadder alone, I fear, that realizes profit from these "desirable acreages," and his neatly baited trap is ever to the fore in the advertising columns of California newspapers. It would be an act of both mercy and statesmanship for the Government to withdraw from entry these delusive tracts, whose very poverty makes their fascination for the impecunious — at least until official experiment has shown whether they can ever be made to repay cultivation.

Nearing "Two-Bunch" (for brevity the third syllable is dropped in common usage) I came upon the tiny store that serves this ungrateful land. Here a young Englishwoman was wrestling with fate, struggling to make ends meet by merchandising on the microscopic scale. Her clients are as varied as they are few — Indians, cowboys, prospectors, chance travellers like myself, and such other unconventional folk as are content to seek health, wealth, or prosperity under circumstances that most people would think intolerable. For example, this young woman (far from Amazonian in physique) for lack of a well fetches her water day by day per burro from a mile away, herself going afoot — and it is along no shady lane or boulevard either. I took a new view of chickens when I heard her speak bitterly of their heavy demands for liquid, and felt respectful sympathy when a scatter-brained young rooster upset the water-pan.

The two "bunches" of palms that give the place its name grow near together on a little bluff, where the level desert breaks to the foothills of the San

Bernardinos. A spring of good water issues below the smaller group, and here I made camp. A settler has built a small cabin above the spring, and as he was absent I made his house my windbreak.

On my first visit here, some years before, I found an old scarecrow of a fellow in possession, living in a kind of burrow or dugout. A more Crusoe-like object I never expect to meet, weird as many of these "desert rats" are to the view. He could not be said to be clad, but antique rags were hung about him, and he wore a scrap of débris on his head, under the delusion that it was a hat. His hair was snow-white, long, and plentiful, his skin like that of a well-roasted fowl, and his eyes bright and very blue. The blue eyes gave an infantile touch, and somehow half prepared me for his proud announcement that he was a poet. What more he was or had been I never fully knew, though I learned that he had known such spheres of life as teamster, preacher, prospector, with others perhaps less blameless. Once only I got a taste of his poetic quality, but of that all I recall is a frequent loud roar of "O Isrul!"

A noticeable thing on the desert whenever one is in the neighborhood of water is the quantity of broken pottery that meets the eye. About Seven Palms the ground is littered with fragments in many places, and a number of fine unbroken specimens have been found by the cowboy settler. Here again broken shards were plentiful, and I have often been surprised at meeting these evidences of bygone populations in the most unlikely places. The pottery, of the common red sort, but sometimes decorated with colored designs, is so light that the fragments remain on the surface, not buried by the wind. It was the custom of these desert Indians to burn the bodies of their dead and bury the ashes in a jar or *olla*, often along with such articles as baskets, stone or bone implements, and beads. Excavation in these places of old habitation often yields interesting treasure trove.

Two-Bunch Palms has one of the finest outlooks on the whole desert. On the west, Mount San Jacinto stands near at hand in gray severity of granite, with many a league-long buttress, gallery, precipice, chasm, and livid avalanche scar, from the vast apron of Chino Cañon that casts its burden on the desert floor up to sky-piercing, splintery crag and high-hung glimmer of snow. The topmost cliffs have a fine cathedral look, with their fretted coigns, and dark-niched, brooding pines.

Separated from the northern spurs of San Jacinto by the San Gorgonio Pass rises another magnificent mountain, San Bernardino. With its height of 11,485 feet[1] it slightly overtops San Jacinto, but being rather more distant it makes from here a less majestic though not less beautiful impression. The twin mountains stand like portals for the traveller's gateway to the fertile coast, the Western ocean, and the new-old world of the Orient. When, in winter and spring, they are hooded with snow, they make a memorable sight, and when a ruddy sunrise sets them aflame they seem torches, lighthouses of a continent, beacons of the old westward march.

[1] The mountain has two main peaks, San Gorgonio, 11,485 feet, and San Bernardino, 10,666 feet.

At evening I climbed a hill for a sunset view. A curtain of murky gold hung over all the west. The sun had set cloudless behind the pass. In clear silhouette the mountains cut the glow, all their ruggedness of contour lost in shadow, leaving only peaceful line and quiet color to charm the eye. Near at hand the palms pointed upward with a gesture of tranquil hope.

The western gold grew duskier; the world seemed dying, life passing again into its first unity. It was such a desert hill as this, I thought, that was once the favorite haunt of the Son of God. Often He must have taken joy, like me, in the full, calm glory of the evening star.

Forage for Kaweah was limited to burro-weed and a scant picking of galleta grass, that stand-by of the desert horse: but I had brought a little barley for emergencies, and Indian frugality had to make up the balance. The breeze was broken in the shelter of the house, and I took a couple of hours of campfire comfort before turning in. I slept unharassed by wind, and when I awoke, the morning star was above the eastern divide, beaming on me like a promise for the day.

That morning, however, proved one of the worst, in the way of heat, that I ever experienced. There was something positively blasting in the air, a deadly quality, as though all oxygen were withdrawn. The light itself was a sickly whitish glare. I should think this sort of morning must forebode vast eruptions such as of Mont Pelée and the Soufrière. I breakfasted, packed, and then changed my mind and declared to Kaweah that we'd be hanged if we would move so long as that state of things lasted. So I off-saddled and lay all morning with canteen at hand watching ominous clouds pile higher and higher over San Jacinto, then spread north and south over San Gorgonio and Santa Rosa. A storm was certainly coming, one of those sudden violent bursts that fall on this region at long intervals in summer, brewed almost in an hour in the furnace of the desert sky. A hundred yards in front of me was a palm that had lately been struck by lightning, and was now a ghastly, headless stick, like a skeleton finger pointing at its murderer the sky. At Seven Palms I had seen others like it, carrying scars that told the story. Being the only objects of height on the desert the palms are naturally marked for attack. The first boom of thunder seemed to be a warning, but I could not bring myself to move.

By noon a little freshness crept into the air, and I gathered energy to eat my cheese and hardtack and make a start. We were now at the back of the great sand-hills, and I turned eastward toward where a long gallery opened between them and the higher San Bernardino extension ridge. The storm still held off us and seemed to be pouring its wrath wholly on the western highlands, a thing that often occurs, resulting in those sudden floods of water from apparently dry cañons that are so dreaded by desert men. When the clouds extend in summer over the open desert, rain may often be seen falling, yet never a drop reach the earth, all being evaporated while passing through the heated air.

I knew of a settler who had an outlying holding in the direction I was taking, and presently came in sight of his homestead, where I hoped to camp for the night and replenish my canteens for the long stretch that would come before I should reach the next water. It was mere luck that my hope was realized. I had taken for granted that I should find a well at the place, but it was a rash expectation. Like others hereabout, this devoted settler brings his water in barrels from miles away, and had he not been at home we must have turned back to our last camp. As it was, we received a hearty welcome from man and wife, and were made as free of their precious water-barrel as though it could be replenished by a word. I was even invited to supper and phonograph.

I can never get over a sense of the marvellous with regard to this invention. I don't mean the thing itself; it is the improbable places where one finds it that staggers me, the contrast of this appendage of artificialized life with surroundings often the most primeval. Canned beef we look for everywhere, and find it a commonplace at Lhassa or the Pole; but "canned music" sounds wild on these terms; yet it is pretty sure to accompany the other. Probably the Lama is already tired of the latest Raucotrola, and only refrains from passing it on to the monks of Kinchinjunga lest it might seem odd to send anything so old-fashioned.

I never saw so spectacular a thunder-storm as the one that broke on the peak of San Jacinto that evening. By sundown the clouds had gathered their total forces. Sulphurous and terrific they piled almost to the zenith, until it seemed that when the stroke fell it must crush the mountain out of being. There was the usual pause; then Jove gave the signal. A spear of lightning shot through the murk, and the battle was joined. By the incessant flash and glitter we could see what seemed a perpendicular shaft of solid water falling from the black vortex of the clouds upon the head of the mountain. It was as if a volcano had opened, and that dark column was spouting upward from a huge crater and spreading mushroomwise into death-dispensing clouds.

It was quickly over: indeed, it could not last long at that rate. Then, after that concert of the Thunderer's best, my host turned on "Dem Golden Slippers," as more suited to our capacity.

The storm had done its work and the morning came clear and, by comparison, cool. I left my hospitable friends early, and riding southeast was soon well into the long pass. A remarkable regularity of slope, as well as of level, is one of the desert's common characteristics, and one that contributes greatly to that sense of austerity which is its universal effect on the mind. There is seldom any modulation between mountain and plain. Rock plunges into sand with startling abruptness; or, where some cañon debouches, the rock wall will meet at sharp angle a *bajada* [1] that may run for miles in even grade at a

---

[1] This Spanish word, signifying a long, downward slope or apron, is one of those useful terms that California has kept alive from the former régime. Like *mesa*, it fills a real need in briefly naming a characteristic element in Western physical geography. Hardly will one find a desert landscape in which the *bajada* is not a feature.

slant of from five to twelve degrees, and the slender
angle where it joins the dead level will even then be
clearly marked. Nature's love for the curve is abandoned here: she works with T-square and mitre-box
instead of with the free hand that rules elsewhere.

For mile on mile we marched up this roof-like
slope over a surface mainly gravelly, but sprinkled
with boulders and varied with river-like stretches of
unmixed sand where washes came down from the
northern mountains. Cactus, encelia, and creosote
rang the changes on creosote, encelia, and cactus,
and animal life was at a minimum. In several hours
I saw but three birds, all cactus wrens, though I
heard perhaps as many more talking plaintively, it
seemed to me, of the loneliness of this post-nesting
season. Even lizards were few, and a red racer was
the only member of the serpent tribe to enliven the
way; nor he for long, for these fellows are like the
Ghost in "Hamlet"; one can barely say "'T is
here!" "'T is here!" when "'T is gone!"

At last we came to the divide and could view the
other side of the roof. The downward slope was as
smooth as the one we had climbed, but plainly much
longer. On the north still ran the brick-like wall of
mountain; on the south a jumble of sand-hills and
gullies, most Arabian in look; and ahead mountains
on mountains, drab in near distance, purple in
farther, with blues in ever-paler tone as range receded beyond range. In the flickering heat they
seemed as if painted on a canvas that wavered in
the wind. This, indeed, is a common feeling in view-
ing a desert landscape. In the intense light, so much

stronger than normal, all seems visionary; the very ground underfoot lacks solidity, with its pale lilac shadows.

Of all those thin, spiritual hues that make the color-charm of the desert and that painters find so baffling, lilac is the prevailing note. It is the most ethereal of tints, hardly to be termed color, and seeming more of the mind than of the eye. Yet, once realized, one finds it universal. Between you and the gray boulder three feet away you half see, half feel a veil of lilac light, and the distance is suffused with it in varying degrees. Overlying the reds and browns of the mountain walls it makes its delicate presence felt, and covers the crudest facts of geology with a film of fancy, a touch almost of faëry.

Desert shadows fall into the same high tone. There is nothing of darkness in them, no weight, no sense of dimness, but always that aerial tint of lilac infinitely thin and refined. Over wastes of sand aching and throbbing with light one catches the same faint hue, lilac, always lilac.

Cañons opened here and there into the hills on my right, and in some of them I thought I caught a hint of palms. A prospector who includes this route in his wanderings had warned me against being misled by these, but as a group of palms was to be my landmark, these appearances tended to doubtfulness and kept me a trifle uneasy. I had a fair idea, though, of where I was making for, so kept on hour after hour, alternately riding or leading my horse, but always in a little question whether I had not passed my point — awkward, if so, on Kaweah's account, for there was no prospect of forage or water for him except by our striking the one right place in this maze of possibilities. The heat was severe, though short of yesterday's intolerable degree. It was about noon when I saw a dark spot miles ahead, which I guessed to signify my palms. By two o'clock we were there and found that the palms grew at the head of a long cañon that should open on desert level. It was Thousand Palm Cañon, the place I wanted.

From under the palms a feeble stream trickled away, its margin white with alkali; but water is water, and an absolute requisite. There were scraps of fair pasturage, too, making it, for the desert, a desirable camp. It was good to see Kaweah go to work at the juicy tules and water-grass, and it stimulated my own appetite, jaded by hours of heat. I brewed some flat, spiritless tea, made a scratch meal, and then lay in palmy shade watching Kaweah's ribs fill out and enjoying a kind of Lotos-Eater's ease. The temperature was just at century point by my little thermometer, and the whole place was kept on echo with drowsy coo of doves and cautious whistle of quail. Smaller birds formed little bathing parties of sixes and sevens, turning on the shower-baths with what seemed criminal extravagance.

At sunset I wandered half a mile down the cañon. The drab mountains changed suddenly to rose, then crimson, then furnace-red. It is fortunate that these transformations come at the hour when one's spirits are rising in prospect of the coolness of the approaching night: otherwise they might be wasted, meeting a listless, heat-burdened mood incapable of enthusiasm or even interest. The great twin mountains were hidden from me here, but the San Bernardino spur was close enough for its four thousand feet to show to advantage. But though these drought-cursed mountains are admirable for color, one's pleasure in them is limited, since for mountains to be merely admirable is almost for them to be failures. The cañons yonder, bathed in indescribable hues, have no enticement for the imagination, for one knows that no streams are there, no trees, no birds, no ferny pools, nor spouting cascades: only uncouth boulders, scant, unfriendly shrubs, threatening reptiles, snarling wild-cat and slinking coyote. Such mountains never reach one's love.

The night was warm, though a breeze rattled the palm fans over my bed. Once I was roused by the approach of some large animal and was barely in time to beat off a couple of mules that were making for my saddle-bags. There is some instinct in these brutes that guides them unerringly for miles on any errand of depredation, yet drives them away from where their presence is desired.

Toward morning, raising myself on elbow for a drink from the canteen (which, on the desert, one keeps at one's bolster, as King Saul kept his cruse of water), I noticed the odd appearance of a star that was just rising in the east. It grew quickly to a little horn, and in a few moments announced itself as the moon, nearly at her monthly finale. By the time she had climbed to where her light fell among the ribbons of the palms, it was dawn; and I rose promptly in order to get breakfast before my unwelcome comrade, the sun, arrived to keep me company for the day.

CHAPTER VIII

A DESERT RIDE: THOUSAND PALM CAÑON TO
COACHELLA VALLEY

Stately palm groves — Desert holly — A settler's camp — Hospitable Edomite — Sand-dunes — Novel tobogganing — Smoke-trees — The edge of cultivation — Burlap-and-hose luxury — Effects of erosion — Unique home-sites — Coachella Valley — Camp in a mesquit — "The Twelve Apostles" — Heat *minus* fatigue — Indio — Desert farming: dates and figs: phenomenal growths and profits — The Romance of Agriculture — Sleep and dress on the desert — Hot baths and watermelon.

THIS was Sunday, and I was glad that the pasturage would allow of keeping it a day of rest — a thing not always possible, even with the best of intentions, in these regions where necessities of forage or water often drive the unwilling traveller on. During the morning I explored my surroundings, and was delighted to find myself among the stately groves that give this cañon its name of Thousand Palms. There are several distinct clusters, each of many hundreds, growing at short intervals, and in side ravines are smaller groups, each showing some feature of charm, strangeness, or picturesque arrangement. In one, a narrow gallery of ochre-hued rock that gave wonderful depth to the complementary blue of the sky, I came on six palms that grew in a compact block, as wide and thick as it was high, thatched to the ground with dead, hanging fans. One could cut into the mass as one would into a cheese, and a fine cell could be carved out of it by a desert hermit who did n't mind scorpions and tarantulas for neighbors.

I climbed a hill to the east, from whence I could overlook a good part of the palms' territory. They stood like an army, an actual forest of palms, as unique a sight as can be found in our country, and as beautiful in its strange, fascinating way. No other plant grows with them: the straight, dark pillars stand solidly on a floor deep laid with dry, fallen leaves which slide and crackle under the foot. As I moved among the stiff, uniform shapes I felt a sense of that old Egyptian awe, the awe of overpowering mass and repetition, of monotony carried to the point of terror. It would have seemed quite in place to meet here one of those nightmarish processions we see on obelisks, or to discover faint hieroglyphs carved on those red, pylon-like shafts.

In this cañon I first found an attractive little plant, *Atriplex hymenelytra*, which I have seen sold on the streets of Los Angeles at Christmas under the name of desert holly. It is a low shrub, with stiff, holly-like leaves and the characteristic brittleness of desert brush. The whole plant is dead white, and looks much like a branch of true holly that has been dipped in whitewash.

The day was warm — 106° by two o'clock in the afternoon. I drank often of the irresistible though unpleasant water, and even managed a bath, which left me with a sensation of being made of old india-rubber. In the evening the mystery of the night-wandering mules was explained when two men came up the cañon. They were surprised to see me, having had no idea of there being any one in that direction for twenty miles. I learned that they had ranches, or rather claims, in the valley below, and were engaged in "developing" water with a view to irrigation. I was hospitably urged to move down to the camp where one of them was working, a mile or so down the cañon, and strong inducement was held out in the promise of better water.

Accordingly in the morning I moved. My friend's camp was pitched at the edge of one of the palm groves, and consisted of a roomy tent, a forge, a rough stable, and a mountain of débris, the accumulation of three years of "baching." For that term he had lived here, most of the time alone, working at his "water right"; tunnelling, sinking shafts, running drifts and ditches, gradually gathering up the underground flow that was betokened here and there by seepages and beds of tules; a life of cheerless solitude plus hardest labor plus purgatorial heat. His task was nearly done, he told me, for he now had two hundred inches of water almost ready to be piped to his "half-section" of land down in the valley at Edom — significant name! — where he hoped to grow dates, figs, and early grapes for the tables of millionaires. If spontaneous kindness to a stranger deserves reward, my good Edomite's acres should soon be as fruitful as the land of Goshen.

I was struck by the Arabian look of this locality. High-walled gullies of red or ochre earth meet and interlace, their bottoms filled with coarse gravel and boulders mixed with blue-gray smoke-bush and stunted mesquit and cat-claw. Among birds, only the raven seems to tolerate this desolate spot, and his morose hue, tragical voice, and general graveyard air do nothing to enliven one's impression. The eye, discouraged by the crudity of the scene, instinctively dwells upon the palm whenever it is in sight, overlooking its sameness of form for the relief of its grace, finish, and appearance of culture.

From Thousand Palm Cañon I struck southwesterly into the open desert. My friend's little brook rippled for half a mile out of the cañon, then suddenly sank into the sands. San Jacinto was again in view, but purpled by distance. His load of snow seemed noticeably less than at my last sight of it only four days ago.

A few miles to the west there is a tract of dunes that looked worth visiting. A huge quantity of almost unmixed sand has accumulated here, and has been worked up into remarkable forms. Wind and the principle of cohesion operating together have resulted in an arrangement of domes, half domes, waves, crevasses, all the shapes that snowdrifts take, but with the characteristic wind-ripple in addition. The glistening whiteness of the sand carried out the likeness to snow, but the sharpness of the breakage lines is what made the sight so interesting. Long curves, beautiful in their ease of contour, led up to keen, clean-cut rims from which steep slopes ran down at sharp angle. From these edges there was always blowing a wavering veil of sand, as fine as the spume stripped by the wind from wave crests at sea.

It was fascinating to stand in that universe of

sand. The Scriptural phrase, "like the sands of the seashore for multitude," seemed almost weak in view of these great billows like the storm waves of mid-ocean. Here was not only a shore, but a sea of sand. The scene stamped itself strongly on my mind — the strange contours, differing from those of other materials; the shadow masses of clear blue; the amethyst of the nearer ridges of San Jacinto; the deep afternoon purple of the great mountain itself; the gleam of mingled snow and cloud along its crest; over all the glowing sky, too luminous and aerial to be fairly expressed as blue.

I had been among these dunes once before, when a youngster from a ranch on the farther side had guided me to the edge of the tract. I was busied with camera and notebook, not noting my companion, when a patter of charging feet and a Comanche yell made me jump. It was only my guide enjoying a desert toboggan-slide. He raced to the edge of a thirty-foot dune, threw up his heels, and took a header down the sharp incline. Running sand at every pore, he pronounced it bully, and recommended me to try it, adding that it was one of his and his sister's regular forms of exercise. But I was past twelve, and found it easy to refrain.

My way lay now more to the south, where, a dozen miles away, was the little railway town of Indio. This lower northwestern arm of the desert, into which Thousand Palm Cañon issues, was intended to be named the Conchilla Valley,[1] from the myriads of little shells that powder the ground,

[1] Spanish *concha*, shell; diminutive, *conchilla*.

mixed with some of larger size — relics of the brackish lake that for a long period filled this great depression. By some error the name got upon the maps
as Coachella, and the blunder has been retained,
until it is now signed and sealed beyond hope of
correction.

A botanical feature hereabouts was the smoke-
tree, *Parosela spinosa*, which appeared in great numbers. It is the most prominent plant of the dry
desert water-courses, and in some of them grows so
thickly as to form an apology for a forest, though a
forest of strange kind and serpentine form. It was
at this time in full bloom, carrying a multitude of
small, pea-like blossoms of dark, bright blue, from
which the plant is sometimes called "indigo-bush."
I have heard it called "desert cedar" also, though it
would be hard to imagine anything less like the
sumptuous cedar than this spectral thing, blanched
and leafless. The other name, smoke-tree, describes
it well (though it is more bush than tree, seldom over
twelve feet in height), for the resemblance to a column of smoke is plain enough at a little distance.
At this season it made a beautiful sight in its dress
of gray and blue. Each plant was humming with
wild bees and other insects that were making the
most of the honey harvest, and the fallen blossoms
had gathered in every hollow like drifts of blue
snow.

A few miles brought us to the edge of cultivation.
A small farm appeared, isolated in the waste, but
looking thrifty and attractive. Glad of a chance to
exchange words with my kind, sure to be interesting

now that they were so scarce, I halted at the gate till the good man appeared. He seemed as keen as I for a chat, inquisitive, moreover, as to my business, and would have me dismount and come to his shady veranda. Good man, indeed, I should name him, heartily pressing me to put up for the night, or in fact as long as I would! When I accepted the smaller offer, "That's all hunkydory then," he cried, and seizing his hayfork led the way to the stable, Kaweah close at his heels, for he knew the omen, and hay already had the pensive charm of "the good old days." The wife proved as kind as the husband, and I shared their supper and breakfast, as well as the hopes, trials, and prospects of their desert farming venture.

Their water-supply was a well and pump, operated by gasoline engine. Through all the centre part of this valley water is plentiful at no impossible depth. The water is pure, soft, and good (that from the deeper wells is usually warm, often as much as 100°), making the greatest of boons to the much-enduring folk who live and work under conditions for the most part decidedly onerous. An illustration of these people's hardships had comic details. The wife was going to the coast for the summer in a few days — the rule with desert women-folk, though not an invariable one — and must leave her husband alone to face the heat and keep the farm alive. But she had a plan, which she confided to me, for his comfort. She would send down from town a quantity of canvas or burlap, which was to be strung on wires along the windward side of the veranda. The poor, panting man was to take his seat there, lightly arrayed, and spray water on the screen with a hose. The resulting evaporation would temper the breeze to a fair degree of comfort. He might even, she pointed out, have pipe or newspaper in the other hand, a sybaritic touch that strongly appealed to me. In the following weeks, when warmth was plentiful and water scarce with me, I thought many a time with envy of my friend sitting with hose and pipe in solitary luxury, or perchance comfortably soaking in the barrel at the corner of the house, which he had pointed out to me with pride as forming a simple but admirable bathtub.

The burlap-and-hose combination, by the by, plays a prominent part in desert household economy. Where ice is not to be had the housewife resorts to the home-made refrigerator: nothing more nor less than a skeleton box or frame provided with shelves and covered with burlap. It is placed in a shaded outdoor spot, and water allowed to drip on it so as to keep it damp on all sides. The evaporation is so rapid in this dry, hot air that the temperature within is lowered by many degrees, and even milk or butter may be kept good for a reasonable time. No doubt it was this simple invention that gave the good lady a clue. If a pound of butter could thus find relief, why not a farmer?

Along the foothills that extend in a dull, mud-hued wall along the east side of the valley, groups and files of palms grow in almost continuous line. A visit to them proved interesting. The erosive effects of the storms that fall (usually in late summer) on the mountains are seen here in sharp *bar-rancas* and ravines filled with water-worn débris. The curiously seamed face shown ˌby these hills at a few miles' distance becomes on near approach a wilderness of rugged gullies that meet and cross at sharp angles and at gradients steep enough to make the short climb quite laborious. Huge blocks of rock, carried by storm-hydraulics from the higher back ranges, lie embedded in the local clay. Vegetation is scanty except for the flourishing clusters of palms.

Standing in picturesque fashion in alcoves and on benches, these suggest, even to a mind with no bent for real-estate speculation, the thought — What ideal sites for houses! From the shade of these elevated groves the fortunate owner would look out over the wide, sunny levels to where in the south the Salton Sea matches the turquoise sky, or, more westerly, to where the great peaks of Santa Rosa, San Jacinto, and San Gorgonio rise in fine succession. There is attraction, too, in the thought that under the progenitors of these palms, which mark the shore-line of the ancient sea, the Earliest Californian may have moored his canoe while he landed to feast on prehistoric clam and turtle.

In one alcove a recent hurricane had overthrown a number of the palms, strewing the ground as if with ruined monuments. From the eagle feathers that littered the place it seemed that the bird of solitude finds these silent groves with their vast outlook a congenial resort.

Continuing toward Indio I came to one of the young date plantations that in the last few years have become a prominent feature of the Coachella Valley, and that seem to indicate that a decade or so hence this region will be one great date-garden. The chugging of a gasoline engine guided me to the place. It was so good to see the generous stream of water that was being led in furrows to the thirsty young Deglets and Khadrawis that I asked the friendly caretaker if I might camp near by. The request was freely granted, and a shady thicket of mesquit pointed out as the best spot. The thicket turned out to be one great, house-like tree, which I shared with a family of quail, a pair of thrashers, a rabbit or two, a rabble of rats and mice, and an Egyptian plague of flies. It was idyllic at dusk to listen to the dozy murmurings of quail, apparently confessions of penitent cheepers answered with maternal forgiveness; while the evening star rose above the gloaming mountains and the breeze came cooler from the graying east.

I may remark here a noticeable fact regarding the climate of the desert. Even on days when the thermometer, hung in complete shade, would register 105° to 110°, walking was not specially fatiguing; and this in spite of the drawback of the looseness of the soil. It is to be explained, of course, by the dryness of the air, through which the sun's rays strike with scorching yet not oppressive effect. It is a sharp, direct heat, like that of a fire and not in any degree like that of steam. Perspiration is profuse, but evaporation keeps pace with it; and when shade is reached, coolness at once enwraps the traveller in an air bath as soft and grateful as evening dusk.

A strong wind blew all night from the northwest.

Rats made my mesquit thicket undesirable as a sleeping-place, but I spread my blankets in its partial shelter and passed a comfortable night, awaking occasionally to enjoy the moderate breeze, which came in playful puffs and sifted me lightly with sand. Kaweah, picketed close by, stood stoically, tail to the wind, until dawn, when he responded promptly to my whistle and whinnied for his morning sugar.

All next day the wind blew without cessation, filling even the higher strata of the air with sand, until in the north and west only the snowy heads of the twin mountains remained in view. They seemed like floating clouds anchored aloft to mark the Pass of the San Gorgonio for the sailors of the new aerial world-routes. By mid-afternoon they too had faded behind the brown sand-haze, and sunset came with a bar of turbid crimson, sharply met by the usual aquamarine of the summer evening sky. Young and slender, the moon moved gracefully down the field of lucent green, a lily princess in a Caliph's garden.

The little town of Indio is an example of the many California settlements whose hopes have been blasted by the rise of an upstart neighbor. Indio is old, for a California town and a desert one, and has existed as a "division point" since the building of the New Orleans to San Francisco railway. But when, a few years ago, desert settlers began to arrive in earnest, and the fight commenced which has already turned considerable tracts from gray to green, a new town, christened Coachella, was started three miles to the south, and has measurably prospered, partly at the expense of the older place. I stayed for a day or two about Indio, finding barely tolerable quarters at a wretched hotel. The sleeping accommodation consisted of a cot bed, with mattress and sheets, on an upper veranda. My request for a blanket for emergency apparently was considered unreasonable, for the article was not supplied (and in fact proved not to be needed at this season of early June).

Indio supports a weekly newspaperette, and my arrival, as a stranger, being duly announced, I was looked up by an old Los Angeles acquaintance, now turned desert farmer, who urged that I make my next stop at his farm. Here again a mesquit thicket made an ideal camping-place. The only drawback was the presence of a horde of the insects locally called locusts, really cicadas. These pests kept up all day a shrill, monotonous hiss, like the falsetto shriek of imps, which I soon came to loathe. There was compensation, though, in the friendship of the kindly people and the sight and sound of happy children. I do not forget, either, the melons and cucumbers, tomatoes, *chiles*, and egg-plants, that for a notable week displaced my daily round of beans, rice, and dull, insipid flapjacks.

The country hereabout is the pick of the Coachella Valley farming region. Looking south and west from camp I saw little but greenness; only isolated spots of gray gave token of the desert. On all sides ranks and clumps of fast-growing cottonwoods outlined the stations of farms; and everywhere along the roads one came on bands of chattering Mexicans or silent Indians at work in shady corners, sorting and packing into crates heaps of onions, cantaloupes, or tomatoes: or met wagons creeping to the railway with juicy freight of watermelons. Plantations of young dates met the eye on all sides, and here and there were palms already bearing clusters of ripening fruit so suggestive of the ancient Assyrian fashion of hair-dressing that I think the idea must have been copied from this source.

One hears wondrous tales of the profits that are being made by the owners of these first fruiting palms. The pioneer date experimenter, Mr. Fred Johnson, showed me four trees from which he had realized in the previous year between four hundred and five hundred dollars. (It must be remembered that in these early days of American-grown dates they bring the price of a novelty, as much as a dollar a pound for the best fruit, which is a temporary condition, of course.) Tempted by these phenomenal figures, desert farmers are raising seedling date-plants by hundreds of thousands, while those who can afford it are planting "offshoots"; that is, young palms imported from the famous regions of Tunis, Algeria, Arabia, and Persia. The industry is well past its experimental stage, and my forecast of the future of this valley is that twenty years from now it will be a waving forest of palms, with millionaires competing for acreage in the renowned date-garden of the United States.

From this locality come also the earliest of figs, apricots, melons, and grapes. The growth of these crops in this once despised soil is truly miraculous. I saw figs of ten or twelve years, monarchical in trunk and houselike in spread of branch; while vines at one year from planting were bearing promising clusters.

At the Government Agricultural Station I found some novelties which are still in the experiment stage; for instance, jujubes, pistachios, even cocoanuts. Both official and private enterprise are engaged on these problems, and from all sorts of out-of-the-way places strangers are constantly arriving who will be encouraged to become "good American citizens." Not only plant strangers either, for other questions arise, such as that of the *Blastophaga* wasp, an insignificant-looking insect who possessed the secret of why that best of figs, the Smyrna, refused to mature its fruit in this country, and who for many a year played hide-and-seek all over the Levant with our agricultural experts. It is the romance of agriculture that one sees here, in process of becoming the commonplace of the future.

The devices to which the white population resort for comfort in the hot months are various and amusing. Beds lurk in unexpected places. Wherever shade, or coolness, or protection from wind is to be had, there a cot, with mattress and sheets (seldom more), may be looked for. In a garden at Indio I noted what looked like a rather roomy rabbit-hutch but proved to be the six-foot-six sleeping-room of the owner of the place. At a near-by farm there was a more elaborate arrangement, a large, well-furnished room, electric-lighted and fitted with telephone, the roof and walls being all of wire screening, and the bed shaded from early morning sun by a broad-leafed castor-bean plant. Everybody, of course, sleeps out of doors, to escape the heat which during the day-time fills the timbers and furniture of the house to saturation point, to be slowly given off into the cooler air during the night.

Dress is cut to narrow limits, especially by those who work outdoors and who are fortunate in having the kind of skin that the sun tans instead of flaying. I recall two young Swedes whom I met at a ranch near Indio, who made quite an artistic effect in brown and blue. Curly-headed, hatless, and encum-bered only with "shorts" of blue denim, their skins were of a fine, pie-crust brown that almost made my mouth water, and their bright blue eyes were matched to a shade by the hue of the brief cerulean garments.

My heavy sombrero was often the subject of re-mark, the comment being that I must suffer from its weight. True, I did so; but in spite of that I feel sure that this thick, close felt, which thoroughly shuts out the sun, is far better than the thin straw helmet which is in general favor, and through which the sun rays pass only half disarmed. To my half-pound "cowboy" I owe it that, though constitutionally a sun-hater and a lover of cloud and fog, I stand the desert summer with much less discomfort than I might reasonably expect. I offer my experience for what it may be worth.

The dusty street of Coachella yielded one or two characteristic items, such as a humorous placard which offered "Hot Baths at the Ice Factory"; the spectacle of a bed hung in the air above the community water-tank at three storeys elevation; and a fleeting vision of the local banker, in rolled-up shirt-sleeves, returning from lunch bearing a wedge of watermelon with him into the financial shades.

CHAPTER IX

A DESERT RIDE: COACHELLA VALLEY TO PIÑON WELL

The "Coral Reef" — Sand-wraiths — Belts of desert vegetation — Vanished races — *En route* for Virginia Dale — Mexican camps — Sunrise — The Mud-hills — Erosion again — Taciturnity of Western men — Heat and drought — The sidewinder — Scene of a tragedy — Hot drinks — Wholesale suicide of bees — A kindly "freighter" — Arsenic water — Joshua trees, junipers, and piñons — A "salted" mine — Hard pulling — View of the Mojave — The desert's challenge — Piñon Wells.

A FEW miles to the south of Indio there is a rocky outpost of the mountain wall known (of course incorrectly) as the "Coral Reef." A ride over to view it at close range proved well worth while. At intervals I came upon farms with fields of alfalfa, acres of grapes or melons, and rows of thrifty young dates. Between farm and farm lay stretches of untouched desert more dreary than ever by contrast with the cultivated areas. In the distance pillars of dust, the genii of the whirlwind, moved in ghostly dance across the view, like dervishes ceaselessly whirling.

The haze of summer had by now settled on the desert, and to-day it almost obscured the mountains. San Jacinto's top was marked by scratches of white where the last of the snow lay in shaded clefts and cañons, while San Gorgonio's slightly higher crest showed in broader streaks and splashes: both seeming to hang without support in the pale cerulean sky. The hot, fitful breeze, the dreamy mountains, and those gliding, melancholy dust-wraiths threw us both into a drowse, broken unpleasantly when Kaweah stepped on a ground-rat's or squirrel's burrow, with resulting jerk and snort, or when, passing a mesquit, clouds of locusts came charging at us with goblin eyes and banshee screech, squirting their vile artillery.

Shells covered the ground, mostly tiny spirals smaller than rice grains, with a few three-inch, clam-shaped ones that gave an iridescent coloring to the surface. Pottery fragments were plentiful, plying the fancy with visions of strange aboriginal things. An occasional litter of cans or bottles raised the reflection that future ages, judging us by our débris, will conclude that we were an ugly, uncouth lot, much inferior to the race we displaced.

On a near approach the mountains on this southern border of the valley showed a more than usually forbidding aspect. Rising abruptly from the sand-level, their forms are almost grotesque, with suggestions of plesiosaurus and pterodactyl in their vast, ridgy backbones. Yet it is these brick-like shapes that at a distance and with sunrise or sunset coloring take on a look that can only be called heavenly. Perhaps it is one point of the analogy between Nature and the mind of man that in retrospect, life, even if it has been unlovely, like these crude rock masses, may gain a quality of beauty from that which enfolds all, the universal Goodness that is God.

The "reef" itself is an isolated hill, close to the main rise of the mountain, noticeable for the strongly marked beach-line, which is seen in a broad band of

dark brown that reaches ten or twelve feet above
the level of the soil. Above this line the rock is
lighter, the ordinary granite weathered to red and
ochre. The so-called coral is what geologists call
travertine, really calcium carbonate, which in a
sort of sponge-like formation encrusts the rock that
was once submerged. Little shells are embedded in
the substance, or remain as they lodged in the inter-
stices when washed there by some wave of the vanished sea.

The hill is cliff-like in steepness and almost bare
of vegetation. A *biznaga* or two lean out as if curious
to see the rare visitor, and a few thin creosotes wave
drearily in the wind. At the rear of the reef the
ground rises to a bench of gravelly soil in which one
notes at once a different set of plants — the smoke-
tree, palo verde, several sorts of cactus, bright-
green creosote, and the odd sandpaper plant. There
is always this well-marked difference between the
vegetable life of tracts above and below sea-level,
the difference being based, of course, upon the distinct characters of the soils. Above the old sea-line
is sand, gravel, and rock, with a varied range of
desert growths; below is a fine silt whitened with
shells and with little vegetation beyond dull clumps
of atriplex and suæda. This lower belt is much the
drearier region: yet it is this selfsame silt which,
where not rendered sterile by alkalinity, shows
such amazing fertility under cultivation. It is Lower
Egypt over again, with the Colorado taking the
place of the Nile.

A little distance to the west I noticed a small

cove, with beach of pure white sand. It was strange
to think what manner of children once played about
it, and how many centuries had silently passed since
their voices ceased with that of the Sea. Now the
hour is close at hand when children will again make
its crannies ring. Will they also "have their day and
cease to be"? And after lapse of other centuries,
will some other fashion of mankind again come,
again to vanish into silence? Above all, shall we
know and watch the recurring drama? — In the
desert one is prone to such aimless dreams. The solitude, the vast unbroken levels, the wandering, idle
wind, perpetually turn one's thoughts inward, yet
seem to lead them out in vaguest reverie. If the
reader finds too much of such matter in these pages,
I can only say that the fault is inherent in the subject, as humanity has ever found. It was always to
the desert, if possible, that the hermit fled when he
meant to waste his time.

The long ridge of mountains that bound this arm
of the desert on the north and east, and the question
of what might lie beyond them, had been on my
mind for a long time. That locality could best be
reached from the Indio region, so this was my opportunity. All I knew of it was that a road, of a sort,
ran that way into the old mining districts of Twenty-
nine Palms and Virginia Dale, and that water was
scarce and forage scarcer. By luck I heard of a
freighter who made periodical trips over part of the
distance, hauling supplies from Coachella to a mine
in these mountains. I hunted him up, and arranged
to accompany him as far as our road was the same,

buying fodder for Kaweah from the supply he carried with him for his own horses.

At four o'clock of the morning of the last day of June I left my mesquit bivouac. A camp of Mexican onion-pickers was already astir as I passed, fire was twinkling under coffee-pot, and men, women, boys, girls, and dogs, to the total of a score, were loafing and yawning with that air of entire leisure which is a mark of their race, and which I, for one, find rather enviable. I like to come on these camps, especially at evening. There is in them a touch of the patriarchal — *padre* in blue "jumper" beneath some rustling cottonwood, rolling and smoking eternal cigarettes: Juanitos and Conchitas in troops clambering over him like caterpillars or tumbling in congenial dust: *madre* an attractive figure in *reboso* or with splendid unbound tresses, preparing *frijoles* or *chile con carne*, or, more likely, Yankee canned beef: and Alberto picking out the latest ditty on his mandolin, wherewith to capture the heart of Encarnación, at the neighboring camp, after supper. Rarely does one hear any word of contention, for family affection runs strong in the blood of our lightly esteemed neighbors from over the line.

At the cross-road I halted to wait for my teamster and enjoy a sunrise. The morning was half cloudy, and the sun threw shifting lights on the mountains to south and west, bringing to view cañons and abysses that I had never known were there. These bare walls have a trick of concealing important features in a way that is impossible with wooded or brush-covered mountains. Some momentary rela-

tion of sun and cloud may any day give you a topo-
graphical surprise, even after years of acquaintance,
as if, some breakfast-time, you should learn from
your paper that the agreeable elderly gentleman next
door was an experienced cracksman long wanted by
Inspector Bucket.

My friend's caravan, signalled by distant clouds
of dust, at length came creeping along — a huge
wagon with seven-inch tires, loaded with a ton or
two of mixed merchandise, ranging from soda-pop
to Bob Milligan's new suit and a case or two of
dynamite. In the jockey-box was the week's mail
for the score or so of men at the mine, and, what
was of most concern to Kaweah, on the tail-board
were piled sacks of barley and bales of hay.

Crossing the railway we turned northward toward
an opening in the so-called "mud hills" which make
a feature equally fascinating and repellent in this
part of the desert geography. In dreariness they sur-
pass even the great sand-dunes which now lay far to
the westward. Their ashy gray is the most hopeless
of hues, and their few scraps of brush are almost
ghastly. The fascination lies in the strangeness of
the shapes into which the material has been wrought.
The cutting and carving, scoring and scraping, twisting and twirling, gouging and grinding that has gone
on here for ages has given an almost unreal look to
the region. A romancer of the type of Jules Verne,
wishing to depict conditions on the moon, or on this
planet when its turn comes, can here find material
to his purpose, "local color" bleached to the appropriate monochrome.

There was not much opportunity for conversation. To ride alongside the wagon was to be enfolded in the dust from sixteen scuffling hoofs, for at our slow gait it was much as if we stood still while the horses milled up dust for our benefit. Moreover, these teamsters of the desert roads are of a silent breed, and Emmons was true to type. Yet I knew he was glad of my company, and I have often proved that a heart kindly to man and beast may beat beneath a taciturn waistcoat. Occasionally he would call to a shirking horse — always a single word and with an odd way of dropping the leading consonant: thus "Ete," "Ill," "Aise," and "Ooze" stood for Pete, Bill, Daisy, and Suse — and the slack trace-chain never failed to straighten when these monosyllabic shots went off.

The creeping pace and the unknown, spacious desolation into which we were imperceptibly moving gave me the feeling of starting on some lifelong enterprise. A faint breeze came now and then from the west, but it was dry and parching, and brought no refreshment. The sky was overcast with a haze which diffused the sunlight to a blinding whiteness that was more trying than the direct rays, and that seemed to intensify the heat by giving it power to attack equally on all sides at once. There was something of the same deadly quality in the air that I felt at Two-Bunch Palms, though not to the same degree. We resorted often to our canteens, while the horses were treated to frequent rests, though short ones. On this kind of day one realizes easily enough how imperative is the need for water to the desert traveller. One feels that, without drinking constantly, one would shrivel, and perceives with horror the fearful nature of such an end as death from thirst.

The track — it could on no terms be called a road — after passing through an opening in the mud hills at a point where curious caverns, pinnacles, and arches occur, turned westerly into a long valley that divides these foothills from the main mountain wall. Silt was exchanged for sand and gravel, and the vegetation changed automatically with it. Creosote, burro-weed, and lippia made a scanty show, with tufts of the interesting white "holly," which at this season takes on pale tints of seashell pink and lavender, almost iridescent. The going became slower than ever. I relieved Kaweah by walking, but there was no amelioration for the straining team that now could hardly keep way on their huge load, though they were splendid animals and in the pink of condition. Looking at my watch I was astonished to find it was only seven o'clock. I should have said we had been five hours on the road.

Little as there was of vegetation, there was still less of animal life. Birds there were almost none, for the distance to water ruled them out. Jack-rabbit tracks came now and then, for Jack is almost a total abstainer. Lizards there were, for they are everywhere; and I noted plentiful tracks of the dreaded sidewinder, *Crotalus cerastes*. This is a small, asp-like species of the ordinary rattlesnake, found most often in the sandy or silty desert, whereas the larger rattler likes rocky country and the neighborhood of water. Two little protuberances over the eyes, like

sprouting horns, give the sidewinder an extra devilish air, and his small size makes him the more dangerous, because less easily seen and heard. His track,
however, is unmistakable, owing to his peculiar
mode of travel, which seems to be by looping himself along in spiral reaches, so that his trail is not
a continuous line, but a series of short, diagonal
strokes, about nine inches apart. For some reason
he enjoys wheelruts, and always takes advantage
of them: but as he moves mainly by night he is not
often seen by the traveller on the road.

It is a strange fact, of which I have been assured
by more than one person who has put it to the proof,
that a sidewinder kept exposed to direct summer
sun will not live longer than a few minutes.[1] The
explanation must be that the thin skin gives no protection to the cold reptilian blood. Certain it is that
the sidewinder is rarely seen in the open by day, but
is almost always found coiled in the shade, usually
about the roots of brush. It would be a praiseworthy
act of Sol, one for which I could forgive him much,
if he would one day turn on for a short time such a

[1] I have recently had an opportunity to test this on a sidewinder
that I brought in to camp for photographic purposes. It was a full-
grown specimen, and was not in the least injured in process of cap-
turing. I turned it into an enclosure of boxes, in the open sunshine.
It was as vicious and full of life as ever at first, but after three or four
minutes became languid, then ceased to move. Soon the head drew
back and the mouth opened, as in the attitude of striking. In ten
minutes it was dead. The month was September and the temperature
at the time 106° in the shade. With a midsummer temperature, ten
or fifteen degrees higher, no doubt, the time would have been much
shorter, perhaps two or three minutes only, as reported to me by
another experimenter. It is certainly remarkable that a desert creature should be so constituted.

torrid blast as would cook the whole sidewinder tribe where they lie snoozing in fancied security.

Hour after hour went by in a sort of trance of heat while we still toiled up that furnace-like valley. The wagon ground its ponderous way through sand or slid screeching over boulders. At half-past nine we reached the point where my teamster was to water his horses. Here he kept several large iron drums of water, which he refilled when necessary at the mine. He unscrewed the plugs with a spanner, and then bucket after bucket was given the eager animals, Kaweah participating. Next we fed them, and then, while we ate our own lunch, Emmons casually mentioned that this was Dead Man's Point. Why so called? "Oh, a Mexican was found dead over there, year before last. At least, part of him was found; not much, on account of coyotes. He'd come out afoot from the mines, — the Lost Horse, think it was, — got thirsty and wandered around some, and then give out. Name was Lopez — no, though, that was another feller; well, any way, some fellers found him up that gully a little ways: saw his tracks going round and round crazy-like, and trailed him. Reckon there ought to be some bits of his clothes up there yet if you've a mind to look. Yes, it's dry-like around here."

As we screwed up the drums I had a vision of a raving wretch — myself? — tearing at the immovable plug with bleeding fingers, striking at it with swollen, lacerated feet, hearing the water gurgle within: — in vain, in vain! Heavens! I felt faint at the thought, and was glad to mount and leave

Dead Man's Point to the coyotes and the murderous sun.

Here we turned up a narrower cañon leading directly into the mountains. The grade became steeper and the vegetation more varied. Cañon after cañon debouched into ours, dozens of them, all dry, baking, shivering with heat. There is no need to describe the country in detail; it was all alike. We ground our way on and up, the sun, now clear, reflected upon us from the rocky walls. My canteen, replenished after lunch, soon grew too hot to be put to the lips with comfort, while the water itself was at a temperature of over 100°, I am sure, and every drink threw me into immediate perspiration.

At three o'clock we came to the next watering-place and halted for the day. We had made just twenty miles in ten hours of travel. A well is maintained here, after a fashion, by the county authorities. There was the usual camp litter, also a rough bed and a stove, Emmons's property, for this was one of his regular stopping-places. A little way back he had inquired whether I liked bees or minded being stung: also asking Kaweah's sentiments on the same point. On approaching the well I caught the bearing of his question. The place was literally alive with bees. The air was like a swarm in flight, and the well itself resounded with the buzzing of thousands down there in the dark. However, water must be got for the horses, though we had enough for ourselves in the canteens, which was fortunate, for bucket after bucket came up covered with dead bees, and the liquid had a fetid smell from the myriads of decaying insects. So we hauled and skimmed and ladled till the animals had got their fill. The cañon thereabouts must be well sprinkled with bee-caves, and some one who enjoys the sort of thing might find exciting bee-hunting, with honey by the barrel.

Then Emmons stripped to the waist and went to work with curry-comb and brush at his horses while they fed. No doubt they earned the care he lavished on them, but it is not every faithful animal's master that will take his turn and sweat for them as they have sweated for him. When supper-time came he would not hear of my drawing on my saddle-bag stores. "Say, I'll have to call you down," he said genially. "If you'd carried your blankets forty years, like I have, you'd know better 'n that. How many eggs do you eat, that's what I want to know? Will four do you? That's my figure." And when next day it came to settling our accounts, he was scornful at the idea of my paying for what I had eaten of his supplies. "It's all right about the hay and grain, they cost money," he argued; "but eggs and such truck — oh, shucks!" And shucks it had to be, at risk of giving offence. Profane my friendly freighter was, alas! at strenuous moments, but it was not profanity of the usual gross type, and seemed almost automatic. Experience makes me wonder, indeed, if there has ever been a really successful Western teamster who was free from this vice.

Waking about midnight, I noticed Emmons get up, light a lantern, and again water his animals, taking them one by one the hundred yards to the well and back; after which he threw them down more hay. Seeing this, I could do no less for Kaweah, though I claim no credit for it. (I found it easy to excuse Emmons for an occasional outbreak of "cuss words" next day, when I remembered how he not only "regarded the life of his beast," as the righteous man will do, but looked to its comfort as well, and at no small sacrifice of his own.) Being up, and the night warm and still, it seemed a good time for a smoke, so we took a pipe apiece, then a pull at the canteen, and so to sleep again till four o'clock and dawn.

By half-past five we were again moving up the cañon. It became constantly narrower, steeper, and rougher, the wagon bumping and lurching along in a dogged kind of way, serenely confident in the soundness of hickory and wrought iron. Our surroundings became more interesting now that we were well into the mountains. There was no outlook, for we were shut in on both sides by walls that rose steeply for hundreds of feet, and the cañon was ever twisting; but bushes of fair size began to appear, and bird life too came in. It is the open wastes, where nothing is and nothing is to be expected, that wear one's spirits down.

One hears a good deal on the desert about arsenic water. Prospectors especially are full of tales of arsenic springs, where death snatches the traveller unaware. I believe competent authorities deny that arsenic in dangerous quantity exists in any of the desert water, and account for the fact that men have died from drinking the water of certain springs by the theory that the men in question, arriving at the suspected spring suffering from thirst and perhaps weak from hunger as well, drank too freely and succumbed to the excess, which, likely enough, was rendered more dangerous by the unwholesome substances often found in the water of these desert springs. (It is a common experience to find one's expected water-supply contaminated with dead coyotes, foxes, birds, or snakes, and water-holes that are seldom visited, and therefore seldom cleaned out, may become poisonous even from decaying vegetable matter.) I have not the means of giving a personal opinion, but one knows the hold that poison legends, like those of lost mines and buried treasure, take on popular imagination: and prospectors as a class are notoriously open to any touch of mystery or superstition.

I found my companion infected on this subject. On leaving our last camp I had filled my canteens, using water that had been boiled to prevent ill effects from dead bees. Emmons had no particular objection to decaying bees, but warned me gravely that there was arsenic in the water. He had found it poisonous himself, he said; but when I asked how he knew that it was arsenic that had upset him, he replied that every one knew there were arsenic springs on the desert, and he figured that this must be one of them. However, I reckoned that if a horse could take several gallons at a draught without any bad effect, I ought to be good for a mouthful now and then: so I drank, at first carefully, then freely, and noticed only that the supposed arsenic left lips and throat gummy, so that there was an inclination to drink almost constantly.

The cañon became a gorge, with yet higher walls, the strata split and upreared at all manner of painful angles. Wild-looking shrubs leaned out overhead and stared down at us with startled air. Strangest of these were the so-called Joshua trees, *Yucca brevifolia*, that now began to appear. Nothing in the vegetable world is more unprepossessing than this scarecrow, all knees and elbows, with handfuls and mouthfuls of daggers for leaves. The name is said to have been given the plant by the early Mormon emigrants to California, in reference to its heralding their approach to the promised land. There seems to be no great compliment involved in having this spiteful-looking object for a namesake.

Next to appear was the ever-interesting juniper. I like our California hero, Fray Junípero Serra, all the better for his choice of a monastic name, though it came second-hand (from that one of Saint Francis's band of whom the Saint cried admiringly, "O that I had a forest of such junipers!"). There is some very wholesome quality about this plant, even in its stunted desert form; and Pliny may be more reliable than in some other items of natural history when he declares that serpents shun this tree and men may therefore safely sleep in its shade.[1] For fuel qualities, anyhow, it has no equal, and I always hail the chance of a juniper camp-fire.

The piñon also soon came in, another of my favorites, gnarly but cheerful, a sort of Puck of the pines. Then appeared small oaks and willows, links with

[1] "Juniperus arbor est crescens in desertis, cujus umbram serpentes fugiunt, et ideo in umbra ejus homines secure dormiunt."

scenes and lands far different from this. All these old friends looked wonderfully kindly, and when I halted and listened to the breeze humming in the piñons it cost me a pang to think that I was in for months, possibly years, of life in a treeless land, and I wondered how I, whose ancestor must have been a dryad, should ever tolerate it.

At a point where a side cañon ran off to the west I noticed a weather-beaten sign-board showing that the Dewey Mine lay up there. This "mine," it seems, was a notorious case of "salting" (that is, baiting a worthless "prospect" with pieces of rich ore), a fraud that nearly came off, but not quite. Even costly machinery was installed in the effort to carry the bluff through. Emmons could not recall the fate of the promoters of the swindle, but we agreed in hoping that the "darned skunks" were at that moment unpleasantly engaged with a pile of oakum.

We were now close to the summit of the ridge, but the steepest rise remained to be climbed. Emmons rested his team while he looked carefully over the running-gear of the wagon: then attached brake-logs to the rear wheels. When all was ready he climbed to his perch, gathered the lines, cast a shrewd eye over the "road" that rose at a sharp angle ahead, and remarked in a casual tone, "Now, gals," at the same moment throwing off the brake. The well-drilled team responded. The trace-chains grated, the wheels screeched against the boulders, and the huge wagon crawled up the grade for twenty yards. The brake came on with a thump, the horses stopped in their tracks, and the wagon settled back against the blocks. Two minutes' rest, and another twenty yards: and so on for eight or ten spells. We reached the top, and crossed the pass at 4600 feet.

A fine outlook opened from the crest. Far to the west lay my brace of giants, San Jacinto and San Gorgonio, a sort of Gog and Magog. Behind and to the east was a jumble of brown ranges, with pale slips of desert showing here and there between them. To the north I looked out over the Mojave Desert, the twin sister of the Colorado, from this point a wilderness of mountains, arid, aerial, almost phantasmal. Beautiful, too, they were in their elemental solitude, their delicacy of tone, and most so in their air of mystery, their magnetic drawing on the imagination. "Come," they seemed to say, "we are waiting for you: have waited since eternity began. You long to know us: you cannot guess what wealth we hide. Come and take it if you dare: we dare you." Yes; and if you yield, and go, you may indeed learn their secret, perhaps a secret of gold such as never yet dazzled man's eye and betrayed his soul: but remember, you may never return to this other world, the world of men, trees, brooks, all the companionable sights and sounds of homes and towns of common people.

A mile of down grade brought us to Piñon Well. Here is an abandoned, worked-out mine, with old buildings and a scattering of other effects — tools, pipe-lines, and so forth. The old well with rusty pump is still in order, and now again we tasted good water; and how good good water is, perhaps is only known to men who travel the desert. We made a hasty meal, for Emmons had still a few miles to cover. My road left his not far from this point, so I decided to stay here for a day, enjoying the mountain air, pure cool water, and picturesque surroundings; resting Kaweah also, who was accommodated with a few feeds of hay from Emmons's store. Lunch over we bade one another good-bye and good luck, and I watched the wagon crawl away down the cañon toward the lonely camp somewhere in that gray wilderness, where a score of men (with never a woman) were dragging the deadly gold out of the grasp of the Sphinx.

CHAPTER X

A DESERT RIDE: PIÑON WELL TO MECCA

I WOULD willingly have stayed for days at Piñon Well but for that annoying trait of the human mind that renders ease uneasy so long as there is an unpleasant task ahead; and there are enough unpleasant possibilities inherent in an unknown stretch of desert to debar the traveller from freedom of mind. The rats that haunted the old house played havoc, too, with my scanty food supplies. They infested everything, even the coffee-pot, of dimensions that might be named Homeric, that hung on the wall, and in which I had thought my bacon would be secure.

Accordingly, after a day's rest we left at half-past five in the morning and took the road down the cañon for a mile, to where a wide valley began. My route soon left the main track, striking directly north into a strange looking country, a sloping plain broken by abrupt hills that looked as if they had burst up from below in some recent explosion. My friendly trees ceased at once at the foot of the cañon, leaving only the Joshuas, which always seem to have been arrested in the midst of some uncouth antics, brandishing daggers like a juggler. Deer tracks were plentiful, and within half a mile I met the three varieties of quail, mountain, valley, and desert, or Gambel, a thing I have never noted elsewhere. Far to the east rose a ragged range, even odder in skyline than the rest.

Another road went off now to the left, leading to the Lost Horse Mine, and my own route became a doubtful sort of track, with little sign of travel. In a pile of rock that I skirted I had been told I should find one of those natural tanks of water (*tinaja* is the common Spanish word) on which the desert traveller often has to place precarious trust — precarious because they are mere rain catchments. This one is known as Squaw Tanks. I easily found the place, being led to it by my nose. A small quantity of slimy liquid remained, nauseous with putrefying bodies of birds, rats, and lizards. A man perishing of thirst might have brought himself to drink it, but would probably not have survived the draught. It was no disappointment to me, for my canteens were newly filled, but the incident had a moral for me, nevertheless.

At the crest of a long rise I looked out over another great plain studded with brick-red rock piles and carrying a thin growth of Joshua trees that spread to the horizon, a ghastly pretence of forest. In the shimmer of heat they seemed to claw the air.

Here yet another track went off, turning easterly to a mine, or erstwhile mine, called the Desert Queen, and leaving me to a sort of phantom trail which still ran northerly mile on mile through the spectral forest.

Presently this trail also forked, sending off a branch to the east, and I came to a standstill in doubt. I had made careful inquiries at Indio and Coachella, and of Emmons, as to forks, crossroads, and landmarks, and had been duly warned as to the roads I had already passed; but this new turn-off had not been spoken of by any one. However, I knew that my direction for Twenty-nine Palms was northerly, and the trail in that direction seemed a trifle the better marked, so I resolved on that and started.

In a cactus bush I chanced to notice a scrap of board, loosely stuck as if it had been tossed there. Going over to investigate, there seemed to be faint scratches on it, apparently made with a nail. I turned it this way and that, but for some time could not make even a guess at what was written. At last, by patching possibilities together, the scratches took on vague coherence, a questionable "2," a hazardous "9," and a conceivable "P." The fragment as found pointed toward the easterly trail, but from the casual way it hung there it might have been twisted hither and thither by the wind, so it seemed a matter of chance which direction it was meant to indicate. It was one of those puzzles that may bring one into serious trouble in this country where distances are so great, water and food so far between, and travel so scanty that it was probably a month, possibly three times as long, since the last person had passed or until the next one would appear.

I resolved to trust the dubious sign and take the eastward track. There was difficulty in following it, for it was often so faint as to be mere guesswork. It is this sort of thing that takes the pleasure out of desert travel. The county of Riverside, in which I now was, has lately done useful work in the placing of metal guide-posts at the main desert road crossings, but a good deal more needs to be done, while other counties quite ignore this need of their desert populations. Unfortunately, the maps of the Geological Survey do not cover the greater part of this troublesome region: and such as are to be had, cheap "county" or "miners'" maps, are little better than none at all.

Persistently eastward ran my elusive trail. It was nearing a mountain range, the Pintos, and must soon turn either north or south, so I kept on, though in considerable doubt. At last, when close to the hills, it ran into a better travelled track, and with relief I found a sign-post with Twenty-nine Palms on its northern arm and Cottonwood Springs thirty miles to the southeast.

At this junction, as marked on my map, there are supposed to be, near together, two more water-holes, Stirrup Tanks and White Tanks. I searched for signs of them (the usual signs being the trails made by animals going to drink) but failed to discover either. I learned afterwards that one of them is half-a-mile away in the Cottonwood Springs direction; of the other, nobody that I have met has any

knowledge at all. Fortunately, I had an ample supply of water, but Kaweah had to be satisfied with a
promise payable fifteen miles farther on. He is an
intelligent fellow, and quickly grasps the bearing of
any indecision that may arise on the matter of trails.
On such occasions he watches every movement of
mine with almost human anxiety, and plainly reflects my own doubtful frame of mind. He had been
as pessimistic as I ever since we left the forks, but
brightened up when we found the road, and made
the best of a dry tussock of galleta while I ate my
lunch: and when we were ready he moved off with
alacrity and surprised me by offering to canter.

We were now on a gradual descent, the southern
rim of the Mojave Desert. From time to time there
opened vistas of volcanic-looking ranges, with
glimpses of shimmering gray level or splashes of
pure white where dry lake-beds glistened with alkali.
For hundreds of miles this strange dead land extends
to north and east, known only to venturous prospectors, a scientific man or two, a few surveyors, a
handful of miners; to the rest of the world as foreign
and unimaginable as if it were some territory of
Mars. Yet what wealth lies locked in that great desolation, for it is, as indeed it looks, a veritable treasure house of mineral. Looking out over it one easily
imagines "goblin or swart fairy of the mine" at
work on veins of wondrous ore under those gaunt
hills, ashy gray, livid purple, or dull red as if they
had been roasted.

At last, five miles down the slope of a narrow valley, I saw a speck that might be a building, perhaps

a ranch-house, though no trace of greenness was in
view as far as eye could see. I pushed on towards it,
indulging thoughts of eggs, "stove" bread, milk,
perchance a lettuce. But these hopes faded when
the supposed farm-house turned into the grouped
shanties of a small mine. However, I was welcomed
heartily by the three men on the place, and Kaweah
was entertained with barley and water — the latter
no trifling gift, for their supply must be replenished
at Twenty-nine Palms, four miles away. I was
eagerly questioned for news, for my items were only
five days old, while their last "news" had passed
into history two weeks before. The six men who
were concerned in developing the mine had formed
themselves into two shifts of three a side, taking
alternate spells at the works and "inside" (the term
used by desert men to signify the cities and the coast
country). The other shift was some days overdue,
ensnared by the charms of Los Angeles, and these
poor fellows were continually scanning the horizon,
like marooned sailors, for signs of the relieving party.

Evening was coming on, so I soon took the road.
Tracks led off to other small mines, reminders of the
lively days of the seventies, when this Twenty-nine
Palms district was a "camp" of renown. Before long
the palms came in sight, and we ended a long day's
march soon after sunset. I off-saddled under a cottonwood that stood near a deserted house, and found
pasturage for Kaweah in a little *ciénaga*, or marshy
spot, formerly the site of a village of Chemehuevi
Indians from the Colorado River. I do not know
who now owns the land, and, what is of more ac-

count, the water; but when I come on these abandoned settlements of the Indians, at places where
they would no doubt have wished to remain, I take
them for links in an old but still lengthening chain
of wrong.

The population of Twenty-nine Palms at the time
of my visit numbered two, so that my arrival, on
the eve of the Fourth of July, seemed to cast an air
of festivity over the scene. The two, one a prospector
and old haunter of the locality, the other a consump-
tive from "inside" who was sacrificing every comfort of life for the sake of the dry air of this lonely
spot, received me cordially enough, but remained
convinced, I think, in spite of my plain story, that I
was "lookin' up mineral, ain't you now?" They
felt it an insult to their intelligence to be asked to
believe that any one would come to Twenty-nine
Palms in July for the sake of seeing the country and
"them old pa'ms." "Country?" said the sick man,
waving toward a sunset landscape that would have
thrown Turner into a frenzy — "Country? Th' ain't
no country round here to 'mount to nuthin'. You
ever see any, Mac?" And Mac sententiously replied, "Durned if I ain't forgot what real country
looks like, anyways."

Nevertheless, the country was satisfactory to me.
To lie at dawn and watch the growing glory in the
east, the pure, dark light stealing up from below the
horizon, the brightening to holy silver, the first
flush of amber, then of rose, then a hot stain of crimson, and then the flash and glitter, the intolerable
splendor, of the monarch, Phœbus Superbus, tyrant

of the desert — and of me: I jump up hastily and hurry through my morning cookery, but not before he has taken toll of my day's store of energy.

Our Fourth was celebrated with make-believe shower-baths. At intervals we resorted to the *ciénaga* and ladled water over ourselves from a tepid pool, and I may say that with a temperature of 112° I found it more exhilarating than some displays of gunpowder and rhetoric that I remember. Between times we talked "lodes" and "pockets," or my friends would grind up some bit of "float" and pan it out at the spring, with brief excitement over "grades" and "colors." Toward evening I walked a mile up the slope to the west and enjoyed a memorable sunset. By some peculiarity of the light, the landscape had much the quality of a wash drawing in black and white, seen through a thin purplish haze. The line of palms made a charming foreground, each one a study of airy grace; beyond rose the Bullion Mountains, dark dull gray with splashes of white where sand had lodged far up, as if it were snow; farther to east another range, the Sheepholes, of the dead hue of volcanic ash; and over all the luminous arch, infinitely remote, with flecks of snowy cloud like sheep straying in the blue pastures of the sky. Spaciousness and solitude were the elements of the scene, and reacted with trance-like spell upon the mind.

As the sun went down a blood-red light suddenly came over all the view. I never saw anything more startling and instantaneous in its coming, or more theatric in its intensity of hue. For the few seconds that it lasted I held my breath. The mountains burned as if they were incandescent: Bullion? no, the lava of rubies. Then in a moment it had paled and like an expiration was gone.

As I walked back to camp I noticed a small enclosure, almost hidden among arrowweed. It marked the grave of a young girl, most likely one who had been brought here in hope of a cure for consumption. There is something inhuman in choosing such a place of burial for a girl. Nature sets a difference even in death, and it seemed a brutal thing to leave a girl's young body here.

Some tokens of old inhabitation at Twenty-nine Palms may be seen in remains of shacks and dugouts. One of these had been the den — it is the only word — of one Wilson, the former *habitué* of the place, who held on here in more than pagan squalor until he was lately forcibly removed by the county authorities. The hut of old Jim Pine, the last of the Twenty-nine Palms Indians, stands open to sky and gaze, and shows a litter of "rock" specimens (for Jim was something of a miner in his day). But mining camps are in their nature evanescent: why build a house, when to-morrow the rush will move on to a newer "strike"? But Twenty-nine Palms is still a base for prospectors in the desert ranges, on account of its water, which is plentiful and good, and by reason of being on one of the roads to the still important mining settlement of Dale.

Thanks to the remains of Jim Pine's alfalfa patch, Kaweah was in good form when we struck eastward next morning toward Dale (or, as it was called in days when it was famous, Virginia Dale). It was a long, tedious march, the country becoming more barren at every mile, and the ground a tiresome alternation of sand with wide expanses of a sort of pavement, made of small bits of stone, reddish or black, polished to a slippery degree and set as if in a mosaic. It was the first time I met with this peculiar condition, though I often encountered it afterwards. I am still puzzled to account for it: one would almost think the fragments had been fitted together by hand and rolled down by a road engine. Little can grow in such a region. Even the creosote grew sparse and stunted here; it is a marvel, indeed, that it can exist at all. A few starved encelias showed white against the dark ground, and in the sandy washes spectral smoke trees quivered in the flickering air. Birds were entirely absent except for the road-runner, who is a sort of Esau, and whose peculiar imprint, like a St. Andrew's cross, one meets in the most impossible places.

Ahead ran the ashy Sheephole Range, to south the Pintos (a word signifying spotted, though I saw no reason for the name in the barrier of uniform reddish rock that kept me company hour after hour). Once I caught a glimpse of a high distant ridge that I knew must be the Cockscombs, they fitted the name so exactly. One or two tracks led off to nominal mines, active only to the extent of the assessment work which must be performed yearly in order to keep ownership alive. This rite, as it may be called, makes the excuse for the owners to set out annually from city or ranch, with burro, grub, pick, shovel,

and rifle, for two weeks' work on their claims. Naturally, summer is not the season chosen, water then
being scantiest and heat most trying, so I saw little
of these pilgrims of hope: but in winter and spring
there will be many such parties, ones, twos, and
threes, creeping about this vast territory wherever
man, horse, or burro may go (automobile must now
be added, for the automobilist's maxim is that man,
with an auto, can go where man has gone before.)

After six hours' travel, a dot in the distance that I
had been speculating upon for an hour past began
to take the shape that I hoped it would — an odd
shape to find in this wilderness, viz.: that of a windmill of the modern iron type. It marked Lyon's
Well, which is a watering station for stock, though
the traveller may see no sign of cattle for days together. On nearer approach there appeared a few
scraps of adobe wall, all that remains of the first
settlement of Virginia Dale. Of all materials for
building used by civilized man, adobe is the one
soonest effaced. Once the roof is gone the rest goes
quickly "back to the ground from whence it
sprung." Fifty years after its palmy days I could
barely find shelter from the wind in what was left of
Virginia Dale. The historian of a mining camp must
be early on the scene if he is to find anything more
than the ground on which it stood.

The pump was out of commission, but I managed with rope and bucket to supply Kaweah's
needs. A strong wind had begun to blow, adding
discomfort to tedium, as we turned southward up
a rocky slope toward a low divide. My next land-

mark, the buildings of an abandoned minc, were a welcome sight, for I confess that though I had had some experience of Western travel I was often anxious on these desert wanderings, where questions of forage and water might render a mistake a serious matter.

On reaching the divide, a row of little buildings came in sight, two miles away against the foot of a mountain. This, I thought, was Dale, and headed Kaweah toward it. As we came near I was wondering at the deserted look of the place when, turning a point, I saw the real Dale perched on the skyline far above me. The other place was a sort of parasite, whose only reason for being was to help the miners of Dale to get rid of their money — a matter which in a mining camp should be accomplished as speedily as possible and with as much detriment to one's self as circumstances allow. No means of attaining these ends has yet been found that can compare with investing in chemical whiskey or "dago red" at fancy prices, getting gorgeously drunk thereon, and then playing monte or poker with a sharper. But now, prohibition days have fallen on Riverside County, and only one, or perhaps two, "blind pigs" grow fat on what they suck from the pockets of the miners of Dale.

One soon comes, in the West, to modify one's qualms over acceptance of hospitality from strangers. Emmons had urged me, at Piñon Well, to accompany him to the mine he was bound for, and told me gravely that "the boys" would n't like it if they found that I (whom, of course, they had never heard of) had passed so near without paying them a visit. It would cost me nothing, he assured me: the boys would regard me as a boon and take care of me as long as I would stay. So, too, I found it at Dale. At the first house on the stairway-like street I asked where I might find lodging, supposing that there must be something in the nature of an inn. "Well, the Superintendent is away," I was told: "you'd better go and see the cashier. He'll fix you up." That friendly chap at once took charge of me as of an expected guest: insisted on my taking his room for my own, and quartered Kaweah in the Company's stable. Other conveniences were offered by the resident doctor, and in effect I was made free of the camp.

This Dale, I learned, was Dale the Third. As old "leads" or veins of ore "peter out" and new ones are discovered, the mining camp "follows the lead" in a literal sense. The present camp is about a dozen years old, and is supported by one good-sized gold mine, named the Supply, though there are a few smaller mines in the locality. Fifty or sixty men, half a dozen women, a half-score of children, and one badly spoiled baby made up the population at the time of my stay. The mine is a highly organized affair, with electric-lighted buildings and a water supply pumped from wells six miles away. Day and night the whirr and crash of engines goes on unceasing. It was strange to wake at night and hear the roar of machinery in that remote place, all the more so after weeks of Nature's quietude.

The village consists of (beside the mine structures)

a score or so of temporary looking houses and cabins, spotted about without any pretence of order. A store, with kitchen and dining-room attached, and a cashier's office of stone are all the buildings of any size. The post-office shares quarters with a Clubroom containing an antique pool-table, the felt worn to a curiosity and the pockets as hopeless as a bachelor's. Relics of the Fourth remained in the shape of a wire cable stretched across the street with fag-ends of rockets and Roman candles still attached.

I do not know how the place got its name, whether through some Virginian who thus showed his loyalty to the Old Dominion, or perhaps by way of compliment to some charmer of a sentimental Argonaut. However that may be, the present site, encircled by steep, rough mountains, is really a kind of dale; though it brought a pang to think of Martindale, Grisedale, Ravenstonedale, and other old Lakeland nooks, flowery and green where this was harshly red and gray. Yet when I climbed above the village at sunset, and the light came warmer on crag and gully, the shadows more tender in the hollow of the pass — yes, that might be Glaramara, and that Coniston Old Man; in that winding gorge Ullswater might lie, or, scarcely less solitary than this, lonely, lovely Wastwater.

The view to the north was memorable as an example of the ultra-desolate. Beyond the ragged brown foreground lay the pale gray expanse of a dry lake, whitened near its centre by the alkaline deposit from its vanished waters. Beyond that rose the ashy wall of the Sheephole Mountains, quite lunar in their look of geologic age and dreariness. A thread-like line that skirted the lake bed and faded in a gap of the hills marked the road to Amboy, forty miles away, Dale's shortest link with the rest of the world.

Capping their hospitalities to me, my good friends would not allow me even to settle for Kaweah's provender, saying that "the Company" expected to take care of little things like that. It is unlikely that these pages will meet the eye of the Crœsus who counts this bagatelle of a gold mine among his numberless "properties" — his name is one at which Wall Street holds its breath — but anyway I hereby make acknowledgment of my obligation.

We left Dale amid the good wishes of a score of the men, who were gathered before the eating-house ready for the stampede at sound of the breakfast bell. One or two of them I met again at later stages of my journey, and was amused to learn what droll rumors had been in circulation regarding my object in coming to Dale. Your miner must have his little mystery, and if needful will hatch one for himself. I was even credited with being the agent of mighty financial interests, perhaps — solemnizing thought — Crœsus himself in disguise.

The "blind pig" of the suburbs was already astir as I passed, and was as portly a pig as could be expected. The few sentences that passed while I watered Kaweah showed that he was a suspicious pig too, which was not surprising in these times when even deputy sheriffs sometimes are unfriendly to pork. My road led eastward through a narrow cañon where every hillside had a metallic look at the most casual glance. Everywhere were prospect holes, or deeper workings where the mountain had spewed out piles of glittering gray rock. Here and there were scraps of machinery, old windlasses and boilers, dragged here at enormous expense, now mere rusty monuments to the ruling passion; though, to be fair, one must say to man's energy, hardihood, and determination, as well.

The stony track made rough going for Kaweah. Fortunately I had had him shod (a new experience for him, though he was rising nine when I bought him) at Indio, in anticipation of the rocky country we should meet in the mountains. I was glad when the cañon opened southward upon a wide plain, a dozen miles or more across, through which the road ran straight to vanishing point. The sun was unusually severe; the scanty vegetation gave no relief to the eye; and all there was of variety for mile on mile was the alternation of glaring sand with darker pavement-like stretches that reflected the sun gleam with added intensity. The air was in a tremor of heat, and under my sombrero my eyes ached so that I often closed them and left Kaweah to pilot us alone. Sometimes I dismounted and walked in order to relieve him, but this was a signal for him to slacken his pace to almost a standstill; so having no mind to drag half a ton of horseflesh I soon mounted again, whereat he sighed, eyed me with soft reproach, and stood waiting till a touch of the spur urged him to a spiritless shuffle.

Still far to the east rose the Cockscombs, ghostlike

in the flicker and haze. On my right was the Pinto Range, now showing a patching of light and dark masses that gave point to the name. Ahead were the Eagle and Cottonwood Mountains, into which the road vanished as if there it must end. Hours passed in stupefying heat while I alternately dozed in the saddle or dragged the apathetic Kaweah along at snail-like pace. The creosotes moved listlessly when for a moment the wind came with furnace-like breath. There was little comfort in the canteen, for the water was unpleasantly hot, and the vacant shell of a tortoise, or bleaching ribs of cattle, were objects not interesting to a jaded mind. The spry white lizards seemed the only things that kept any touch of energy, I might almost say of life.

By early afternoon we reached the entrance to a rocky pass that led into the mountains, and stopped for rest and lunch. I had saved a feed of barley for Kaweah, which he munched with indifference and then dozed with drooping head, too fagged to crop the scraps of galleta that I pointed out to him. Loath as I was to move on, I could not afford more than the regulation hour, for there were many miles ahead of us before we should reach the next water.

The wash that issued from this cañon was filled with a dense growth of the smoke tree, looking like a column of men in light gray uniform winding away in close-shut ranks across the plain. The flowering season was nearly past, but the ground was colored deep blue by the fallen petals. Plant life became more varied as we gained the higher ground, as is always the case in these desert cañons, bare as they look from the plain. I saw yuccas of three species, the lycium with its ruby-like berries, the simmondsia, which bears a nut of good flavor, the curious salazaria, covered with quaint little bladders, even the wild buckwheat common on the coast, to say nothing of the eternal cat-claw and the common desert growths. There appeared also a plant or two of the rare *Nolina parryi*, their tall flowering-stalks bearing masses of yellow seed-vessels that reminded me of hydrangea bloom.

Soon after crossing the divide I noticed a rude cross close beside the road. Later I learned that it marked the grave of a man named Riley who died here of thirst a few years ago. He had left the Dale mines intending to walk to the railway at Mecca. The footprints showed that he reached a point almost within sight of Cottonwood Springs: it may have been dark or dusk, so that he failed to see the spot of green a mile farther on that marks the water. He turned back towards Dale, but soon turned again, staggered as far as this, and here died. A brother of his is said to have lost his life in the same way soon afterward on the road from Dale to Amboy. Similar tragedies occur every year in these deserts, and it would seem that the county authorities, or the State, or the nation, might afford out of our millions of taxation the small sum that would suffice to set up guide-posts on these roads, indicating where water is to be found, the distance to it, and if necessary the marks by which the exact place is to be known. It is now quite possible for some wretch to perish in the tortures of thirst within so short a distance of water that by a final effort he might have reached it.

It was just sunset when I caught sight of a cotton-wood in a cleft of the cañon wall. In a few minutes we were at Cottonwood Springs, among shady trees and with excellent water in abundance. We had made thirty miles of extra tiring travel, and I resolved to stop for a day and enjoy the beauty of the spot. But when, after we had drunk our fill, I searched for pasturage, the pleasing prospect faded. I had been told that I should find grass in plenty here, but except for a few scraps of half-dead "fila-ree" there was nothing to serve for forage. For to-night we must make the best of a bad job, and in the morning push on to Mecca, twenty-five miles away. With compunction I picketed Kaweah for the night on his meagre billet, he watching me with anxious gaze as I moved away.

I ate a cold supper, drank about five gallons of water, smoked a pipe, and turned in, not before enjoying a shower-bath of the desert sort, by means of my tin drinking cup. With musical rustle of cotton-woods I was wafted to luxurious sleep.

As I was saddling up for an early start, a Crusoe-like figure appeared on the hill above a doorless cabin that I had decided to be uninhabited. The old man proved to be a caretaker in charge of the machinery which pumps water from this place to a mine eighteen miles to the east. (Such are the difficulties that must often be overcome before these desert mines can be worked.) Crusoe seeming friendly, and urging a longer stay, I explained my case, when he mentioned that in a locked building near by there was a little store of hay, the property of a Mecca man who occasionally made trips to a claim in the Eagle Mountains. He also offered the opinion that "a feller's hoss had n't oughter go hungry when there was hay layin' aroun'." Enough said: I could pay the owner when I reached Mecca: so I took French leave, off-saddled, and treated my surprised Kaweah to a hearty breakfast.

Under these circumstances I returned to my former programme and passed an easy day, revelling in shade, cool sweet water, and leisurely meals at which Crusoe bore me company. Cottonwood Springs is one of the few desert watering-places at which the traveller would wish to stay longer than necessity requires. Some bygone hermit had planted a few apple trees, which promised a tolerable crop, and there was even a garden patch where Crusoe cultivated radishes, beans, and tomatoes for the benefit of the local quail and jack-rabbits. An old *arrastra* (the primitive means of crushing ore in a circular pit, by dragging heavy weights over it, with horse or mule for motive power) spoke of old times and timers, and the samples of rock scattered about would have furnished several museums with specimens. My friend's conversation bore all upon mining affairs and was Hebrew to me; while mine no doubt was equally worthless to him, for the desert had dried out every interest but one, and turned him into a sort of mineral.

While I was deep in slumber that night I had a sudden alarm of rumble and shouting, and jumped up just in time to escape being trampled by a pair of horses that failed to see me until they were almost on me, when they reared and backed on the heavy wagon. It was the owner of that hay, come at midnight as if to avenge his wrongs. At the moment, that seemed to be his mood when he heard my story: but in the morning he felt better about it, and became quite friendly when he pocketed his scandalous overcharge.

Sunrise found us on the move down the cañon, in shadow of high walls from which came ever and anon the haunting call of the cañon wren, as charming as that other

> "Sweet bird, that shun'st the noise of folly,
> Most musical, most melancholy."

The air in these desert cañons at early morning, before the sun shines in, is about the finest in the world, cool, light, mildly energizing, pure as the upper ether. It was enchanting to ride in ease and shade, not now too wearied to feel the finer glory of the sun-ray as it roused the dull tone of common rock into living flush of color, kindled the upper cliff to a beacon flame, trimmed each coping and pinnacle with tremulous fire. The cañon sides here were high and precipitous, and weathered at the top into fantastic confusion. Outlined with toppling crags and turrets on an almost overhead skyline were spectral yuccas and ocotillos, their rigid shapes fully in keeping with the crude rock forms among which they appeared.

In the cañon bottom a few palo verdes were still in blossom, along with desert willow and cat-claw.

I here began to meet the *palo fierro* or ironwood, a tree that to me has always an interesting, friendly look. I had hoped to find it in flower, but it was a month too late, and the apple-green foliage was sprinkled thickly with brown seed-vessels. This locality seems to be about the northwesterly limit of the tree's growth.

To the cañon there ensued the usual expanse of gravelly plain, somewhat relieved here by a remarkably fine growth of ocotillos. Their short season of beauty was over, the leaves had fallen and left the thorny canes skeleton-like and gray, and the fiery blossoms were dried to the color of rust. But in size many of them far exceeded the ordinary. Some were over twenty feet in height, with butts as thick as well-grown oaks. The typical contour of the desert mountains also is specially well marked in this locality. The steep slope of the rock wall meets the horizontal abruptly, with no conjoining curve; but from every cañon a long straight tongue or *bajada* runs out at low angle, and even then the junction with the line of the plain is clearly marked. That is the desert: no suavity, grace, or curve of beauty, but always a stark construction of right lines and angles, repeated to the point of obsession.

A higher mass at length came in sight to the south, and I recognized Santa Rosa; then, more westerly, San Jacinto swung into view: both faintly drawn in the haze, mere bands of uncertain blue hardly darker than the sky. A few more miles, and far in the west I caught a glimpse of what seemed a white iceberg, showing above the long, sea-like horizon of a distant mesa. It was the topmost crest of San Gorgonio, the thousand feet or so by which it over-tops the two-mile mark.

I was now again approaching the so-called mud hills which here form the inner barrier before reach-ing the open levels of the Colorado Desert. Presently the road passed into a gorge framed by high white cliffs. In this peculiar formation the elements find free play, and they have made the most of the oppor-tunity. One can hardly credit those plodding work-men, water, wind, and frost, with these spectacular forms, which seem more in the style of Vulcan's art. Thunderbolts might have riven these vast perpen-dicular scars, these crumbling turrets and threaten-ing towers, which hint more of dynamics than of slow erosion.

A mile down the cañon we found ourselves at Shafer's Well. It was only mid-morning, so there was time for a good rest. I threw off the saddle and left Kaweah to pick what he chose out of a scatter-ing of hay that some prodigal team had wasted, while I niched myself into a scrap of shade and watched, between dozes, the antics of a troupe of chipmunks. These jolly little scamps, hardly bigger than mice, are the most entertaining of the whole Sciurus tribe (which is a good deal to say when one remembers the Douglas squirrel of the Sierra). Their impudence is delicious, quite in the style of the Artful Dodger. They are practical jokes incarnate, and there is something positively wicked in the cock of their tails.

The cool of evening was still some hours away

when we took the road for the last stage of this part
of our travels. The gorge became narrower, the walls
higher and in places vertical. I have changed my
mind so often with regard to the possibilities of temperature, whether greater in cañons or in the open,
that I hesitate to say that the heat that July afternoon marked a new record in my experience. The
winding of the cañon shut off all chance of a breeze;
the white walls and the white sand of the bottom
reflected the sun's rays mercilessly; the cañon
seemed to reverberate with heat and light. Once or
twice it grew almost insupportable and I fancied I
felt warnings of vertigo. I have no doubt that the
thermometer, if a shade reading could have been
taken, would have shown 125° or over. Kaweah,
like a true Indian, pushed doggedly on through the
yielding sand. Bronco he may be, but I have found
every ounce of him good staunch horse.

The cañon widened, and at a turn — behold! the
Salton Sea lay across the opening, faintly blue, mysterious, romantic, pictorial. At the same moment a
breeze met us; not cool, oh no, but bringing at least
a touch of life into the stagnation, even a momentary tang of good salty ocean. Beyond the line of
blue rose the opaline barrier of Santa Rosa, and far
to southward, Superstition Mountain, hardly more
than a shadow on the sky.

Passing into the open I looked westward up the
valley. Dark clumps of cottonwoods marked the
sites of the nearest ranches, five miles away: a trail
of smoke, like that from a steamer far out at sea,
showed where a train was running down from the

Pass: hazy in distance, the places of the little settlements of the Coachella Valley could be guessed: and over all, though now low on the horizon, San Jacinto and San Gorgonio kept the gateway of the Pacific. Mecca, a nondescript hamlet and railway point near the northern margin of the Salton Sea, was now only a few miles away, and at evening we came to rest and welcome at the ranch of a friend who grows the earliest grapes of the season, at appropriate prices, for "such as choose to buy them." Here we enjoyed again for a few days plentiful hay, cultured society, newspapers, music, and, what seemed the consummation, the sight and sound of water gurgling day and night from artesian wells.

The round I had made since leaving the valley had taken me about a hundred and fifty miles, roughly in a circle. Ten miles away was Coachella, whence I had started a week before.

CHAPTER XI

A DESERT RIDE: MECCA TO FIGTREE JOHN

Painted Cañon — Complicated shapes and strange colors — The Heroic Age of Geologics — Work of earth-sprites — Solitude — Hot drinking-water — A date plantation — Erosion once more — A "low-down" newspaper — Camp at Toro — A friendly *capitan* — Martinez Indian village — Cahuilla Indian wells — The old fish-traps — Alamo Bonito Indian village — A thunder-storm — The Oasis Ranch: a swimming-pool — The Salton Sea, its origin — Engineer *vs.* River — Pelicans — Figtree John — Valuable archives — Duke of Conejo Prieto — Hair-ropes and rattlesnakes — A sophisticated "sitter" — Camp at Figtree John Springs — Evening colors — Night and coyotes.

A FEW miles to the north of Mecca a cañon opens into the Cottonwood Mountains that is remarkable for the contour and the coloring of its walls. It is known as Painted Cañon. A view of it well repaid the discomfort of the ride on a July morning with the thermometer at 110° in the shade. A broad horizontal band of red on the face of the mud-colored foothills plainly marks the point of entrance.[1]

These foothills never fail to rouse my curiosity by the complicated shapes into which the material has been wrought. The material is earth, not rock, and is mostly of a pale gray hue, approaching white. Erosion, supplementing the work of some violent original upthrow, has produced a most intricate medley of forms. At a mile or two, the light and shade effects are so eccentric as to seem artificial. Creasing,

---

[1] It is not the cañon that opens directly into the red formation, but the next one to the westward, that is most notable.

pleating, braiding, dovetailing, are carried to the point of confusion; yet on this vast scale it has a look of orderliness that is unnatural: and under sunset light this whole foothill range for leagues becomes a chequer of red and purple, a charm of color, a mystery of design.

On entering the cañon the sides are at first not high, and are built of whitish earth. But as one goes on the walls increase in height and verticality, and in strangeness of form, while the cañon narrows to a gorge, then a defile. Novel colors appear. Cliffs mainly of dusky red are banded and splashed with lavender, chocolate, bright ochre, purple, gray, ashy dark green, and brilliant lighter red. Clefts only a few feet in width wind away from the main cañon. Curious shapes are met — gullies, cirques, domed recesses, tunnels, perpendicular walls of unbroken smoothness topped with turrets and spires in perilous balance. There has been wild work here in some Heroic Age of Geologics: enormous mud eruptions, I suppose, succeeded by cooling conditions almost equally violent, and these followed by ages of varied though slower play of elements. Even Kaweah was impressed, and stared about him like any tourist.

The passage way became yet narrower, the cliffs more vast. I do not think five hundred feet is an overestimate of their height in some places, and the nearness of the walls to the beholder doubles or trebles their towering effect. One feels as if he were at the bottom of a well. A feature that interested me was the formation, in places, of a sort of lace-work, curiously fashioned of earth, which hung in perpendicular valances from projecting ledges where water had trickled over the cliff face; the work, one might fancy, of some race of gnomes or fairy cliff-dwellers, who inhabited the crannies of the wall and wove this airy grill to screen their privacy.

After some miles I dismounted and sat down in the strip of shade at the foot of the cliff. The silence was profound. No breeze penetrated thus far, no rustle of wing, piping of insect, nor hint of delicate footfall broke the trance-like stillness. The dead air and the pressure of heat in that confined space added to the feeling of absolute solitude. Only the swing of an eagle across the narrow ribbon of sky told of life, motion, the sentient in Nature. On the sand near by lay the carcass of a raven. Then, momentarily breaking the spell, from some ledge far overhead came a shower of pearl-like notes, the sweet, unvarying phrase of the cañon wren, plaintive, beseeching, like Orpheus's farewell to Eurydice.

At this season there was no water in the cañon, though in winter a feeble trickle is sometimes forced to the surface by an outcropping ledge of granite. My canteen supplied my own needs, but Kaweah seemed unhappy and must have longed to drink. So I refrained from exploring farther than some four miles of the cañon, which continued to wind on, apparently into the heart of the mountain. On the return I noted a few clumps of the rare *Aster orcuttii* still holding their large lavender blossoms, the only flowers and almost the only plants that the place afforded.

Halfway down the cañon a hot wind met us. It

had a fierce, stinging quality that made the skin smart, and seemed as if it would wither the eyeballs through the lids. The water in the canteen became so hot that it was only while in the act of drinking that thirst was allayed. Kaweah hurried along without need of spur, and when we reached camp drank until I feared the water resources of the valley would be endangered and made him stop. I poured what remained in the canteen into my canvas washbasin, and on using it several minutes afterwards found it uncomfortably hot. Its temperature by the thermometer was 108°.

When a friend who had a date plantation near Thermal — an over-modest name at this season — a few miles up the valley, invited me to visit his place, I was prompt to comply. Months of solitary travel lay ahead, and I did n't miss any chance of society while I could get it. My friend himself was absent, but the jolly young Canadian foreman and a delightful Mexican family who worked on the place made my stay pleasant and profitable. The owner is one of the pioneers of the date industry, and an importer of the palms on a large scale from the African and Asiatic date regions. The plantation was a picture of thrift and perfect cultivation, and the young Algerians, Arabians, and Persians seemed as comfortable as though Santa Rosa Mountain, across the valley, were Ararat, Sinai, or the Atlas.

One of the neighboring cañons gave another example of the fantastic in natural carving. The walls are in places wrought to almost a cathedral look of fineness, and with their whitish color take on, at a

little distance, almost the look of old ivory. Deeply
worn trails of bighorn marked the hillsides here and
there, and once the silence was broken by a far-off
bleat that only augmented the sense of solitude.

It was a sultry, half-cloudy day when I moved
southward across the valley to the old Indian village
of Toro. There was little token of desert in the green
fields of alfalfa, willow-shaded reservoirs, and flocks
of water-loving blackbirds that I passed; but along
the mountain-side ran the ancient sea-line, reminding me that I was in one of Neptune's cellarages,
pumped dry by the sun. There used to be a little
newspaper published monthly at Thermal, that bore
the heading, "The Coachella Valley Submarine,
published 122 feet below sea-level." A humorous
sub-heading described this inoffensive sheet as "the
most *low-down* newspaper on earth." I know of
others to which such a character might be attributed
seriously enough.

Arrived at Toro, I sought an interview with the
capitan. He bore the unromantic name of Joe Pete,
but was a good-looking, portly, friendly fellow, who
willingly showed me a good spot for my camp in a
grassy corner of his little farm. There were evidences
of thrift in his neat house of cement blocks and in
flourishing rows of grape-vines, cantaloupes, and so
forth; also in his wife, busy with the blackberry
patch. Two boys and half-a-dozen dogs made it their
business to interview me, and I was put through a
short but sharp examination: — "What your name?"
"Where you come from?" "Where you go?"
"When?" "Where you get you pony?" "How

much?" "Can he buck?" and "What you do, you prospect?." When my turn came there was not much to be got beyond shy grins and much shuffling of dusty feet: but I learned that one of the boys was Joe Pete's godson, and that he lived with his godfather in preference to staying at his proper home, close by: which seemed to speak well for the big *capitan*.

There were heavy clouds and vivid lightning that evening to the north, and I guessed they were catching it up at Dale and Twenty-nine Palms. Once or twice in most summers an electrical storm breaks over these mountains, but the rain seldom reaches the open desert. It may sometimes be seen falling but is likely to evaporate in mid-air and return unspent to the parent cloud. Joe Pete, who came over while I was breakfasting to present me with a melon, promised two months of what he called "Little warm, like this" (it was then about 95°, less than an hour after sunrise).

In the morning I went on to the next village, Martinez, a short distance down the valley. Somewhere hereabout there were to be seen until lately examples of the wells dug by the Indians of olden days. I got an intelligent young Indian to pilot me to the sites of three of them, but they were now shapeless pits filled with mesquit and other brush. The water supply is now the commonplace one by pipe and bucket, no longer *per* squaw, marching picturesquely with *olla* through thickets of arrowweed and mesquit to draw from the pool at the foot of the earthen stairway, returning with plentiful germs of typhoid fever. I have inquired for these old wells in other parts of the desert where formerly there were large Indian settlements, but have failed to find one remaining in tolerable condition. I am told that these Indians, the Cahuillas, are the only tribe known to have solved the water problem by digging wells.

At the foot of Santa Rosa Mountain, a short distance from Martinez, there is an interesting relic of aboriginal times that is fairly well preserved, though it must be of very great age. A number of years ago there appeared in a Los Angeles paper an account of the discovery of remains of a prehistoric city in this locality. The story had all the marks of a mare's nest, but I fancy that this that I refer to may have been its foundation. The object is hard to find, being indistinguishable until one is on the very spot, and even then it might be overlooked. Yet it is as unmistakably man's handiwork as the cliff dwellings, when once the eye grasps it. In a little recess or bay, perhaps three hundred yards wide, at the foot of the mountain one sees a curious arrangement of the stones that litter the slope. They seem at first to be grouped in circular formation, as if they marked the outlines of small round huts. The circles are not complete, however, but are like horseshoes, with the openings on the upper side. The slope is covered with continuous lines of these horseshoes, nearly touching one another, the rows extending almost from side to side of the recess. The diameter of the horseshoes is six or eight feet, and there are several rows, one above the other, like terraces along the foot of the slope.

When one observes that these stone horseshoes are placed just at the level of the former sea, their nature becomes plain. They were simply fish traps. Whether the entire set was built when this was a tidal shore, and the sundry rows were meant to serve for higher or lower tides, or whether the traps date from more recent times when this was an inland (and therefore tideless) sea, and the ranks were built downward in succession as the water line gradually lowered, I must leave to heads more archæological than mine. When I spoke of the place to one of the Martinez Indians he knew at once what I meant and referred to the objects unhesitatingly as "the old fish-traps."

A short ride from Martinez took me to Alamo Bonito,[1] another Indian village, taking its name from the trees that mark its location from miles away. It is ruled by Jake Razon as *capitan*, and to him I applied for permission to camp near the water, and for Kaweah's rations of hay. At first he was suspicious, for which I did n't blame him, especially as my military saddle and other traps gave a half-official look to my coming. I had broken in on a family watermelon party too; but after talking me over while they finished the melon, Jake relented, and again all was *hunkydory*, as a former host had phrased it. He came over after supper for a chat; but his Anglo-Indian-Spanish was too abstruse for me, and was complicated by one or two original compound idioms that found place in every sentence, for instance, "Sometime-anytime" and "You-

[1] Spanish, *alamo* = cottonwood; *bonito* = beautiful.

see-you-bet." I gathered, however, that some local authority was bent upon breaking up the few remaining tribal customs of these harmless people, such as the periodical *fiesta* and the use of their Indian language. It seems odd that Indian officials are so enthralled by the repressive idea, which may be summed up as "See what those confounded Indians are doing and make them stop it."

I slept well with Jake's scanty hay pile for mattress, but was aware once or twice of thunder, lightning, and sprinklings of rain. Just before dawn there came a splitting crash right overhead. I jumped up and found a partial shelter, which only enabled me to soak piecemeal instead of going in for a whole-hearted sousing at once, which would have been much more comfortable. A mare and colt that had been my neighbors all night, gradually nibbling my mattress away, dashed wildly about at every flash and roar. Kaweah was not interested; he had hay to attend to, and munched on, sloppy but happy.

The farthest outpost of civilization in this direction is the Oasis Ranch, a flourishing spot where, owing to plentiful water, desert life is almost luxurious. I had meant to camp there for one night, but the cordial welcome I met from the caretakers and from some friendly people who owned adjoining land was too much for me: though the oranges, grapes, and melons, with the charms of a reservoir big enough for swimming-pool, also had weight. It would be my last taste of such pleasures for a pretty long spell, and I willingly succumbed to a three days' stay. Pasturage moreover was plentiful, and

the fig season at its prime. At evening we all took
to the water, and for an hour the welkin rang with
shoutings, splashings, and barkings. When I retired, cooled to sleeping point, repose was enlivened
by big over-ripe figs that dropped on me at intervals through the night.

My route now was for a few miles near the margin
of the Salton Sea. This body of water is well worth
a paragraph, and the more so, perhaps, for the reason that it will probably find no place on the maps
of the next generation of schoolboys. The central
part of the Colorado Desert has long been known
to be below sea-level, a fact, indeed, plainly stamped
on the face of the country in the water line of the
ancient beach. The means by which Neptune lost
this corner of his domain can be stated in few words.

In far distant times the point at which the Colorado River debouched into the Gulf of California
was not, as it is now, at the head of the Gulf. The
sea then reached farther northward, to the limit
shown by the old shore line, so that the river's
mouth was some distance to the south of the sea's
northern boundary. In course of ages, the great
stream (then no doubt engaged in the carving of that
marvellous cañon that ranks perhaps first among
the geographical wonders of the world) built up
with its silt a dam which in time extended com-
pletely across the Gulf, leaving the upper part cut
off from the ocean. This isolated part (which was
over two thousand square miles in area, and by
geologists is named Lake Cahuilla, from the Indian
tribe that inhabited its western side) receiving

practically no supplies of water, tended to disappear by evaporation.

From time to time, however, the river must have broken in, with the result that the lake became brackish. Thus, the shells that are a noticeable feature of all the below-sea-level area are of kinds native to fresh or brackish waters. The shell-remains of the original sea epoch are now found high above sea-level, betokening some great upheaval in remote times. It is to the brackish period that the deposits of travertine (calcium carbonate) are due. Proof can be seen, in marks of old lake beaches at various levels, that there was a succession of complete or partial fillings and emptyings of the lake basin, the inflow no doubt usually coming from the river, but perhaps sometimes from the Gulf.

From Indian tradition it would seem that for a long time prior to recent years the lake bed as a rule has been dry. Great deposits of salt occupied the deepest portion, and, a few years ago, were being worked on a large scale. In 1891 there occurred a relatively small inflow from the river, creating a shallow lake of some two hundred square miles: but in 1905, through the weakness of levees and headgates of the canal system that was carrying the Colorado River water on to the lands of the new Imperial Valley settlement, came a greater flood which caused serious loss and threatened a wholesale disaster. For over two years the water rose, until it seemed as if it would entirely fill its old basin. It was not till early in 1907 that the Engineer finally conquered the River. (I say finally, but after all that is a word man should never use for his little victories over physical nature.) At that time the lake was over four hundred square miles in area, with a depth of more than eighty feet — an imposing body of water.

That is the so-called Salton Sea. Evaporation has somewhat reduced it, and in about twenty years, should there be no new inflow, it will probably have disappeared, perhaps forever. To-day it is still a great expanse, which looked at over its farthest extent appears a veritable sea, with no horizon of land to mark its bounds.

Near the western margin of this geologically romantic lake my road now ran to the southward. The water, faintly blue and ideally calm, looked, in the summer haze, like a water-color drawing, and the mountains beyond, the Cottonwoods and Chuckwallas, might have been an "insubstantial pageant" instead of the uncompromising reality that I had lately experienced. The Chocolate Range, farther to the south, was a mere dream of air tints, quite phantasmic. On the nearer shore a white and grisly rank of dead mesquits stood like skeletons. They had been killed by the flooding of the basin and had but lately emerged as the water receded. Here and there among the branches were many nests of pelicans, which make this inland sea, swarming with fish of one or two coarse species, their home and breeding ground. The effect upon the mind was of a Dead Sea, with horror veiled under a Circean smile. Nor did the sight of the old beach line, with its hint of vanished ages, of countless generations long passed away, at all lessen the impression.

The Indian patriarch of these parts is old Juan Razon, or, as he is better known, "Figtree John." In former times he lived, far from whites and other Indians, at a spot a few miles to the south. It is to be known by a few fig trees and is marked on Government maps as Figtree John Springs. When the Salton Sea submerged his little estate he moved to another spot, called Agua Dulce, on somewhat higher ground. I already had a slight acquaintance with him, and was pleased now to meet him as he was leading his horse to water. When I had surrendered the can of tobacco with which I had come prepared, he invited me to share a watermelon with him at his house. I hastened to agree to this excellent idea. The mellowest *sandía* was brought from his little patch and bisected with a rusty hatchet, and we sat in shade of the *ramada* and chatted while the cooling hemispheres rapidly melted away. To my regret, Mrs. John was coy and would not join us, nor would a huge girl who gloomily watched the melon's effacement through peepholes in the brush partition.

From a chummy, almost fraternal, tone, John became impressive. An old satchel was produced, and proved to contain archives that revealed my friend in higher rôles. First was a photograph, tenderly wrapped, of himself *en cavalier*, wearing a police uniform the feature of which, apart from a certain roominess of fit, was its double rows of gleaming buttons. The severity of a stove-pipe hat gave effect to an attitude of martial rigidity which he had thought proper on the occasion of being "taken." A possible defect of topheaviness was off-set by bare feet which corrected any impression of overdress. The steed, appropriate for a desert chief-tain, was a minute donkey, whose dramatically pointed ears betokened a deep sense of responsibility.

Next an aged document was perilously unfolded and spread before me. In clerkly hand and formal phrase it set forth that Cabezon, the last great chief of the Cahuillas, did thereby name and appoint Juanito (= Johnny, or Little John) Razon to be *capitan* of the Agua Dulce Tuba village, and to exercise authority in the name, place, and stead of said Chief Cabezon; and called upon his people to render respect and obedience to said Johnny in all said Johnny's lawful commands: etc., etc.: "given under my hand this so-and-so," and signed with a cross in presence of a witness. Then came some ragged maps, apparently rough drafts of surveyors. These, he held, made him owner of all the territory shown, running from the last low ridge of the Santa Rosas (the ridge was named Hiawat on the map, evidently an Indian word, though John could not translate it into Spanish) as far as Conejo Prieto or Black Rabbit Peak. No wonder he eyed me closely while these valuable papers were in my grasp.

Before I left I bought of him a *mecate* or rope of plaited horse-hair, of his own making. The price to others would have been four dollars, he said, but on grounds of friendship I should have it for half the sum. This statement warned me that the article was not worth the price he asked me for it, but I was glad to carry away this souvenir of the dusky

lord of Conejo Prieto. There is a legend, the truth
of which I may some day put to the proof, that the
rattlesnake will not cross a rope of this sort. Many
cowboys and others are convinced that this is a
fact, and John also affirmed it stoutly. I have sometimes, in specially snake-infested districts, laid the
rope round the place where I spread my blankets,
and can assert that I have never been bitten. This
may not be thought convincing, but I doubt if any
cowboy has better evidence to offer.[1] There is, however, a reasonable theoretical basis for the belief.
Any one who has handled a hair rope knows that it
is about as uncomfortable an article to the touch
as a thistle. The arrangement of the belly scales of
the rattlesnake is such that in the act of crawling,
the prickly hairs would certainly prove annoying —
perhaps enough so to cause the snake to change his
course.

When I suggested a picture it was made plain to
me that the great do not receive but confer a favor
in being photographed. John demanded a round
sum, which in this case seemed not to be modified
on the score of friendship. When that was arranged
he took the position and expression of one who
bears intense pain with determination. Then the
great girl would be taken with her pet goat. No need
for any formula of "Look pleasant, please," with
smiling Juana. When I asked how I should address

---

[1] I have recently made the experiment with a sidewinder, which is
a small species of the rattlesnake. It passed over my hair rope three
times without any token of discomfort. Each time, however, the
snake was moving backwards. It is possible that in forward motion
the effect might be different.

her in sending copies of the picture, she sedately gave her name as Mrs. So-and-so, Post-Office box so-and-so, at Mecca; thoroughly up in the ways of the world. No doubt her children will be little Bills and Bobs, Sadies and "Soosies," with chewing-gum and all modern improvements.

An hour's easy ride brought me to my camping place for the night at Figtree John Springs, no longer obliterated by the flood. The water is good though tepid, and a few small palms and a cottonwood or two make the spot attractive. The margin of the lake is now half a mile away. I walked over to it, and found an uninviting beach of slimy mud, the surface baked by the sun into large curving flakes like potsherds. A few dead trees were all that broke the melancholy expanse, if I except the decaying bodies of fish that added no charm to the landscape or the breeze. From the many coyote tracks it seemed that this sort of diet is much to the taste of that broad-minded animal. Far out, pelicans in groups of three or four were fishing for supper, one of them now and then launching itself with mighty splash upon a school of prey.

The sunset color was unusually fine, though of extreme delicacy. One might suppose that desert conditions would work for crudity and staring distinctness in form and color. The reverse is the fact. The most ethereal tones in Nature are those of desert landscapes. The mirage itself is hardly more elusive than the reality of these plains and mountains, faint, vague, mystical. And when the light comes level, as at evening or early morning, there is a quality in the scene that makes it ineffable, almost subjective.

I slept beneath the palms. Overhead the stars played hide-and-seek as a gentle wind moved the leaves and brought low sounds from the lake, where tiny ripples plashed on the beach. Once a deeper sound came, as if by subterranean ways, to my ears: a heavy train was rumbling down the valley to Yuma. I sat up and watched the speck of light from the engine, ten miles away across the water, and fancied I heard the ghost of a whistle as it neared the Salton siding. There was no doubt in the case, however, when the coyotes began to sing grace over their fish bones. Such a hullabaloo came from the shore as one would think must signify some "vast immedicable woe." But no, that is the coyote's way of enjoying himself. As a rule I enjoy it too, but now I wanted to sleep, so fired my revolver to see what the effect would be. There were ten seconds of sweetest silence: then the hubbub was redoubled and mounted to a crisis. Well, I would have it a smoking concert, at least, so lighted my pipe and talked to Kaweah until the performers grew tired and took their way homeward, their farewells coming in touching *diminuendo* from some distant cañon.

CHAPTER XII

A DESERT RIDE: FIGTREE JOHN TO BOREGO SPRINGS

Travertine Rock — The desert's dead-line — A desolate region — Fish Springs — "Fill up" the word — Tom Sawyer and Huck Finn: an unhopeful venture — A Miltonic sunrise — Doubtful trail — The dreary Salton — A vacant land — Mirage, ants, and antelope — A missing spring — Economizing water — Sign-board but no sign — Seventeen Palms — Vile water — Arabian surroundings — Watering Kaweah — Bad-lands — Devil's house of the Indians — Stone curios — Difficult trail-work — Nearing the mountains — Borego Springs, and water.

A NOTICEABLE landmark, less than a mile distant from Figtree John Springs, is an isolated outpost of Santa Rosa Mountain that from its coating of calcium carbonate is known as Travertine Rock. Standing ringed about by the sandy ocean, there is a suggestion of a battleship in its turreted shape, an idea further carried out by the strongly marked sea line near its top, as if that were the deck level, the gun turrets and other upper structures contrasting in pale gray of granite with the darker bulk of the travertine covered hull.

In the morning I walked over to examine it at close range and climb it for a view over the Salton Sea. Close to camp I noted a bench-mark of the Geological Survey, giving a *minus* elevation of 197 feet below sea-level. (The lowest part, now of course under water, of this depression has been found to be 287 feet below the sea, eleven feet lower than the bottom of Death Valley, on the Mojave, which is dry.) But the testimony of bench-marks was discounted by that horizontal line, still far above my head when I reached the base of the rock, though the ground I had walked over sloped slightly upward. It was like a dead-line, warning me that I was out of bounds, and drawing my attention to the fact that the whole bulk of the earth's oceans was dammed up a hundred feet or so overhead, a few miles away. If, I thought, Nature should decide just now to shift things round once more, and should knock a hole in the dam, I wonder what would happen? Something startling, for certain. It would be the Johnstown flood multiplied by billions.

In climbing among the huge boulders that lie tumbled round the foot of this ancient island, I was surprised at the thickness of their coating of travertine. In places where it had scaled off I saw blocks of the stuff a foot and a half through. I do not remember any such thickness at the "Coral Reef" or other points where I have found the travertine. Perhaps the exposed position of this rock, which, standing out in the sea-way, must have caught the full wavewash in times of storm, may account for this excessive deposit.

A little way from the foot, on the northeast face, I found a narrow cave, twenty yards or so from front to rear. Fragments of pottery showed that it had been inhabited, probably as a place of refuge. It can hardly have been used as a regular dwelling, for the floor was very uneven and the sides and roof showed no traces of smoke. The rock has hardly any plant life: only a few scraps of vegetation find foothold where a handful of soil has lodged. About the base an unthrifty palo verde here and there holds on to life, its smooth greenness, more like paint than verdure, looking stranger than ever in this stark spot. For animal life, one small brown wren flitted silently among the rhomboids of this natural pyramid.

The view proved worth the climb, though that was a warm experience. From here the Salton looked like a narrow bay, the head of which was near at hand though to south no land horizon was in sight. The few cultivated spots on the opposite side showed black rather than green, by contrast with the pale hue of sand or the white of patches of alkali. The mountain barrier beyond was a mirage-like band of neutral tone, giving no hint of the color flood that would come when the sun passed the zenith, to culminate at evening in the pageantry of sunset. Far to south the Chocolates paled imperceptibly into mere sky. Behind, the great mountain rose in leagues of barren rock, tremulous with heat but unmistakable as to reality. The sky was pale hard blue, no least film of vapor softening its aching glare. Out over the water, sea-birds wavered in rhythmic manœuvre, like some ghostly, impossible snowstorm.

In the afternoon I moved on a few miles to Fish Springs. The road ran near the lake margin, sometimes on land that had until recently been submerged. There was little of interest in the long levels through which we plodded. Pale drab of dried saltgrass — the ugliest grass that grows — alternated with stretches of alkali where Kaweah's hoofs broke through the white crust and sank into gray slime.

Rounded bushes of atriplex, repeated without variation of size, color, or outline, and shapeless clumps of sour-smelling suæda, followed one another with dreary monotony. A bit of arrowweed or a stunted screwbean was a boon by comparison. Ghosts of drowned mesquits made a phantom procession by the water's edge, and seemed, in the tremor of heat, to be up to some weird antics, like skeletons playing leapfrog. The vague shape of the Superstition Mountains, on the southern horizon, gave the landscape an extra touch of horror, recalling tales of men, not a few, who have perished in attempts to reach the treasure supposed to be hidden in that waterless labyrinth.

Fish Springs is marked by a growth of mesquits and small cottonwoods, spread over a few acres of damp land close to the border of the sea. The road, or rather track, I had been following is used occasionally by travellers to the Imperial Valley. The usual mode of travel nowadays is by automobile, which can cover the long distances quickly and, barring accidents, without danger from lack of water. It was significant of the sort of country I was entering to find beside the road a sign-board pointing to the water, with the warning, "Fill up. Last convenient water for 45 miles." At Fish Springs itself the water is brackish and tepid, nevertheless quite fair water for the desert. In the pool were numbers of tiny fish about the size of tadpoles.

As I neared the place I was surprised to hear a gun fired and the shot come peppering near, so I let out a whistle; but I was more surprised when I saw the gunners. By the edge of the pool stood two boys, a long and a short, both about twelve years old. On the ground were a scrap of blanket, some bits of food, and a half-gallon can of the lard-pail kind. The boys were poorly dressed, one shoeless, and neither of them in the pink of condition. It was near sundown, and if these were their preparations for supper, bed, and breakfast (to go no further) they seemed inadequate, especially in view of their surroundings. The smaller boy held a long, single-barrel gun and the carcass of a dove.

There was an air of uncertainty about the youngsters as if they had been discussing their next move. I asked whether they were camping there for the night, and the half-hearted way in which they "guessed so" seemed to show that they did n't know what else to do. When I inquired where they came from — "Indio," said the smaller and shoeless boy, who seemed the captain of the enterprise. As he glanced disconsolately this way and that I caught sight of the stock of an old-fashioned revolver projecting from the pocket of his ragged overalls. "How did you come?" "We walked," was the reply. (Indio was about forty miles away.) "Is that all the grub you have?" "No, I just got a bird" (exhibiting the dove). "Well, you nearly got a man, too. Where are you going?" "Borego Valley — I guess." "Do you know how far that is?" "'Bout ten miles, ain't it?" "Do you know the trail?" "No: I know where it is though; over that way." "What do you carry water in?" "That" — the little lard-pail. "Do you know how far it is to the next water?"

"No." "I'll tell you then. It's twenty-five miles to Seventeen Palms, and when you get there you can't drink the water. Then it's a good twelve more to Borego Springs, and five more to Borego Valley. Now, do you think the two of you can make nearly forty miles on that can of water?"

My youngster was visibly impressed as I rubbed in the water question, and now asked what I thought they had better do. In reply to my question of what had started them on this wild errand he opened up and explained that his father "knowed a feller" who had taken up land in Borego Valley, and they were going there to work for him. Had reached Fish Springs last evening, camped, and in the morning started on, carrying the pitiful little pail of water. Got a few miles along, water half gone; met two Mexicans, who were thirsty and drank the rest of the water; felt tired and hot, so went down to the lake and had a bath and drank a lot of the water. Felt bad and guessed they'd come back to Fish Springs to camp for the night.

"Now," I said, "there's just one thing for you boys to do, and I want to see you start to do it. Roll up your blanket and things and start back for home. I'll give you a note to the people at the Oasis Ranch, and they'll see that you have something to eat and a place to sleep. Then get back to Indio as soon as you can, and never do such a foolhardy thing again. It's a thousand to one you'd have got lost and died out there if you'd gone on. Will you do what I say?" They promised.

It was Tom Sawyer and Huckleberry Finn to the

life, to see those poor little scamps as they started up the dusty road. Over the big boy's shoulder the long gun waved vaguely to and fro; the little fellow carried the can of water, with the bit of blanket professionally rolled and slung by a cord at his back: the revolver-butt protruding from his flapping overalls in comico-pathetic fashion. As I gauged it, it was a case of running away from home. The Mexicans by drinking their water had very likely saved their lives. There is little doubt as to what would have been the outcome if they had gone on. They would have used up their water in the first ten miles: would almost certainly never have reached Seventeen Palms, which is not easy to find even had their strength held out so far: and if they had reached it they would have drunk their fill of the half-poisonous stuff and promptly succumbed. More likely they would have wandered about on a hopeless search for Seventeen Palms and would have run the usual course of thirst, delirium, insanity, death.

To-morrow's march would be a long one, so I turned in early. Mosquitoes were such a nuisance about the spring that before long I had to move two hundred yards away. Awaking after an hour or so, I could hear Kaweah stamping restlessly, and had to go over and rescue him also. The night was unusually warm and sleep unwilling to oblige. At last, the murmur of the ripple on the shore and the rhythmic chant of frogs sent me into an intermittent doze, from which I arose by moonlight at half-past three, not particularly refreshed.

I gave Kaweah a hearty feed from the little store

of barley that I had brought for helping him over the hard spots in the near future, and before five o'clock we were on the move. A heron rose from the lake as we started, and flapped slowly alongside for a hundred yards, etched Japanesquely on the brightening saffron. In a few moments the sun rose in his old tyrannic splendor, and our heron steered away as if it might have been one of the "yellow-skirted fayes" of that quaint idea of Milton's —

"So when the sun in bed,
  Curtained with cloudy red,
  Pillows his chin upon an orient wave,
  The flocking shadows pale
  Troop to the infernal jail,
  Each fettered ghost slips to his several grave,
  And the yellow-skirted fayes
  Fly after the night-steeds, leaving their moon-loved maze."

This time his chin was pillowed on the Cotton-wood Mountains, and his first shot at me came in a blaze of red across the dreary waters of the Salton.

The road (if it could be called a road) continued southward, paralleling on one hand the sea and on the other a long southeasterly spur of Santa Rosa. The spur ran out at last in a tongue of yellowish rock of the *malpais* kind, cut by many gullies and *bar-rancas*. Round this spur, which is known as Clay Point, my route lay. It seemed as if we should never turn that point. The going became worse, loose sand and gravel for hour after hour, and travel was slow and tiresome. It was a relief to reach the place where we must leave the road and strike westward across unbroken desert. The only mark of this spot was a heap of stones, and I felt a little anxiety on seeing that no tracks came in there, lest it might not be the turn-off for Seventeen Palms but only some prospector's sign leading into the bad-lands or the mountains. I had started with full canteens, of course, but though a gallon and a half may seem a good deal of liquid for one person for a day, any one who has travelled the desert in summer knows how quickly that quantity will be used. In this parching land to be without water for a very few hours means disaster. Hence, a mistake of direction, requiring retracing of steps or leading one into country through which it is difficult to find one's way, is a thing to be dreaded (and, I may add, is dreaded all the more as one gains in desert experience). It was the thirtieth of July, and the summer heat at its climax, reaching most days 115° to 120°, shade temperature.

I stopped Kaweah and glanced back at the Salton Sea, which I was now leaving for a time. It is at best a rather cheerless object, beautiful in a pale, placid way, but the beauty is like that of the mirage, the placidity that of stagnation and death. Charm of color it has, but none of sentiment; mystery, but not romance. Loneliness has its own attraction, and it is a deep one; but this is not so much loneliness as abandonment, not a solitude sacred but a solitude shunned. Even the gulls that drift and flicker over it seem to have a spectral air, like bird-ghosts banished from the wholesome ocean.

> "E'en the weariest river
> Winds somewhere safe to sea";

but for the Salton the appointed end is but a slow sinking of its bitter, useless waters, a gradual baring of slimy shores, until it comes once more, and probably for the last time, to extinction in dead, hopeless desert.

My outlook ahead and to the south was changed now that I had turned the shoulder of Santa Rosa. Before me to the west stretched one of the most forbidding tracts of the desert, grayer, more dreary than the rest. The shrubs grew smaller and more sparse; even the greasewood seemed ready to succumb. For mile on mile one sees no animal life either of beast, reptile, or bird, hardly of insect. Once I noted the track of a sidewinder, but this is a creature that moves by night: desert-dweller though it is, the desert sun is deadly to it. Far in front was the line of the Peninsular Sierra that runs on southward down the long length of Lower California. On the left, across a glistening alkaline expanse, rose the pale uncertain shapes of the Vallecitos and other ranges, fading into the Cócopa country beyond the Mexican border. Close at hand on the right was the southern face of Santa Rosa. The shells that whitened the ground told that I was still on the *minus* side of zero in elevation.

I looked carefully for tracks that might show I was headed rightly for Seventeen Palms. At long intervals I came on some faint wheel mark or doubtful shape of horse-hoof, but they were disjointed fragments, signifying little. Every rain storm brings down fresh sheets of sand from the washes of the mountain cañons, and every wind storm distributes the sand afresh; so that whatever travel there may

be must break its own road. The amount of such
travel may be gauged from the reply of the storekeeper at Mecca to my question whether he knew
of any one thereabout who had lately crossed this
piece of country and could give me directions.
"Seventeen Palms?" he said. "No, I have n't
heard of any one coming that way for six months."
The only guiding marks I saw were, once or twice,
a so-called monument — chance bits of stone which
the trained eye may know to have been placed by
man, not Nature — marking the best route across
the wider washes.

For long hours of glare and heat I pushed on, sometimes riding, sometimes leading Kaweah, who plodded steadily along like the loyal comrade he has
ever shown himself to be. Once a mirage suddenly
grew before me, the common one of a sheet of water
a few yards ahead; and once I saw a flicker of something white a mile away, which may have been a
band of antelope. About ten o'clock I found a few
scraps of blue-stem (galleta grass) and burro-weed
to eke out Kaweah's scanty barley, and we stopped
to rest and lunch. In saying that there was no insect
life in these parts I overlooked the ant. I should like
to know whether Arctic travellers do not find these
enterprising explorers always ahead of them. The
moment I sat down they converged on me. Evidently the word was passed round that a fellow had
arrived and was eating hardtack over by the greasewood, and the speed with which every crumb was
whisked away showed that it was a notable event.

A short half-hour was as long as I could afford,

since Kaweah, after a nibble at the uninviting forage, preferred to doze. On some unofficial map I have seen a certain "Sacaton Spring" marked as somewhere about here. Judging from the name, it would be marked by a growth of sacaton grass, which could be seen for miles in this kind of country. I searched with my field-glasses, but in vain, for any trace of greenness. Fortunately, as I had been unable to find anybody who knew of such a spring, I had not counted on it. Even if it could have been found it might have proved to be like that of the next spring to the south, which is too strongly impregnated with soda to be usable.

We took up our march. Occasionally a wandering breeze blew for a moment, and I opened my shirt and my heart to it, but it quickly died away, and again the heat struck fiercely down. It was impossible to maintain any interest in the view, but that was no loss, since nothing changed, hour after hour. The mountain profiles merged and emerged imperceptibly, and that was all. It seemed a week that I had been creeping over this unending plain. Somehow I felt unreal, as if I were a picture of a man in my position, and wondered vaguely whether the man ever got anywhere. The sole distraction was in counting the time for my periodical drinks, two mouthfuls per half hour, the first one held for a few seconds in the mouth before swallowing.[1] The reason

---

[1] I have since learned a good dodge from an Indian with whom I was out for some days in dry country. A little plug of the creosote (greasewood) bush, say three quarters of an inch long and a quarter of an inch thick, peeled, held in the mouth, is a good palliative of thirst, much better than the regulation pebble.

for this economy was not that I feared running short of water, but there is always the unforeseen to be reckoned with. I found that this small but regular ration kept me going, and I had already accustomed myself to drink only for necessity, not for comfort or luxury.

The appearance of a sign-board (a fragment of box-lid tied to a stake) raised hopes of a word as to direction and distance. But whatever information it may once have carried was gone as though it had never been there. Sun had bleached and sand had scoured till not a mark could be made out. This sort of thing is as aggravating as a practical joke. I was tempted to kick the thing sky high, but refrained when I reflected that it might be named as a landmark to some future traveller.

At last appeared, miles away to northwest, a few dots that showed black against the pale yellow foothills. If they were palms they were my landmark. I turned toward them: lost them and found them again and again: but finally knew that they were my palms; not my destination itself, but a guide to the place. Tracks became more frequent and converged toward a point in the clay hills that fringe Santa Rosa's southern base. A faint trail grew out of nothing, and led into a winding gallery of sand and boulders, where strange wind-worn and sand-worn cliffs showed at every turn. The palms appeared again, now close at hand; and in half an hour I caught sight of another group (once, I suppose, seventeen, but now only six or eight) that marked our halting place for the day.

The water at Seventeen Palms is a mere seepage, found in two small holes. If the holes were kept cleaned out for a day or two, probably the quality of the liquid would improve, though at best it would be strongly alkaline. At this time they were slimy and ill-smelling, and the water, which was brown, bitter, and nauseating, would have been dangerous to drink unboiled. Kaweah, however, drank eagerly when I had cleaned out one of the holes, though he is a gentlemanly horse, quite fastidious about his water. My small canteen was still full, but as it must carry me on to Borego Springs I used this unpleasant stuff, carefully strained, for my cooking. Rice boiled in it was thoroughly disgusting in color and taste; no amount of sugar could render it more than just bearable. The tea had a dirty gray curdle and a flavor like bilge, and when I tried cocoa as an alternative the mixture promptly went black.

Traces of former visitors were a rusty stove, abandoned, I guessed, by some survey party who travelled *de luxe* with cooks and water-barrels (perhaps the Government surveyors whose token I found near by in the shape of a bench-mark recording 417 feet); and an assayer's card nailed on a palm. The usual cans and bottles were in evidence, but in no such profusion as at most of these old camping spots. The locality does not attract prospectors, being, I fancy, scanty of valuable minerals; there is little to interest hunters; and the bad water, with scarcity of forage, puts a general ban on the place.

A few small mesquits with meagre show of beans, and a nibbling of salt-grass, helped out Kaweah's supper. With my back to a palm I hugged the shade till the sun went down, then climbed to smoke a pipe on the hillside and view the surroundings. Without having been in Egypt or Arabia, I could easily imagine myself to be looking down on a *wady* of the Red Sea region. The abrupt gullies with banks of sun-hardened clay, the gravel-strewed sands, the shapeless brown foothills, the sparse thorny scrub, the solitary group of palms, made up a scene much more suggestive of Arabia Petræa than of any part of the American continent. Not less so was the Oriental splendor of a gold and crimson sunset.

A strong breeze began to blow down the cañon about nightfall. I found a hollow in which I spread my blankets (first despatching a warlike scorpion that rushed out at me sparring away like a little prizefighter) and slept excellently till daybreak. My cold breakfast was despatched while Kaweah ate his barley, and we bade farewell to Seventeen Palms with almost as much satisfaction as we had felt on arriving.

For safety's sake I filled the large canteen, though heartily hoping I should not need to draw on it. Kaweah refused to drink before we started, preferring to fly to ills he knew not of rather than repeat the one he had tasted. However, to-day we had only half of yesterday's distance to make, with prospect of good water at the end. It was sometimes exasperating to have Kaweah thus refuse water, especially at the beginning of a long day's march. When he thus washed his hands of the responsibility, confident that I would not get him into serious trouble,

I wished I could make an incision in his hide and pump him full, willy-nilly.

I determined to-day to make a particular effort to keep the "road." The start was plain enough, for there was only one outlet to the cañon that could lead in my direction. It was a long ravine similar to that by which we had come, winding among strange shapes of clay, the dome being the most common. Red and yellow were the prevailing colors, with mud-hued grays and drabs for background. Ocotillos, always interesting in their weird way, had come in as I entered this clay country, but they looked starved and haggard, the shrivelled flower heads a rusty relic of their vivid spring. There was little other brush to be seen, and all looked at the point of death.

This clay formation, wherever found on the desert, is the last extreme of the barren, dreary, and dangerous. The vast network of gullies into which it becomes worn may easily become a death-trap for the traveller. Sense of direction is quickly lost: in the deep sand and gravel of the bottoms a trail is almost as evanescent as if marked in water. I was recently looking down again on this tract from the mountain country to the west. The Indian who was my companion pointed to the hazy yellowish patch, twenty miles from where we stood, and said, "Cheechlicsh'-noo-ah, devil's house, we call that. Very bad place. Man get in there no can get out never. One time some of our people camp there. Night time one get up and go for drink. He die, never come back." A white man's chance of escape from this "devil's house" might be, say, one twentieth of an Indian's under equal circumstances. It is just as well, perhaps, that there are few attractions to draw travellers to Chee-chlicsh'-noo-ah.

Reaching more open country we entered on a tract littered with curiously shaped objects of stone. Dumb-bells were a common form, and accurately circular plates and rings, balls, symmetrical ovoids, and many more — among them grotesque figures of men, quite as realistic as some pagan idols that one sees in museums. The region is well above sea-level, but probably water was the chief factor in shaping these oddities, perhaps at the time when the oyster-shell beds were laid down which are now a thousand feet up on the adjacent mountain-side. Paralleling our course a mile or two to the north ran a level bluff of clay, colored in pale tints of rose, lavender, green, and ochre, its face marked with vertical scorings as neatly drawn as if they had been engraved by a machine.

It was the last day of July, and seemed to me even hotter than the day before. Again I measured my water in half-hourly gulps. I found my thoughts turning constantly on water, as Arctic explorers' dwell on beef-steaks. Ride for an hour and lead for an hour was the programme. I had kept the trail pretty well, missing it often in crossing wide washes where the gravelly soil held no mark of travel, but picking it up again in softer places. To keep it at all, one's eyes must be "peeled" every moment. For long distances the only indication was the powdery dead leaves of the brush, which collect in the faint depression. The trained eye, looking ahead, can trace this dubious clue, though meeting it at right angles one would see nothing and might cross it a dozen times yet fail to recognize the trail one is seeking.

Slowly the line of the western mountains grew higher and darker. The tint was not, however, that mystical azure that gives to distant mountain prospects the usual wistful charm, but a smoky, furnace-like hue as if the range were built of slag. I tried to believe that I saw the appearance of timber against the sky. Could that be my old friend the Cuyamaca, or the Volcan? It was cheering at least to imagine the green-plushed firs, the singing cedars, and wise, sober pines up there, looking down with pity, surely, on the blanched, sun-drained desert, so old, withered, and gray.

I felt pretty well withered myself, baked through and through. The interminable ridge of clay danced when I glanced over at it, as if bent on giving me vertigo. At last we crossed a wider wash that I guessed to be the channel of the San Felipe Creek, one of those phantom streams that for nearly all their course run underground, if they run at all. Tracks began to come in from some mysterious origin in the southeast. Then a patch of green appeared a mile ahead, which I knew must mark Borego Springs. I halted by a palo verde that had somehow got lost out here, and recklessly drank my remaining Fish Springs water. It was hot, of course, and stale and flat, but to drink freely, with no grudging of table-spoonfuls, was genuine dissipation.

It was only early afternoon when we reached the

oasis of mesquits and arrowweed. I found the spring of good cool water, and we enjoyed ourselves for ten minutes before unloading. On the bank above the spring there was an old cabin and behind that a fine mesquit. Here I off-saddled, then picketed Kaweah among the mesquits, which were at their best fruiting stage, and left him to a dinner of unlimited beans, followed, if he chose, by a siesta to match.

CHAPTER XIII

A DESERT RIDE: BOREGO SPRINGS TO LOS COYOTES

Cows and cowboys — Peg-Leg Smith and his mine — Patron saint of prospectors — Legend or fact? — Following the gleam — And reaching the goal — Dregs of Uncle Sam's domain — Anza's expedition of 1774 — A question of fact — In Anza's footsteps — Hell-hole — Alkali flats — Desert cattle-range — A Borego Valley homestead — Devon and desert — "A beautiful climate" — Modest request for lard — Cholla cactus — Coyote Creek Cañon — Ocotillo houses — Agaves — A lost trail — Happiness in trifles.

BOREGO SPRINGS is one of the important watering-places on the Colorado Desert. Lying near the mountains, it is a strategic point in the operations of cattle-men whose ranges extend over the Santa Rosa, San Felipe, Volcan, and Cuyamaca country, and who once in a year or two may have occasion to drive cattle into or out of the mountains by the desert route. These drives are often for long distances, say from Arizona or Sonora, and in large herds, so that only the few spots that furnish abundant water are of service for resting and watering the stock. Borego Springs makes a convenient one-day stage before entering or leaving the mountains.

When I was camping here with some friends on another occasion, we were disturbed in the middle of the night by the arrival of a "bunch"[1] of cattle

---

[1] Nicety is observed in the West as to the use of nouns of number. Thus, it is a *band* of horses or of sheep, but a *bunch* of cattle, of steers, of yearlings, or whatever the case may be. A concourse of hogs, those flower-like quadrupeds, also are properly spoken of as a bouquet. So, by the by, are fellows. Thus, the leader of a college prayer-meeting has been known to open his petition, "We come, a bunch of fellows —" etc.

that had just "pulled in," *en route* to Borego Valley. In the morning, when the drove was getting under way, we were passing the compliments at the corral bars with two of the vaqueros. Names were exchanged. "And who is that young fellow?" one of us asked, pointing to a lively young "puncher" in red shirt and well-worn "chaps," who was rounding up the stragglers. "That 'young fellow' is this fellow's wife," one of the men answered, indicating his companion. *El habito no hace al monje* (the dress does not make the monk), says the Spanish proverb.

The old house bore testimony to many years of usage by cattle-men, surveyors, prospectors, and other haunters of the open spaces. On the back door I found an elaborate decoration, dated four months earlier. The two men who signed it stated themselves to be in search of that old will-o'-the-wisp of prospectors, the Peg-Leg Mine; and in lightness of heart had drawn a picture representing Peg-Leg Smith himself "looking at Borego Springs from Gold Hill." The great man was realistically shown mounted on a burro, pipe in mouth, pick on shoulder, and "peg" advanced as if hospitably greeting the beholder.

Peg-Leg Smith, who might by courtesy be called the patron saint of California prospectors, deserves more than passing reference. In the course of this journey I came on his tracks so often that at times I felt almost haunted. To be for two hours in company with a prospector and not have Peg-Leg come into the conversation is among the impossible things of life. I heartily wish that some one would find that mine, and put the old eternal anecdotes and theories to final rest. "Well, sir" (this is the sort of thing), "Dutchy kin say whatever he's a min' ter. I claim to know them 'ere Choc'lates purty (blank) well, seein' I've dry-washed every (blank) gully from Dos Palms to Carga Muchach', an' I tell *you* they ain't no *chanst* for that (blank) formation in the hull (blank) lay-out. Why, look a-here: ole Peg-Leg he says —." And off we would go once more into the threadbare history, with changes rung on "buttes" and "monnyments," "ledges" and "bearings," till I remembered to go and water Kaweah, or put my rice to boil, or whatever excuse came easiest to hand.

To make a brief statement of the case, for the benefit of any citizen of the United States who may not have heard it: This particular Smith, Thomas L., conspicuous among the tribe by the circumstance of a timber leg, was a brother of that Jedediah Smith who ranks high among Western pioneers. Thomas L. became the leader of one of those bands of trappers who in the thirties and forties roved over the vast spaces of the West in quest of furs and adventure. (The peg-leg itself was a souvenir of the adventures, he having amputated the natural member himself when it was shattered by a bullet in the course of a fight with Indians.) On one of these journeys the party reached the Colorado River, worked down the stream to its junction with the Gila, and crossed into California, when they struck northwest toward the pass, later known as "Warner's" or the "San

Felipe," which was at that time the only known approach to the southern coast.

Before reaching the mountains, some of the party one evening climbed a low hill near camp, and noticed that the dark outcropping rock was thickly sprinkled with yellow metal. Strange to say, though the men were interested enough to carry away specimens, they seem not to have guessed that they had found gold, until the year of 1848, with the historic "strikes" on the Sacramento, turned all men's thoughts to one idea. Then it was found that the specimens brought from the desert knoll were phenomenally rich in gold.

Smith was then in San Francisco along with the rest of the world. In 1850 he got together a party to make a search for the precious butte. Before getting well started, the loss of some of the equipment of the expedition put the leader out of humor with the affair, and it was abandoned: nor did he ever renew the attempt.

This is all ancient history, and it might seem strange that the legend of Peg-Leg's find, rich as it may have been, should have survived through two generations. But from time to time there have occurred seeming corroborations of the fact of such a wondrous mine in just such circumstances of position and "formation" as are named in the details of the discovery. Indians figure largely in these later evidences, and not merely to the extent of word of mouth. There have been incidents showing that they had access to some rich store of gold in the region of Smith's memorable "strike," and always the hints have been of "buttes" and the mysterious "black formation." These accessory details have not only kept alive the belief in the mine, but have extended the field of believers until the Peg-Leg Mine is a household word in California. From first to last (though the last is yet unreached) the number of those who have gone out on this adventure must run to hundreds, and the tale of those who have never returned is tragically long. Hardly a year passes without two or three parties taking up the search, following some new theory or clue. My predecessors at this old cabin were among the latest additions to the list. I may say here that a month or two later I chanced to meet a man who had recently seen them, safe and sound, but of course unsuccessful, well on their homeward way.

As for me, though I am not of the breed that Peg-Leggers come of, and long ago resolved, following a well-known example, to die a poor man, yet I feel the fascination of the gold-hunter's game, and have sometimes, over my camp-fire, played with the idea of sudden freedom from impecuniary cares by stumbling on a mine. Here at Borego Springs I overlooked the very ground where, if anywhere, Peg-Leg Smith's bonanza is awaiting an owner. From all evidences it could not be a day's march away — a little hill, such as I walk up any day for the view, but — behold! littered with nuggets that one could pick out, like walnuts, with a pocket-knife! It was an exciting idea, and I almost resolved to make a practice of climbing all little hills hereafter. But there came a soberer thought — of the poor wretches who had fallen to the lure, "followed the gleam"; and the gleam had led them on and on, a little farther, to the next rise, the cañon beyond, till the terrible "bad lands" had them locked in their scorching maze, there to wander till, crazed and raving, they staggered and fell: scrambled with frantic terror to their feet and stumbled on (the thought of gold a frightful mockery now) till they fell once more and did not rise again. If ever the Peg-Leg Mine is found, it would not be surprising if there are seen about it the bleaching bones of the fortunate ones who reached the goal. Then it should be renamed "The Death's Head," and christened with the dregs of a canteen of Seventeen Palms water.

Kaweah and I kept Sunday very comfortably at Borego Springs. For him there were mesquit beans in plenty and even a picking of Bermuda grass: for me, shade and the thought of a bad piece of country in my rear: for us both, good, cool, abundant water. A road-runner came round several times to make sure his eyes were not playing him false: lizards with iridescent head and throat crept down the roasting boards and watched me with cunning reptilian stare: a few finches cheeped and twittered — the friendliest sound I had heard for days.

A tour of the immediate neighborhood showed the usual incidents of these old camps — cascades of cans, scraps of rawhide, horseshoes, rock specimens, and stove-in canteens. The corral-gate was decorated with the skull of a steer, a satirical object for the famishing cattle as they shoved their way to the water-trough. Among the names scrawled here

and there were some that have gained a measure of
renown in the story of pioneering in the Southwest.
More recent were the autographs of a party of
Government surveyors, from Lieutenant Tripod,
Chief Engineer, down to "Pete Ortega, Chief of
Remuda." Slowly the mapping of the dregs of Uncle
Sam's domain is being completed — though it is
rash to call anything dregs, when date groves flour-
ish on what a few years ago was marked "Unknown
Desert," dry lake-beds yield priceless fertilizers, and
any day the prospector's pick may strike a blow
that will bring men stampeding in thousands to the
latest El Dorado, perhaps within rifle-shot of where
I stand.

History is always fertile in debatable points for
students to quarrel over. Even in the history of the
West, short as it has been within white men's times,
there are matters of dispute. One of these is a question as to the route of the first Spanish expedition
by land from Mexico to the California coast. This
entrada (to use the Spanish word) was led by Captain Juan Bautista Anza, in 1774, its object being
to make overland connection with the settlements
of San Diego and Monterey, established five years
earlier by Don Gaspar de Portolá and Fray Junípero
Serra.

The party, starting from Tubac, in Sonora,
crossed the Colorado River on the 9th of February
(first picking up that stout old campaigner Fray
Francisco Hermenegildo Garcés, who had already
been knocking about for years among the wild tribes
of the region), and made their way across the desert,

apparently at first keeping to the south of the present Mexico-United States border. On reaching the Cócopa Mountains they turned north and crossed the line somewhere near Signal Mountain, finding water, it is guessed, at what are now called Yuha Springs. Travelling still north, the next camp, March 10, was at a large *ciénaga* where the water and forage were so bad as to cause the loss of several of their animals. This place, which they named San Sebastian del Peregrino, is identified as the Carrizo *ciénaga*.

At this point students of the records fall into disagreement. Some suppose that the expedition, keeping on still north, rounded Santa Rosa Mountain at Clay Point (where I had turned west for Seventeen Palms) and then turned northwest up what is now called the Coachella Valley, entering the coast region by San Gorgonio Pass. Given our present knowledge of the country, that would have been the natural route, and many of the details set down by the explorers suggest that it was the one taken. The other opinion is that on leaving the Carrizo camp the party struck northwesterly up the broad arm of desert (which I had just crossed in another direction) that leads by way of Borego Springs into Borego Valley and Coyote Cañon; that they made their way, by that cañon and a branch of it now called Horse Cañon, up to what is now known as Vandeventer Flat. Whichever route they took they reached high ground with good forage and water, and of the place, wherever it was, the gallant Captain writes: "This *paraje* [station] is a pass, and I named it El

Puerto Real de San Carlos. From it may be discovered some very beautiful plains, green and flowery, and the Sierra Nevada, with pines, oaks, and other trees proper to cold countries. In it the waters are divided, some running to the Gulf and others to the Philippine Ocean."

I do not know all parts of the routes in question well enough to venture a decided opinion, but from what I have seen I think the southerly is likely to have been the one followed.[1] Anyhow, it was pleasant to think so, for in that case I was now on the old Anza trail, and should follow the footsteps of that picturesque company of *padres*, *soldados*, and *arrieros* for a good few miles. On this understanding, my Borego Springs was probably the *aguaje* (watering-place) of good quality that Anza, or the padres, named for San Gregorio, and where the party rested for a day. He notes the fact of an Indian *ranchería* (village), and there is evidence, in the shape of fragments of pottery, that Borego Springs was long the site of an Indian settlement: but that would be sure to be the case where good water was to be found.[2]

[1] My Indian friend, Lee Arenas, tells me that the Cahuilla tribes, inhabiting country adjacent to Coyote Cañon, have a tradition that the first white men came that way, and speak of a fight that took place in the cañon with strangers using swords. Anza mentions no such incident. His record of the natives hereabout is that they were expert thieves, and could pick and steal with toes as cleverly as with fingers: further, that they made much play with their legs and feet, on which account he named them *Danzantes* (dancers). Lee also says that the Indians call the head of the cañon La Puerta, but this is the common designation of any point in the nature of a pass.

[2] It was the *ranchería* of San Gregorio, by the by, that was thrown into consternation, naturally enough, by the racket of the thirsty mules of the approaching party. On the other hand, it is related of the Cócopas that they were quite captivated by the mules of some

I turned in betimes and coyotes obliged with a lullaby. It seemed about twenty minutes afterward that I awoke to see the red pennon of dawn flying on the horizon. It was inspiriting, however, to be now close upon the mountains, with the prospect of being for a few days among them, with genuine trees, grass that is green, not gray, perhaps even a brook to drink from. This variation from my desert programme was for the purpose of getting mail and supplies at Warner's Springs, the only postal point I should even approach until I reached the settlements of Imperial Valley.

I turned now northwesterly, following the route taken (as I think likely) by Anza and his fellow explorers. To my right rose an isolated dark mass called Coyote Mountain, which Figtree John claims as his birthplace. One could hardly imagine a more unattractive place to call one's native spot; yet no, I remember the slums of man's cities. It is there one reaches the *ne plus ultra* of the hideous. On the other side at a few miles' distance were the abrupt foothills of the Peninsular Range, the high ridge of San Ysidro overlooking them and showing on its crest tantalizing tokens of pines.

Near here there is a place that has gained, not

pioneer of about the same period (I think it was Padre Garcés: there were not many travellers on these deserts a century and a half ago). These natives had never seen mules before, and, astounding as it sounds, found them charming. Moved with compassion at seeing the animals hobbled, at night they removed the fetters and led them tenderly away to where a banquet of soothing pumpkins was spread. And when a jack fell into a quagmire, they "all came to his assistance, took him in their arms, carried him to the fire, and warmed and consoled him." This is like the snug experiences of Nick Bottom.

without reason, the unpleasant name of "Hell-Hole."
It is a small bit of country, but so maze-like in its
ramifications that to enter is probably to remain.
I have talked to a man who, with a companion, was
once caught in this death-trap. He narrated with
vivid details the events of days during which they
wandered about, trying gully after gully for a way
of escape, and hourly losing heart and hope. Luckily
it was winter, so thirst, the deadliest enemy, was
not to be feared; and they had food enough for some
days. It was by mere chance that, on the fourth day,
they stumbled out into the world that they hardly
hoped to see again. There is a fascination for me in
these ill-favored bits of geography; but in August,
with a horse and but a gallon and a half of water, it
seemed best to confine myself to guessing which of
those furnace-like cañon-mouths might be the reputed gateway to Hades.

Patches of salt-grass began to appear, mixed
among wide expanses of alkali (*salitres*, as the Mexicans call them) for which this unwholesome grass
has a liking. The country looked as if it had been
flooded with a saturated solution of salt: in places
the very grass-blades sparkled with the salty incrus-
tation, and Kaweah's hoofs kicked the stuff before
us like snow. After a few miles I saw something
ahead which looked like a house and windmill.
This was a surprise, though I knew that within late
years land-hungry settlers had turned their attention to Borego Valley. On close approach the house
proved to be a wagon and the windmill a derrick.
Some one had made an attempt to find water, but

money or patience had given out, and the wagon and tools were left to fall to pieces in the sun. I heard afterwards that the outfit had come by the same route that I had taken, but the men had lost their way after passing Clay Point and had been three days in reaching Seventeen Palms.

Skulls and ribs of cattle, sometimes with shreds of hide upon them, gave token that I was in cattle country. Leg bones, being easy to manipulate by those ghouls the coyotes, are generally hauled off to a distance, but the skull and ribs with backbone usually stay where the poor brute perished, and coyotes, buzzards, and skunks repair again and again to the feast until the ultimate remnant glistens in the sun, a melancholy monument. There is something specially ghastly about the ribs with their hollow griddle look. Perhaps it is because of the resemblance to the human skeleton in this detail that the staring emptiness has a horror all its own: one realizes the fragility of one's own frame, and thinks, with a shock, What, am I such a drum!

A speck of green that I had been watching for half an hour revealed itself as the homestead of a settler. Half hidden by a huge mesquit was a one-room tent-house of fair size. It was surrounded by half an acre or so of cultivated ground, all that was possible with the feeble flow of water yielded by the well. The man was away, but the barking of the dog brought out his wife, a cheery little Devonshire woman, who bade me be seated and "Rest, do ye now." The first question was, "Have you brought any mail?" and great was the disappointment when

I explained that I was bound to, not from, Warner's, which is their mail station, forty-two miles away. It appeared that the postmaster at Warner's was under instructions, whenever he heard of any one going through to Borego Valley (which might happen half a dozen times a year) to press him into service as mail-carrier. The next request was for a newspaper. This was another misfortune: and when I remarked that if I had brought one it would have been a week old, the reply was, "That's nothing. If it was a month old it would be news to us. Never mind, you can tell us the news, anyway." (This I well understood meant news of the war, for Devon is England in little, the county of Raleigh, Grenville, and Drake.)

So we sat and chatted of combe and tor, of Torridge, Dart, and Tavy, and of the importance attaching to "scraps of paper." Then she must show me her garden, the wondrous beans, radishes, and tomatoes; above all, an incredible rose that had borne six blossoms in the spring. "I do wish it had one on now, so you could have it: 't would carry all day if you'd keep it in the shade. I do love a rose, don't you?" she went on: "seems like I never can get my fill of 'em. 'T was four years come Michaelmas we took this desert claim. Yes, I've worked pretty hard over this garden. The jack-rabbits are something awful, and the quail too: I suppose they come for the water. My husband wants to fill up the hole where the water stands, but I tell him 't would be cruel. And doves: they don't do any harm, though; I love to have them come. There must be five hundred, maybe a thousand, come round that little pool of an evening. It sounds like a hundred autos when they fly. This is my second turn at what you might call pioneering. First was in the State of Washington; that was twenty-five years ago. Seems like I strike mostly quiet places. Like it here? Why, yes, I think it's pretty good, and a beautiful climate. Why, 106 is as hot as we've had this summer, and think of them poor folks down in Imperial with 120, and hot nights and poor water."

A whiff as of recent baking led to my buying a loaf of the genuine article, together with a little sugar; also a few feeds of barley for Kaweah. A muskmelon and two tomatoes were added as a present. When I urged her to take payment for these luxuries she refused, but as I was leaving (charged with three letters that had lain many days under the family flat-iron) she became wistful, then said softly, "You wouldn't happen to have a mite of *lard* that you could spare, would you now?" She could not bear to see me depart without asking this one boon. So we divided my little store, and I left with a warning that I must look out for snakes in Coyote Cañon.

For several hours we plodded up the broad gray valley toward the point where Coyote Cañon came in. Other cañons were passed, their mouths almost choked with mixed colonies of ocotillo and cholla. This is the most clannish of the cacti, holding the foothill benches for miles to the exclusion of other growths. These tracts make a strange appearance, as if regiments of soldiers, in uniform of palest gray, were issuing from the cañon and had halted on the slope for a review.

One of these cañons, on the west side of the valley, is known as Palm Cañon (not to be confused with the other Palm Cañon, on the farther side of the mountains to the north). I scanned it with the glasses, but could see no likelihood of water, so reluctantly passed it by. Once or twice paler patches could be seen on the gray distance of the plain. They were the clearings of settlers, but I saw no token of cultivation about these places. If water is obtained, as it may be by deep boring, a similar miracle to that in the Coachella may follow, for the soil seems good, or at least fair, in parts of Borego Valley.

As we neared the head of the valley the ground changed to coarse gravel and boulders. The ocotillo and cholla took advantage of this congenial mixture to make a sort of devil's garden, to which one or two other choice spirits, like the "nigger-head" and deer-horn cacti, were admitted. Once or twice, in spite of our best care, Kaweah got nipped by some imp of a cholla. Much alike as the cholla and deer-horn are, I found that Kaweah had learned the difference. When a bit of the latter caught him, he dislodged it by giving a violent kick, but if it was cholla, he came to a conspicuous halt and waited for me to operate with pocket-knife and pliers.

At last we turned the shoulder of the mountain and entered the narrow cañon. Anza's *aguaje* of Santa Caterina may have been somewhere hereabout, for it is here that Coyote Creek becomes

visible. Below this point it takes refuge underground, in the usual fashion of desert waters. At
this season the stream was a mere thread of intermittent dampness, but in March, the month of
Anza's passage, it would make more of a showing.
Near the neck of the cañon I noticed a cabin built
of ocotillo canes. It consisted of one room of fair
size, seven feet high, and roofed with brush. In spite
of its chicken-house look, it would make a tolerable
dwelling for summer-time on the desert. By the
little pile of hay in a corner I guessed that it was a
cattle-man's house of call.

The ocotillo is a convenient material for such
structures, and is so used by some Indian tribes,
who plaster the walls with mud and so make a house
that answers for winter as well as summer use. This
mud and ocotillo combination has a peculiar result.
When rain comes, soaking the earth in which the
canes are embedded, the seemingly dead sticks
spring to life, put on leaves, and may even break
into blossom.

Two or three miles up the cañon another interesting plant appeared — the agave, a wild type of
the century-plant. Its circle of bayonet-pointed
leaves and ten-foot pole of flower-stalk make it
conspicuous among the low desert growths. Deer,
bighorn, and cattle are keen for the juicy flower-
stem, and few of the plants would fulfil their destiny
if it were not for the *chevaux-de-frise* that protects
the citadel. Growing usually in close colonies, the
interlocking leaves make an almost impenetrable
barrier, so that the inner members of the group

could only be attacked from the air. Thus, the wild desert bees find the agave their best means of support.

The brush became heavier as we made our way up the cañon, until at one spot I counted, close together, ocotillo, agave, desert willow, smoke-tree, cat-claw, and the two kinds of mesquit. We were both on the lookout for water, and when a faint trickle showed above ground Kaweah made for it at once, sucking up a mixture of sand and liquid as if it were nectar of the finest tap. I was not much more particular, for the water in the canteen was too hot to be pleasant.

There is said to be a trail up this cañon, but it was beyond my skill to follow it. Evening found us entering a jungle of arrowweed and mesquit. In this we struggled for an hour, hoping to fight a way through into clearer country. The last daylight left us at an impassable place, the creek close by, but running in a deep channel with perpendicular walls, impossible for Kaweah to descend. We turned and stumbled back for a mile in the darkness, Kaweah getting badly snagged more than once on stumps of mesquit. When we could cross the creek I turned upstream looking for a place to camp.

Reaching a sandy opening among willows I stopped and off-saddled, gave Kaweah a hearty feed, and ate my bread and cheese by starlight. Breakfast had been my last meal, sixteen hours before. It was delicious to lie listening to the ripple of the creek and hearing Kaweah nibble about. These moments gain charm in proportion to their rarity, and the desert traveller meets them seldom. How true it is that happiness consists in trifles. Water, a little bag of barley, a few stars, a loaf and cheese, a tomato, and a cool night coming, that was about all: yet even the mosquitoes could not disturb my tranquillity that long evening on Coyote Creek.

CHAPTER XIV

A DESERT RIDE: LOS COYOTES TO WARNER'S SPRINGS

Kaweah a tyrant — Los Coyotes — A grub-staked miner — Credulity of miners — Prospector and poet — A player of many parts — Snakes, assorted kinds — Vagaries of McSandy — A mountain trail — Flowers and cactus — Indian relics — Stiff climbing — From brush to pines — An Indian patriarch — San Ygnacio — Supper with Mary Jane — Snakes again — An Indian alpine village — Mountain delights — The desert's spell deepest — Kaweah breaks the ice — San Ysidro — Warner's Ranch — Agua Caliente Indians.

I AWOKE to find the sun making a green-and-gold sanctuary all about me, a cañon-wren showering me with cascades of plaintive melody, doves sympathizing from a dead branch overhead, and numerous bumps on face and arms, with mosquitoes' kind regards. Kaweah was watching for my first movement. With little encouragement this comrade of mine would become a tyrant. His annoyance when I am half an hour late is not to be mistaken.

I knew the night before that I was not far from a small bay or valley, about midway of the cañon, known as Collins Valley, or to the Indians as Los Coyotes. This was where I had hoped to camp, and when, after breakfast, I went prospecting for my lost trail, I soon found that another half-mile would have taken us there. It had an attractive look, with a little patch of grass and tules, a palm or two, and many mesquits and willows, even a cottonwood. There was also an old cabin, another evidence of being in cattle country, though one may travel for many a day and see no cattle, to say nothing of implied mankind.

I went back for Kaweah and my traps, and moved to this better camp, where I resolved to stay for a day. As I passed the cabin I heard some one exclaim, "Well, I'll be (so-and-so), here's a man at last! Who are you, anyway?" I glanced in and saw a big fellow stretched on the ramshackle bed that half filled the place. He excused himself from rising on the score of having "durned near worn his feet off yesterday, clambering over these eternal mountains," but hospitably told me to come in and share the *casa*, adding, "There was a rattler around here a while ago, but I reckon he's maybe left by now."

When I had accounted for myself, my new acquaintance reciprocated with the statement that he was Thomas McSandy (the name was not exactly that) for the present a prospector, and that he had been "grub-staked" by a Los Angeles friend who was acquainted with a man whose brother (then in an insane asylum) knew of a gem mine, the location of which, as described to some official of the asylum, was supposed to be somewhere hereabout. On this hopeful quest he had been searching the surrounding country, and his "stake" of grub being about exhausted, he had given up the job and was striking out next day for home by way of Warner's Ranch.

The gullibility of mankind with regard to lost mines or buried treasure is staggering indeed. The number and giddiness of these wild-goose chases amount to a phenomenon. No story is too unlikely, no clue too frail, to gain the belief of men in other respects judicious enough. The "old Indians" who, when dying, have spoken of some wondrous cañon in the Humbug Range; the prospectors found at "poison springs" who at the last gasp have babbled of glittering ledges or placers, abandoned by them under stress of famine; the others who in this or that county hospital have whispered to some attendant the "sure thing" secret of the long-lost Blue Dog, or Holy Smoke; to say nothing of the variegated legends of the Peg-Leg — these must run into hundreds, and their devotees into a veritable host. McSandy was but one of a long list that I myself could call to mind, to whose credulity no absurdity is an obstacle if their will-o'-the-wisp has the glitter of gold.

But McSandy proved to have other erratic ideas. Before we had talked half an hour he boldly announced to me that he was a poet. Nothing odd about that, of course; in these days of *vers libre* we are all poets if we care to say so: but in sounding for his depth I dropped the names of Wordsworth and Byron. "Ah," said McSandy, kindling, "*they* could make poetry. Why, d' you know, I can't put up any better stuff myself than what those fellows did, durned if I can. No, sir."

I looked at him carefully, but, no, there was no sign of humorous intent; candor, regret, perhaps a touch of surprise, no more. I hastily changed the subject, which, luckily, was easy to do, for he had wrongs to relate and adventures to recount that would fill fat volumes. He was amazed, even incredulous, that his name and exploits as a detective in a celebrated case were not familiar to me; was convinced that the other side still thirsted for his blood, and that emissaries of a certain famous organization were even now on his trail. He showed the revolver with which, while a deputy sheriff in New Mexico, he had "got his man"; he had lived everywhere from the Argentine to Alaska, and made and lost "scads of money"; he was full of tales of arsenic springs and poisoned desert waters, and of "close calls" in Death Valley, where he guaranteed a temperature of a hundred and forty-five in the shade. Yet, oddly, with these feats to his credit McSandy showed a total absence of that sense of location which is all but indispensable to the desert man. He was even hazy on the points of the compass.

McSandy preferred to sleep in the cabin, while I spread my blankets near by outside. The night being warm and not conducive to sleep, my friend unfolded new leaves of his career. I learned that he had visited Constantinople as seaman on a United States warship: had also been a Michigan lumberman; and I forget how many other things. In spite of lifelike details, his narrative was an irresponsible farrago that kept me on the edge of an explosion. From Turks we had come to Apaches; when, "I think there's a snake climbing up on the bed," he remarked in the midst of some episode. "Can hear him creeping and creeping, durn his hide. Ain't them rattlers the limit, though? Sure death ev'ry time they get you. Say, d' you think I'd better make a light and look what he's doing?" He struck a match and, no snake being revealed, concluded that it was one of them blame trade-rats. But the snake topic, once started, is ever a prolific one. Did I know how a king-snake kills a rattler? "Well, sir, the son-of-a-gun just naturally jumps on top of him, yes, sir, jumps clean off the ground and lights plum on Mr. Rattler and does him up. Say, he's a son-of-a-gun, ain't he now? Snakes don't jump, don't they? Well, then, how about this? Up in Placer County I killed a rattler one day; cut off his head and two inches down the neck; and *then* that rattler up and jumped two foot clear. Why, they're powerful jumpers, them sons-of-guns are."

He desired my opinion as to the best course to follow in the event of finding a rattler with one in bed. To jump, or not to jump, that was the question. I was strongly for jumping, but McSandy had his doubts: he feared that the rattler would "get" him ere he was halfway to the door, and would strike even in mid-air — yes, sir. I brought up the hoop-snake legend. "Why, yes, sir," McSandy responded, "that's all right. I've seen them fellers many a time down in the Argentine. He puts his tail in his mouth, and starts to roll, and roll, and — say, I'd hate to have one of them fellers a-hooping after me. Joint-snake? — the feller that breaks in little bits when you hit him and then joins up together again? No, I ain't ever seen them do it, but I reckon it's so, all right." Twenty feet was his estimate of the length of red racers that had crossed his path, while as for speed, greased lightning was a weak comparison. He had full belief also in the deadly nature of the tarantula's, scorpion's, and centipede's "sting," with vivid instances to allege in support. When at last we had cooled off enough for sleep his mind was still busy with snakes, and at intervals I heard him softly murmur, "You bet," or, "Son-of-a-gun, *he* is," until final silence fell.

On McSandy's invitation I had resolved to change from my intended route to Warner's, and accompany him by a much shorter trail, passing the Indian villages of San Ygnacio and San Ysidro, places I had long wished to visit.

I bade good-bye, then, to Anza and his band when next day we turned westward and made for the mountains. I had meant to visit Thousand Palm Cañon (a second cañon of the name; the other had been taken early in my journey) which opens two or three miles farther up Coyote Creek; but through the glasses it did not look inviting, showing only the usual vast fan of gravel, boulders, and brush. I suppose the palms are hidden in the upper gorge. There were miles of tedious travel before we reached the foot of the cañon up which our trail ran, but we passed this before the sun was high, and it was still early when we commenced the steep ascent. Agaves and mesquit continued with us, but soon there appeared willows, sycamores, and occasionally a palm or two, giving interesting variety.

After a mile or two of warm climbing we found a spring on the hillside and stopped for a rest and the luxury of drinking without the medium of a canteen. The ground about the spring was ablaze with the superb cardinal flower, *Lobelia splendens*, a plant which surely represents Nature's last effort in intensity of color. Even more charming were a few wild roses. Meeting them here, their frank, innocent look seemed almost touching by contrast with the ungentle desert forms just left behind.

The trail was far too steep and rough for riding. I was close behind McSandy, leading Kaweah, when I saw my supposedly experienced friend stop and draw his hand across a lobe of the common *Opuntia basilaris* cactus, remarking that Burbank was a fraud, for here was spineless cactus growing wild. Mr. Burbank was promptly avenged: it took half an hour to free McSandy's hand of the worst of the hairlike prickles, and when we came to the next water and stopped for lunch he spent an industrious hour in finishing the job.

Though this trail is little known and not given on any map, it is plain, from the depth to which it is worn, that it has long been used by the Indians in passing between their desert and mountain villages. The rock that gave us shade was blackened with the smoke of ancient fires, and in the earth I found beads, scraps of pottery, and yellowed bones some of which had a strong look of *homo sapiens*. Near by were deep holes in the solid rock where generations of squaws had ground their flour.

The trail now became yet steeper, one of the steepest, indeed, that I ever tackled. Kaweah was a good deal worried, and often inquired with earnest gaze if I knew where I was going? We made progress by scrambles of forty or fifty yards at a time, sometimes in the bouldery creek-bed, sometimes on slippery mountain-side.

The changes in vegetation as we climbed were full of interest, though the circumstances were not the best for noting them. In the wet creek bottom grew masses of the same wonderful lobelia, often six feet tall and with flowering heads a foot in length. Sycamores and alders mingled with the willows, yet here and there the desert-loving palms held on, though the altitude was well over three thousand feet. On the open mountain-side the wild plum was common, now hung thickly with yellow fruit. The California sumac, *Rhus ovata*, made blots of heavy color on the pale background of rock. A little higher the mountain mahogany, *Cercocarpus*, came in, an attractive, individual bush, at this time silvery with the silky seed-vessels. Then scrub-oaks appeared, and next the ever-welcome juniper. Yuccas still held their own on rocky ledges, looking strangely out of place. Yet higher, masses of dull gold that had been puzzling me proved to be groves of the interesting *Adenostoma sparsifolium* or false cedar, with bright red bark, slender foliage, and huge clusters of white blossom that were now faded to golden brown. The sturdy manzanita was another goodly sight; but most so of all, on nearing the crest, the pines, often sighed for, who now gave me kingly welcome. On this high sky-line they were finely pictorial and as much the unquestioned monarchs as ever. I have heard that it is a custom in mountainous parts of Spain to brush the face of a new-born child with a twig from a pine. I think something of the kind has happened to me, for among these trees I find that my face unconsciously takes on a smile.

It was nearly sunset when we struggled up the last rise and crossed the pass at about five thousand feet. A short descent brought us to water, but forage was scanty, and tired as we were it was necessary to push on. Two miles farther we climbed a second crest, and looked down on a little green valley. This was the home of old Santiago Segundo, the patriarch of the San Ygnacio Indians. At the house we found Santiago, his son Felipe, three or four picturesque squaws, and half a dozen unfriendly dogs. The old man was a memorable figure. Tall and well built, with features more of Egyptian than of our Western Indian cast, and a bearing of natural dignity, from sandalled feet to thick white hair he looked the ideal Indian chief.

Our request for permission to camp by the stream was refused (the only time I have been denied at an Indian's, but I could not complain, for the Indian has good reason to be suspicious of white strangers). It was dark when we came to a larger valley encircled by pine-clad heights, where we found the *ranchería* of San Ygnacio. It is a romantic situation, like an eagle's eyrie on the craggy crest of the mountains: on one hand is the desert, far and steep below; on the other the long seaward slope, fifty miles as the crow flies, to the Pacific.

Disappointment met us at the first house we tried, which belonged to the tribal policeman; but the next attempt brought better fortune, for smiling Mary Jane Segundo, the very type of good-humor, made us welcome to camp, hay, anything we wished. This was a relief, for the day's travel, perhaps twenty miles in distance, had been equal to forty on the level, and I had not ridden any part of the way. When I made bold to ask if we might share the family supper — "Sure you may," came the reply from the gloom where Mary Jane hovered with fork and lantern over a crackling fire.

It was an excellent meal. Eggs fried to a charm, *frijoles* at their best, wild honey fresh out of the rocks, coffee at perfection, and such biscuit as one seldom meets on this mortal plane. There was *tasaje* too, but not for me. I have had experiences with "jerky" that after lapse of years remain a solemnizing memory. The household consisted of our hostess, her mother (who carried her years so lightly that I took her for a sister), and two cousins, José and Dionysio, the latter a boy. A good deal of laughter went with remarks, in their own language, of which we were plainly the object. It might well have been our appetites that were the joke.

I was able to bring Mary Jane items of news of her relations on the desert. This made us doubly welcome, and it was altogether a pleasant evening that I spent in the smoky adobe. The room itself was worth observing, festooned with ropes of *chile* and *tasaje*, adorned with chromos of religious subjects, and hallowed by a tiny shrine with candle and crucifix.

As there seemed a prospect of rain we elected to sleep in the barn with the rats. My companion again attributed every disturbance to snakes, and twice during the night made a tour of the premises with lantern and revolver. As it happened, I killed a rattler a few yards away on first going out in the morning, whereupon McSandy declared that after this he was going to shoot whenever he heard " them sons-of-guns snooping round."

The daylight view of San Ygnacio confirmed its attractiveness. The little valley was deliciously green, water was abundant, and the surroundings were almost Alpine in boldness and novelty. The air was superb, and the summer climate delightful. Eight or ten families make up the little settlement. Perched on the rocks beside Mary Jane's adobe was the *may'-a-not* or storage basket in which Indian housewives keep their stores of acorns, piñon nuts, or other wild provision. In the house were a number of handsome baskets for various uses; jars and *ollas* of native pottery, without decoration but excellent in form; bows and arrows, with which Dionysio, as he told me, was able to kill rabbits at forty or fifty yards; throwing-sticks for the same purpose; and much of the paraphernalia of the old Indian ways of life. The rumor having spread that a man was taking pictures, the children of the village assembled for this thrilling experience. When I sent them for their bows and arrows, with a view to a characteristic group, some of the young warriors returned with weapons taller than themselves.

Down a steep road that followed the windings of San Ysidro Creek we took our way for Warner's Springs. This wooded country of oaks, pines, and cedars was enchanting to me. It seemed incredible that one day's travel could so change every aspect but that of the sky; though even that was a more cheerful blue, no longer the pale, glary azure of the desert. Grass waved along the roadside — what a contrast to chollas! Late flowers brightened the path, replacing gray burro-weed and snaky ocotillo. Kingly oaks for dull mesquit; winey breath of cedar instead of acrid alkaline dust; frank bird in place of furtive reptile — it was a blessed exchange. And yet, and yet — already I felt the magic, the magnetism, of the old, wonderful desert, drawing me back: back to its dreariness, silence, and secrecy, its cruelty of heat and thirst, its infinite expanse, its ageless mystery and calm, its threat of death, its passionless repose. I am no misanthrope: I love my fellow men, indeed, I eagerly claim my right in mortality. But there is a presence in that quietude, a sense of wisdom and of the sadness that goes with it, which something in me recognizes as brotherhood too. The mountains, the ocean, the forest, go deep in their spell, but the desert goes deepest of all.

McSandy, anxious to reach civilization and supplies, had gone on ahead. Kaweah and I were well content to idle in this elysium of roadside springs, fresh green fodder, and beguiling sights and sounds. Some few miles along, a neat little house appeared, the owner sitting patriarchally under its sheltering oaks. It proved to be Sibimoat, *capitan* of the Indians of San Ysidro. Half a dozen young bucks were loafing on the porch, inert, hardly speaking, simply enjoying the passage of time, while their saddled ponies stood about with drooping heads. I had often known Kaweah to act as mutual friend and breaker of ice when we came among Indians. However far from home, he is spotted at once as of Indian breed, and often recognized as having been present at some *fiesta* or other foregathering. "Ah-h-ha, where you get that pony?" "Francisco Patencio, Palm Springs," I would answer. "Ah, *sí*, I know: good pony you get: how much you pay?" — and so we were launched. Indians and Mexicans never forget a horse, and more easily recall the rider by his horse than the horse by his rider.

The San Ysidro Indians' farming land lies scattered along the course of the creek. For miles I saw below me little fenced scraps of bottom land planted with beans, potatoes, corn, or barley. The barley was being harvested with the sickle, as it has been ever since the *padres* taught the California tribes to supplement Nature's roots, seeds, and game by a little — not too much — exertion on their own part. San Ysidro village itself is a dreary hamlet of a dozen typical Indian houses, a tiny cemetery, and a brush *ramada* for the accommodation of visitors to the yearly *fiesta*.

By now we had left the pines and were travelling through less inviting country, so I was not sorry to approach a wide valley which I recognized as the Valle de San José, or Warner's Ranch. This tract of nearly fifty thousand acres is one of the last of the old land grants to remain unbroken since Mexican times. Over the valley hung the smoke of a forest fire.

The road ran steadily down, opening a view of the timbered Volcan Mountain far to the south. Finding a trail that made direct for the settlement we plunged through thickets of fragrant chamise and glades ennobled with oaks, and at early evening came to what was formerly the Indian village of Agua Caliente. Some years ago the old population were evicted and their neat cottages coolly appropriated by the whites. The place is now known as Warner's Springs, and has become a summer resort on a small scale, the attraction being the hot sulphur springs from which it took its old Spanish name.

McSandy made for his old bivouac, in the dismantled Indian church. Apart from scruples on the religious score, which McSandy thought high-flown, I preferred the open air, so chose a spot beside the warm creek for my camp. It is reported by some old traveller that the Indians of Agua Caliente were in the habit, on cold nights, of sleeping in the creek, with the grassy bank for pillow. At this season there was no need to adopt this simple dodge. Farther on in my journey I found people in Imperial Valley soaking their couches with cold water before going to bed, for better comfort on sultry nights.

On calling at the store for mail and the news I learned that two days after I passed Clay Point a party of three men met disaster a few miles farther south. One perished of thirst, the others barely escaped with their lives.[1]

[1] While preparing these pages at least four cases of this kind have come to my notice in the local newspaper. The latest, a typical one, reports the end of a prospector who was found dying beside one of the so-called "poison springs" on the northern part of the desert. He had reached the place famishing for water and probably had drunk too much. So every year the desert takes its toll.

CHAPTER XV

A DESERT RIDE: WARNER'S SPRINGS TO AGUA CALIENTE

Don Juan Warner — The March of Progress — Desertwards again — The cowboy at home — "A durn boulevard" — Warner's Pass and General Kearny — A pioneer storekeeper — San Felipe Indians: a funeral — Voices of the Night — The deserted village — The Ranchita Mine — Potency of a *fiesta* — Kaweah disgruntled — La Puerta de San Felipe — The Mormon Battalion — Sanguine settlers — Elysium of Indians — The Vallecito — An old stage-station: its memories — A lucky encounter — Carrizo Creek Cañon — Forest fires — Camp at Agua Caliente Springs — Grewsome yarns — Travellers who "stayed" — Sunrise and the Sun — An easy day, and sunset.

THERE is not much of attraction at Warner's Springs. A pathetic interest, however, hangs about the row of adobe cottages, now used to house visitors who come in summer for the medicinal baths. I felt inclined to refuse payment for baths to the present owners and hand over my "two bits" per tub to the first Indian I might meet. Such of the old houses as have not been put to use are far on the road to the quick obliteration that awaits any neglected building of adobe. The church was still intact as regards walls, but cracks were starting, and the roof was fast going to pieces. Inside, paltry tourists have scratched their names, and stray prospectors, like my poet, camp in corners and fry sacrilegious flapjacks at the *padre's* fireplace in the tiny vestry adjoining.[1]

[1] Recently, a year or so after the time of my visit, I received from the Reverend Father Doyle, priest of the Mission of San Antonio at

The ranch takes its name from one John or Jona-
than Warner, a native of Connecticut, to whom it
was granted by the Mexican Government a few
years before the cession of California to the United
States. Of him little is remembered beyond the
legend that to his intimates he was Juan Largo
(Long John); to others it was ever Don Juan — a
vaguely interesting item. The original adobe ranch-
house has wholly vanished: its site was pointed out
to me by a Volcan Indian who remembers it well.
In Warner's days it formed a halfway house between Yuma and the young "Pueblo de Nuestra
Señora la Reina de los Angeles," and was the farthest outpost of civilization, and indeed of humanity, in this direction, being the first house met after
leaving Yuma, well over a hundred miles away.

Warner's Ranch is to-day a vast cattle range.
Leagues of sweet grass, with shade and ample water,
make it a stockman's paradise. There are wide
stretches of arable land besides, and ere long, no
doubt, the real-estate dealer will adjudge it ripe for
his little schemes. A town-site will be platted: the
truthful "folder" will cast the net: free excursions,
perhaps a barbecue, will draw the trustful "sucker"
gently in: and Warner's will proudly join the March
of Progress.

I stayed for two days, by which time I had cleared
the store of its fruits and vegetables. Then bidding

Pala, where the dispossessed Indians of Warner's now live, an invitation to attend the reopening and dedication of the old church. By
the Father's energy, the building has been acquired, repaired, and
restored to the use of such few of the Indian parishioners as remain
within reach.

good-bye to McSandy I again turned my face desert-wards. The forest fire that I had seen burning on the western edge of the ranch had been put out, but another had started in the Laguna Mountains to the southeast. I had meant to take that country on my way, in order to get as much as possible of mountain pleasures before tackling the long desert stretches that lay ahead. This now was barred, and I viewed the distant column of smoke with no little disgust.

For hours I rode south and east through the great valley, the summer-yellowed grass varied with dark-clustering oaks or islands of aromatic brush. From these came the shouts of those jolly pirates the Steller jays, or the guffaws of red-headed blackbirds, like "Laughter holding both his sides." Nearing the eastern edge of the ranch, patches of cactus and cat-claw met us with reminders that beyond the next ridge stretched the thorny, dreary desert. As I ate lunch beside a spring under a hillside oak, thoughts of the torturing heat of coming noonday camps would intrude, but I turned my eyes to the pine-clad heights and revelled in draught after draught of the cool, pure liquid tinkling by at arm's length.

I diverged here to call on an old acquaintance whom I had last known as a *vaquero* on a ranch a few miles to the south. He had now "given hostages to Fortune," and was established as cattleman on his own account. I came to his place about evening and met a hearty welcome. It was amusing to see how the family-man had qualified the cowboy of a year or two before, and to note the air, mingling the old and the new, with which my friend ruled what he termed his "outfit." The baby was addressed in a dialect quite unlike the orthodox — more in the Roaring Camp or Circle Bar vein. A special event was the young lady's first appearance on horseback. This, at the age of twelve weeks, I think beats anything offered in circuses.

The cowboy's liking for unlimited range was illustrated by my friend's complaint that new-comers were crowding him out. A neighbor a mile away in one direction and another four miles off in the other were the grounds of objection; and the road was "getting to be a durn boulevard: there were two fellows went by yesterday." As this is the main route from Warner's to Borego Springs I hoped the swelling tide of travel might brighten the lot of that little Devonshire woman down in the lonesome valley.

A road runs southeasterly from Warner's along the flank of the Volcan Mountain, and by it I took my way next day toward the desert. It is the old Warner's Pass route between desert and coast. By this trail came General Kearny and his dragoons with Kit Carson in company, on his long march in 1846 for the conquest of California; and it was from Warner's Ranch that he advanced to the battle, not much more than a skirmish, of San Pasqual, thirty miles to the west, where he met defeat at the hands of the despised Californians under Andréas Pico. Later, in the early years of American rule, this was the route of the Butterfield Overland Stages, which carried mails and passengers between St. Louis and San Francisco on a bi-weekly schedule, with twenty-one days for running time.

Too soon the oaks were left behind, and with them went the shade. The road trended steadily down, and already the desert seemed to be sucking my vital juices. Before us opened the San Felipe Valley, midway between mountains and desert and showing the characteristic features of both. The moving specks on the gray expanse were cattle, for it was still stockman's country, though rainfall here is unreliable, and disaster often points the moral of the cattleman's besetting temptation, overstocking the range.

An old pioneer, Wilson by name, keeps a pretence of a store on this road, about midway between Warner's and the San Felipe. As a store it is merely a joke, and I take its real purpose to be that of a trap to detain the passer-by until the old fellow has satisfied his curiosity. He is the antiquity of the region, but unfortunately is so deaf that conversation, short of roaring, was impossible. The process of business is simple. The customer walks about and collects what he needs, if he can find it, from the all but empty shelves, while the old gentleman hobbles close behind and keeps the reckoning.

A cluster of decaying adobes at the foot of the mountain marked the deserted village of the San Felipe Indians. This small *ranchería* shared the fate of the Agua Caliente village when the Warner Indians were evicted, fifteen years ago. One or two families, whose instinct for the old home was too strong to be defeated, still live about the locality. A few miles farther on I met a little procession of three wagons. On the seat of the first were two Indian women: one was driving, the other held upright a small wooden cross. In the bed of the wagon was a child's coffin, roughly made and unpainted. The other wagons held Indian men, women, and children, some of whom carried withered flowers and greenery. It was the funeral of a San Felipe boy on its way to the old burying-ground. The sad-eyed women, the lonely road, the sun, the dust, the old, universal errand, brought home to me a sense of gratitude in our common humanity; and as I stood uncovered, I claimed the Indian child for flesh of my flesh, spirit of my spirit, in no empty phrase my little brother.

It was past noon when we came to the San Felipe ranch-house. The old, picturesque house of adobe which I knew twenty years before had been replaced by a pretentious building that was out of keeping with its surroundings. The owner seldom visits the place, which is left to the management of Teodoro, the Indian *vaquero*, with a caretaker for the house. I bought some hay for Kaweah, and camped near the house. The night was enlivened by episodes between the coyotes and the ranch dogs, Bones, a greyhound, and Maje, a mongrel. "Bo-o-o-o-o-o-ones!" went the coyotes in derisive chorus, ending with howls of laughter: then "Ma-a-a-a-a-aje! Ya-a-ah, Ma-a-a-a-a-a-aje!" and again fits of maudlin glee. Out would charge Bones and the Major with robustious challenge, but the enemy, with no stomach for close quarters, were off like the wind. They were back like the wind, too, to break out again the moment the dogs settled down, which they chose to do close by my sleeping-quarters.

From the San Felipe two roads go to the desert, one continuing down the valley, the other, which I took, climbing the shoulder of a mountain to the south, and making a circuit behind it. In a *rincon* or elbow at the foot of the rise lay the hamlet of Banner, a place of some repute thirty years ago, when, with the mountain town of Julian, a few miles to the west, it was the centre of a lively mining region. Now, the population could be counted on the fingers of one hand. The only inhabitant I saw seemed to typify the place — an old, old man, bent and silent, who crept to and fro on the veranda of an echoing "hotel."

The trail here turned eastward, making a sharp ascent. As usual, the change of altitude was at once registered in the vegetation. Sizable bushes took the place of low and scanty brush: tall yucca spears appeared, their creamy candle-flames now long burned out. Then live-oaks began to spot the pale slopes with blots of umber. Shafts of old mines were numerous, and here and there stood decrepit cabins, long unused, surrounded with a litter of rusty shovels, drills, and crowbars, and specimens of mineral.

On a shoulder of the mountain I came upon the remains of a once notable mine, the Ranchita. The machinery was still in place, and the ten-stamp battery stood open-jawed as if begging one more meal of pay rock. There was something ghostly about the place. The engines, the complexity of pipes, shafts, and belts, the assaying-room with its furnace, retorts, and regiments of bottles, all had a look of tragedy, as if some deed of horror had occurred, and caused the whole crew, men and masters, to drop their business on the word and flee the place for ever.

A spring of good water and a few old fruit trees made an inviting halting-place. I had put Kaweah to graze on a precious scrap of grass, and sat down to my lunch, when a man on horseback came clattering down the trail. It is an event to meet anyone on these scantily travelled paths, so to stop and compare notes is the natural thing. This young fellow, coatless and baggageless, had come from some lonely mine twenty miles off and was casually going up to Julian, ten miles away on the top of the opposite mountain, to "take in" a *fiesta* of horse-racing and general hilarity, with a barbecue and an all-night dance to wind up with. To-morrow morning he would light-heartedly start for home, fully satisfied with his little jaunt. He was a friendly chap, and suggested my turning back and "taking it in" with him; and to encourage me he displayed a handbill which declared "every cowboy and cowgirl in the universe" to be welcome. When I pointed out that I did not fall under either head he replied that any fellow that rides a pony was eligible. But my road lay eastward; and with a "Well, then, adios!" and a wave of the hand, he skittered away down the mountain.

An hour more of climbing took us to the divide. Kaweah is never happy in this sort of country. He reminds me of the ingenious excuse of the defeated Syrians: "their gods were not gods of the mountains but of the plain." It is always weary work with him on rocky trails, and puts my temper on a strain. So it was a discontented pair that plodded down that interminable cañon of sand and boulders, jokingly termed a road. The afternoon was sultry, with clouds to south and west portending storm, though eastward over the desert the sun glared down as fiercely as ever.

The cañon opened at last into a brushy expanse called Mason Valley, from the name of some old settler. Through a narrow gateway in the mountain wall to the north, known formerly as the Puerta de San Felipe, the old stage-road climbed up to the San Felipe Valley, and thence to Warner's and the coast. The first vehicles to pass through it were the wagon-train of the "Mormon Battalion," under Lieutenant-Colonel Cooke, in 1847, on their long *trek* from Fort Leavenworth to San Diego. The colonel has given a vivid picture of the difficulties they met at this point, where a way had to be hewed with axes through the rocky pass before the wagons could proceed.[1]

A naturalist friend who makes Mason Valley his occasional home had made me welcome to the use of his cabin and, much more important, his haystack. About dusk we arrived at the place, but

[1] *The Conquest of New Mexico and California*, by P. St. George Cooke: G. P. Putnam's Sons, 1878.

found he was away. Unluckily, too, his well was out
of order, so we had to go on to the next settler's for
water. A rainfall averaging two to five inches would
not seem to offer much inducement to the farmer;
yet here, as at Borego, three or four men have taken
up homesteads, and are holding on in hope that
some day matters will improve, through the striking
of abundant water by deeper borings. Meanwhile
it is mainly the jackrabbits that profit by the crops
planted by the pioneers of Mason Valley, and, indeed, the jacks of this region are giants of their
kind. As they bounded away with that inimitable
grace and ease, I was almost tricked into thinking
they were antelope.

This valley is a natural plantation of agave, and
I saw many traces of the pits in which generations
of Indians have baked *a-moosh'*. These Indians, like
those of Santa Rosa, were happily placed as regards
climate. Within the distance of two or three hours'
travel they had the perfect winter temperature of
the desert or ideal summer surroundings among the
timber and running streams of the Laguna Mountains. With a surplus of game, and a wide choice of
vegetable food, their life, on the physical side, was
far from being one of hardship. The canned beef
and phonographs, "wrappers" and trousers, we
have conferred, have not made them sincerely hap-
pier, and the rattle-trap houses we persuade them
to live in are but a means to consumption and pneumonia. It is seldom a kindness to give anything the
need of which has not come to be felt.

From Mason Valley the road passed over a divide

into a larger valley called the Vallecito. Low mountains bounded it on the north; on the south rose the higher wall of the Lagunas, with pines trimming the edge and seeming to reproach me for the visit I had failed to pay. This long cañon, dropping from valley to valley, is the course of one of the desert's considerable streams, the Carrizo. Only a trained hydrographer would suspect it, however, for the flow is wholly underground for nearly all of the year, and comes to the surface only at times of unusual rain.

The heat was intense, for we were nearing desert level, and the landscape wavered like a picture on a screen. Ocotillos covered the valley closely and the hillsides more scantily, a few struggling up to the crests where their skinny arms moved in the breeze as if signalling of some rare sight that I should come and see.

At the lower end of the valley some arrangement of the strata brings the moisture to the surface to form a *ciénaga*, with a few mesquits and much salt grass and sacaton. Near by stood the long-deserted stage-station, an ample, picturesque building of what at first sight I took to be adobe bricks of the usual kind, but found were blocks of natural sod from the *ciénaga*. It is the only structure of the kind that I know, and the material appears to answer its purpose well, better in fact than adobe. It was interesting to note the rough but solid construction. Not only the walls and the square pillars of the veranda, but the roof, was built of sod, in flat bricks about nine by eighteen by five inches. The rafters were of natural pine, unsquared. On this, crosswise, were

mats of thin willow poles, interwoven with strips of
rawhide now brittle with age. On this, crosswise
again, was a layer of tules: then the sods, closely
fitted together, and cemented and surfaced with
adobe mud. A similar mortar was used in the walls
and pillars.

In the wide sunny silence the old house made a
charming if desolate picture. These structures made
of the very earth have preëminently that air of fit-
ness to their surroundings that is the first command-
ment of taste in building. Hence the peculiar beauty
of our California Missions. Simplicity is inherent in
the material, for elaboration is impossible in adobe.
The low round arch is its highest flight, and the
style accords with our gentle coast landscapes almost as if the building had grown spontaneously
from the soil. Though other fashions of architecture
are greater, statelier, or more ennobled by genius
and imagination, no other is so natural, so coherent,
so familiarly pleasing, in a word, so humane. The
old Vallecitos station, slowly rounding and crumbling back to its original earth, seems in the same
way suited and almost necessary to its place.

I would have given a good deal for the power of
visualizing the scenes that this old place has wit-
nessed. Seventy years is not a long term, and the
Warner's Pass stage-road has at no time seen anything that could be called a tide of travel: but for
grip and interest I fancy that the life lived and the
tales told round that old fireplace would hold their
own against the best that any Wayside Inn could
show. Many of those pioneers, the very last of whom

are now close upon the final destination, came this way, with scars of Apache arrows and notches on rifle-butts that meant stories that would make "movie" men bite their fingers for envy. Here passed bands of jingling caballeros in the ante-Gringo days of the forties, and here came Kearny's dragoons and Cooke's nondescript "Mormon Battalion," and many of those Great Plainsmen to whom every trail from the Mississippi to the Coast was like one's private short cut 'cross lots. Much of the great California gold rush came this way, and a later generation of gold-seekers found this the handiest route for quests into the Superstitions or Cócopas, Chocolates or Huachucas. Engineers, from Lieutenant Emory's 1846 Military Reconnaissance of the Thirty-second Parallel down to the party whom I met near here a few years ago looking out aëroplane landings, have found Vallecitos Springs invaluable as a base of operations. And it may be reckoned that many a fugitive from justice has found this the easiest way to cheat the sheriff by the time-honored method of "skipping across the line," since the Mexican border is but a few miles away.

All the morning I had seen hardly a token of animal life: a road-runner perhaps, but no other bird, nor beast, nor even reptile. Here I found flycatchers and a woodpecker or two gathered in a cottonwood near the water-trough that the county authorities have placed here for the benefit of cattle and cattle-men. Dragon-flies were patrolling over the *ciénaga*, and hornets were busy at their masonic labors on a branch overhead. It was altogether a seductive place, and I had to resist an inclination to let the afternoon slip away in a prolonged siesta.

At a little cabin on the farther side of the *ciénaga* I found a lonely settler who runs a few head of cattle on these dry ranges. With him, as it happened, was a prospector who for years had made this part of the desert his beat. This meeting made my opportunity for seeing a remarkable gorge, known as Split Mountain Cañon, which I had been warned not to attempt to explore without a guide who knew the intricacies of the "bad-lands" that must be crossed to reach it. By good luck this prospector needed to visit certain claims of his near the outlet of the cañon. We agreed to join forces, and arranged to meet next day at a spot a few miles farther on called Agua Caliente — the almost inevitable name for any place in California, or Mexico either, where warm springs occur.

Next morning, then, I took my way again down the Carrizo Creek Cañon. Crossing a divide, the high country I had lately left was soon lost to view, and on either side rose pale, ashy hills that dipped lower and lower till they sank into the level. They looked the very stronghold of drought, a scattering of drab brush only serving to mark their ugliness and hopeless aridity. The ocotillos grew few and small, even the agaves were yellow and stunted. When the road dropped to the dry river-bed, smoke-trees and desert willows appeared as in duty bound, but they had a pinched, last gasp look that intensified the misery of the landscape. The loose sand made the hardest kind of going, and the sun dealt his fiercest stroke. Over the mountains to the south hung the brown haze of a forest fire which had burned intermittently for a week. The thought of those smoking hillsides going up with crackle and roar in league-long sheets of flame gave the final touch to the torture of the heat. I felt as if the skin of my face would crack and shrivel off, and wondered if any mortal man could possibly be fighting that fire that day at close range.

At length I saw against the gray hills a tiny spot of green that I hailed as my landmark. Arrived there I found my man with his two horses already in camp. He seemed surprised to see me, and remarked that he had not expected me to show up: had thought that I should back out and go by the nearest way to Imperial Valley, seeing I was so near. Split Mountain, he considered, was a crazy place for any one to go without better reason than I had named.

The spot was pleasant, for a desert camp. Three springs of good though warm water broke out on the hillside and fed a strip of green grass, dotted with mesquits, palms, and tufts of arrowweed. Some mineral contained in the water has built up mounds of a whitish deposit, giving the appearance of geysers, or miniature volcanoes. As the next day would be Sunday, and the forage would carry us over, we agreed to postpone our start till Monday. In the evening we had a small camp-fire — not for warmth but for the look of it — and Wellson entertained me with episodes in the lives of sundry Coyote Charlies, Shoot-'em-up Smiths, and other local celebrities. He had also grewsome tales of men who had come by their death in the region we were about to visit. The spot where Frenchy's boot, containing a leg-bone and part of a cake of Navy Plug, was found: the "monument" that Newt Dolan must have missed in the dark and so taken the wrong branch of the dry-wash from which he never emerged, and other points of interest, he would show me on Monday if he did n't forget. In most cases, though, there was no memento: they had merely, as he compactly put it, "gone in and stayed."

A case in his own knowledge was a young fellow from Syracuse, who had arranged last summer to meet Wellson at Carrizo Springs and accompany him through Split Mountain Cañon. As he did not arrive when expected, Wellson went on alone, leaving word, in case the other came later, that he was not to try to follow him, but wait for his return. Next day the young man appeared at Carrizo Springs, and, disregarding the advice, started, with a small quantity of food and water, to follow Wellson by his tracks. He had not been seen or heard of since: the bad-lands engulfed him and, like many more, he "stayed."

It was fine to lie at leisure next morning, careless of time, and watch the coming of day. An uncertain pallor stole into the east while the morning star was still low in the horizon. It strengthened imperceptibly to a silvery light, unearthly and shy and holy. A stain of orange came, flushing quickly to crimson; but the color, vivid as it was, did not escape beyond a narrow belt of horizon, and met the indigo of the upper sky, where the stars still shone, with scarcely a tinge of change. Then over the crimson came a glow of gold. The stars grew pale and suddenly were quenched, while the gold gathered into one spot of quivering glory intolerably bright. A moment of crisis, and — up strode The Sun and began flinging abroad his terrible largesse. Well, Tyrant, I am but a puny son of one of thy puny planets, but — hark: I defy thee!

The day was helped along by occasional visits to the largest of the springs, where a bathing-hole has been formed, I do not know whether by Nature or man. A tall rock made a slip of shade where we huddled between times. The horses strayed from Bermuda grass to screw-beans and back, or lay wondering what would be the penalty to-morrow for this unwonted ease to-day. At evening, after watching all day the dull changes on the colorless hills, I was once again startled by the magic of sunset. Leagues of gray slope and plain, that had seemed thrice dead, drained of color, were changed in a breath to hues the most enchanting and spiritual. With no divinity at work, could mere physics, laws of refraction and so forth, achieve this heavenly splendor by blind, automatic result?

CHAPTER XVI

A DESERT RIDE: AGUA CALIENTE TO "SAN FELIPE CITY"

Prospectors' rites — *En route* for Split Mountain — The cavalcade — The *campomoche* — Bad-lands again — Miners' Hell — Digging for water — A spectacular cañon — Gloom at midday — Nightfall in a cañon — Fish Creek Mountain — Impossible water — A "dry camp" — Kaweah in distress — Horse and master — Tragedy again — An optimistic city — Conversational finance — Feats of the sun — A depressing landscape — Approaching Superstition Mountain — A warm cañon — A prospector's "close call" — A waterless region — Evening luxury.

L IKE every genuine prospector I ever met, Wellson had three articles of faith without observance of which no day could hopefully begin: one was flapjacks, another bacon, the third coffee. (The second of them I find it wise to abjure when there is a thirsty day's work ahead.) Thus, though we were up at half-past four, the sun was already hot when we started from Agua Caliente. Our horses carried, beside our other baggage, all the water that we had vessels to hold, viz.: three canvas water-bags and four canteens, giving eleven gallons altogether. At one place on our route it was possible we might get a little water by digging, and in hope of it we had borrowed a shovel from our Vallecitos acquaintance. Failing this, we should not find any till next day, and the horses must have water once at least before then.

The best known entrance to Split Mountain Cañon is from Carrizo Springs, some miles to the

east of Agua Caliente; but Wellson believed he could
find a direct route through the bad-lands that would
save us that détour. We struck directly northeast,
over a rising plain dotted with dwarfed agaves and
ocotillos. Ahead was a high divide formed by the
meeting of the flanks of Vallecitos and Fish Creek
Mountains. It is between these two mountains that
Split Mountain Cañon runs, a mere rift in width,
but deep and clear-cut. To the south there gradually opened a view of Coyote Mountain (not the
peak of that name that I had passed on leaving
Borego Springs), a handsomely shaped block of
dull reddish brown, standing a few miles to the
north of the Mexican border.

Of my companion's two horses, one was generally
used as pack-horse, the other for riding. Now, however, loaded as all the animals were with bags and
canteens of water, we were both afoot. On a gravelly
bench we found galleta grass growing in tussocks
any one of which would have made a meal for a
truck-horse. It was hard to pass it by, but fortunately Wellson had brought along half a sack of barley, from which I would draw rations for Kaweah.

It was here that I first identified an insect of bad
reputation, the *campomoche*. It belongs to the same
family as that ferocious hypocrite, the praying man-
tis, and is a gray, stick-like creature, not easily seen
amid the dry stems of the galleta where it is apt to
be found. Taken into the stomach of horses or cattle, its effect is said to be that of a corrosive poison,
sometimes strong enough to cause death. I am a little doubtful regarding this fatal quality of the *cam-*

pomoche, in view of the tendency to exaggeration in such matters: but the story has come to me from several sources.

Two hours brought us to the edge of the badlands, in the form of a deep, abrupt *barranca*, the first of dozens through which we must thread our way. In we dived: and, indeed, to plunge into one of these mazes is much like diving into unknown water: when, where, or whether one will get out is somewhat a matter of chance. In and out, up and down, we went for hours, scrambling up and sliddering down. Now and then we left the horses and climbed out to get our bearings afresh. It was not reassuring to see that Wellson was often at fault, though it was natural, since he was gauging landmarks from an unfamiliar side.

We reached at length a rim from which we looked out over a still more intricate piece of country. With a sweep of the hand my companion remarked, "There's the worst stretch of country I know, and I know 'most all the bad layouts from Idaho down. More men have got lost in that mess of stuff than any other place I ever saw, and most of 'em are there yet. Miner's Hell I call it, easy to get in and the devil to get out. Well, I know where we are, anyway. I wasn't sure before, but now there'll be monuments, if we can find 'em, so I reckon we'll get through."

It was a remarkable sight. Imagine a cauldron of molten rock, miles wide, thrown by earthquake shock into the complexity of a choppy sea and then struck immovable. Looking down on it one would say that not a stick or leaf of herbage was there, still less any animal life in that sterility of vermilion, ochre, and gray. Life there is of both kinds, but so scant that it is merely the scientific minimum, almost more theory than fact.

Our eyes needed to be on the alert every moment to get the benefit of the monuments. They were sometimes a hundred yards, sometimes half a mile apart, and such casual affairs that without a sort of instinct one would not know them. However, with one or two mistakes we worked our way through and found ourselves in the main cañon. The name of Split Mountain fairly describes its appearance. The spectacular part of the defile begins some distance from the mouth, but already high walls shut us in, and made a narrow corridor with level floor of white sand in which a few bits of brush huddled close to the cliffs for shelter from the blasting sun.

Before getting far into the cañon we came to the place that gave our only chance of water. On a boulder was dimly written in English and Spanish, "Water 100 feet West. Dig": with an arrow marking the direction. Pacing off the distance we looked for a likely spot and went to work. The first hole giving no encouragement, we tried another, then a third: but after half an hour of thirsty work we concluded that it was hopeless, and ceased. Earlier in the year we might have had success: now the water-level had sunk out of reach. Traces of others' attempts could be seen, and I hoped that none of them stood for the last struggle of some fellow mortal.

To us the failure meant pushing ahead at once

instead of exploring a certain part of Fish Creek Mountain that Wellson wished to visit with an eye to mineral. We found a smoke-tree and made the most of its hypothetical shade while we ate lunch and fed and rested the horses. Before going on we gave them each half a bucket of water, which they drank eagerly and asked for more; but it was imperative to ration the whole party more severely than we had intended. A good deal had escaped from the water-bags by leakage, though they had been soaked all the previous day in the spring.[1]

We now entered the most striking part of the gorge, which reminded me of Painted Cañon, near Mecca, which I described in an earlier chapter. The cliffs here, though they have not the variety of color of those in Painted Cañon, are vertical, like them, and equally high. The width of the floor is about the same. There is always a feeling of gloom in these places. Let the sun pour his blinding rays as he will, a chill is on the mind. The walls seem to draw closer about the traveller; the eye itself seems to feel a sense of dread, and shrinks from realizing the threatening height.

The gorge continued for several miles. Now and then some side cleft opened, choked with granite, here old, there freshly broken. The sky-line was torn into wild forms as if by blows of a Titan's hammer. Lean ocotillo or starving creosote stared grimly from

---

[1] These bags, much in vogue in our desert regions, would be improved by providing a heavy reënforcement, preferably of leather, to cover the bottom and extend a few inches up the sides. Without this, the pressure of the water in a large bag forces it through the canvas.

the rim, or shrank back into niches of the unfriendly wall. The only bird I saw was a raven, whose slow wing-beats struck heavily on the well-like air and whose croak as he flew from point to point before us seemed to warn us back, and promise dismal consequences if we followed.

Sunset found us nearing the northern outlet of the cañon. In that deep, silent place, the light as it faded away up the vast walls seemed to be withdrawing for the last time, clinging and lingering on the upper heights with the dull glow of dying lava. Close behind crept like tragedy the ashy shadow. Now only the topmost edge held the rays, as if clutching a last hope. For a moment they brightened, and the spectral shapes looking down moved as if in relief: but on the instant a dark hand passed over, and chilled all color to stony gray.

I pushed on to overtake Wellson before he passed out of the cañon, where I might be unable to follow his tracks in the darkness. I came up with him just as we emerged upon the sloping *bajada,* which is the feature of almost every desert cañon mouth. Brush grew more thickly, and had a friendly look after the barrenness of the gorge. Far across the valley to the north I recognized Santa Rosa Mountain, unmistakable, though showing a face new to me. A dark ridge to the east I knew must be Superstition Mountain, now not many miles away.

We picked our way round the shoulder of Fish Creek Mountain, an imposing mass that even in half darkness showed a metallic look, very noticeable by daylight. I expect to hear some day of fortunes coming out of that mountain, which has hardly been touched by prospectors, on account of the difficulty of taking in sufficient water for a stay long enough for effective work.

Wellson was making for a "dry camp" of his on the way to which we should pass an old mining shaft in which a little liquid was sometimes to be found. This, though quite impossible for human beings, Wellson had known his animals to drink when hard pushed.

It was long after dark when we reached the hole. We hauled up a bucket of the stuff, the horses crowding round for first chance. The stench was atrocious, and it was all I could do to avoid being violently sick. One after another the animals did their best to drink, putting their noses to it thirstily time after time, but it was too foul and they would not take it. We drew bucket after bucket in hope of getting something a degree less disgusting. At last one of Wellson's horses reluctantly drank a little, rolling back her lips after each mouthful to get rid of the filthy taste and odor. Her mate, and my Kaweah, who is unusually scrupulous, could not bring themselves to touch it, though their eagerness was pitiful.

We led the poor beasts to camp, which was in a clump of mesquits near the foot of the mountain. With barley and mesquit beans they were well fed, at any rate. Then we scratched up a meal by the light of a candle-end, threw our blankets on the sand and ourselves on them, and smoked for an hour while we radiated the day's accumulation of heat into the scarcely cooler air of the night. We had made a fifteen hours' march with one stop of less than an hour at midday.

At first daylight we took the horses again to the hole, thinking they would by now be forced to drink. Wellson's animals both drank a little, though with every token of repugnance; but Kaweah would have none of it, though he snuffed eagerly at each bucketful I brought him. Probably the water, besides being alkaline and stagnant, was putrid with dead animals — birds, snakes, possibly a coyote or two. My gorge rises now when I think of the place.

Breakfast almost ended our own water, and the first necessity for all concerned was to get to a new supply. Six miles to the north a settler had sunk a well and obtained a small flow, sufficient for household needs, though not for irrigation. We made for this place, my poor Kaweah in distress and panting hard as I led him.

The relations between man and horse who are much together, especially when for long spells they two are alone, take on a touch of sentiment, on the man's side (and I do not doubt on the other's also), that to some people might seem overdone. The loyalty of the dumb beast, patiently doing his best, accepting his master's will without thought of dispute, and taking for granted that his service will be repaid by care for the needs which he is prevented from supplying for himself — the pathos of this becomes better recognized in the daily sharing of chances. And whenever, as here, my trusty companion has had to suffer, I have had pangs, I don't mind saying, that came near bringing tears. When it comes to magnanimity, few of us can equal the average horse or hound.

Under a greasewood bush I noticed an old shoe. It had belonged, Wellson said, to a man who, the year before, had gone crazy for want of water and had here thrown away clothes, shoes, blankets, everything — the usual line of action — and, raving and naked, had wandered across the desert until, by luck, he came to one of the canals of the Imperial Valley irrigation system, some twenty miles away. There he was found, lying in the water, out of his senses and famishing for food, but too weak to travel farther. In this case rescue came just in time and the man eventually recovered.

The fact that I was again below sea-level was registered both in the shells that sprinkled the powdery plain and in the water-line at the foot of the mountain. To the south, Signal Mountain, an isolated peak beyond the Mexican line, showed near at hand. Ahead was Santa Rosa, and a few miles to the east the haze of the plain shaded to faint blue where the Salton lay anæmic under the fierce evaporation. Behind us rose the spur of the Peninsular Range through which we had yesterday threaded our way.

At length appeared a derrick, and a dot or two beside it. This was our destination. The horses quickened their pace, and as we approached I was relieved to hear a hail, for I had been worrying over the possibility that the place might be deserted and the pump out of order. In that case we should have been in a serious fix, with less than half a gallon of water left and the horses badly used up.

Two young fellows, a Norwegian and an Irishman as I later found, who were watching our coming, first handed us the water-bag as a natural preliminary, then made us welcome to San Felipe City. We hastened to water our anxious beasts, then rejoined the populace, and Felipe the dog, at the pump-house. I had heard of this thriving place before, and was pleased to find myself within its boundaries. Over the door of a shed which adjoined the house was a signboard painted —

SAN FELIPE
71 FEET BELOW SEA-LEVEL
WATCH IT GROW
POPULATION 1920, 1000

It was a good example of Western optimism — generous, yet modest withal, for what California "city," with two citizens already secured, does not set a higher mark than a single thousand for the end of the decade?

Here, as in other places I have described, the hope on the settler's horizon is that some person of wealth, providentially going daft, may be inspired to waste his substance in the reckless sinking of wells which shall tap the water-bearing strata that, as the settler is convinced, underlie his precious claim.[1] Our San Felipe friends, though, had an eye

[1] There are uses to which public money is put that seem less statesmanlike than employing it in experimental borings in these localities, provided the soil is such as to make agriculture profitable if water

also to mineral possibilities. The talk centred on mines and prospects, claims and "jumpings," water-holes and deaths for lack of them; and thousands, hundreds of thousands, or millions of dollars were freely tossed about. Easy Street is the only thorough-fare in the city of the prospector's dreams.

The day was hot, though not specially so: 115° was the highest point touched by the municipal thermometer. The look of our hosts made a commentary on the general temperature. Both were naturally fair-complexioned, but had taken a pleasing tint of *café au lait* wherever the skin showed (and their dress of tattered duck trousers with armless and barely coherent shirt did not leave much in doubt). The Irishman mentioned that, a few days before, the iron head of a drum of water he was hauling was blown off by the steam generated within. He reported also that in his capacity of cook he often found eggs which had lain outdoors partly cooked by the sun, so that they did not fall from the shell when broken for the frying-pan. Readers who have had experience of the summer climate of these regions will not be unduly critical of these stories.

One of Wellson's horses — a raw-boned animal with a kind of pile-driver action due to a case of spring-halt — having become tender-footed, we gave her a day's rest at the ranch while we paid a visit to Superstition Mountain. This low range hardly deserves the name of mountain, for it does not rise to

were found. Good land would be brought sooner into use, while set-tlers would be saved the spending of years upon tracts intrinsically worthless.

a thousand feet, and is merely a long ridge, mainly interesting for its deadly reputation among both Indians and whites. From this side it had a peculiar piebald look, unlike any other range I have seen.

We rode southeasterly toward a low clay ridge beyond which lay the Salton Sea. The ground was a dead level of silt that rose in puffs and lingered in the nostrils like acrid smoke. Shells glittered everywhere, almost the only thing for the eye to notice, for the vegetation was reduced to an occasional hummock of mesquit of which only the topmost twigs showed above the mound of soil that struggled to engulf them. I tried to imagine some addition or subtraction by which the landscape might be rendered more depressing, but had to admit that the maximum was reached: it was wholly, conscientiously bad.

Sand and gravel succeeded to silt as we approached the ridge. Pebbles of unusual colors were strewn about, mingled with odd-looking bits of black baked clay, some like fragments of tile, some in large balls or grotesque shapes such as children make from a lump of plaster. Large flakes of mica glittered here and there, objects of awe to the simple Indian mind, which, I notice, takes brightness in any form to be significant — good or bad medicine. I looked for animal life but saw none, except, rarely, the track of a lizard. Even flies were absent; as a matter of fact, they almost disappear from the desert during the hottest weeks of summer.

The black clay continued for miles, usually as a capping to layers of red and yellow. Turning southward we made direct for the mountain, picking our way through gullies of sand and boulders bleached almost snow-white by the terrific sun. The glare from the ground was even more intolerable than the direct blast, and the heat was intensified by the scarifying dryness. The effect on the eyes was acutely painful; indeed, it is surprising that such a sensitive organ can endure these conditions without lasting damage. Aqueous humors were never meant for this sort of thing. As we neared the mountain I found that certain white patches that had puzzled me were splashes of sand that had been swept far up the slopes, as waves rush up the face of a cliff. Along the base appeared again the curious shapes of clay, many of them as perfect as if turned in a lathe or cast in a mould.

By a narrow pass we turned into the heart of the mountain. Precipitous walls, as in Split Mountain Cañon but not so high, shut us into a winding defile where we could not ride abreast. It was midday and the place was like a furnace, the temperature not less, I think, than 150° in the sun. The formation looked like red clay, but the loose rocks that strewed the cañon were of varied kinds and colors, prevailingly igneous and many with metallic lustre. I saw that my companion occasionally added a bit of rock to the museum he carried in his hip pocket. It is hard to keep one's mind off the subject of mines and metals in this locality where something striking in the way of minerals appears at every turn, and every lonely cañon looks just the place to be hiding ledges of "the right stuff."

We rode along looking for shade, but it was a mile

or two before we found it under the overhang of a
boulder, and then our feet projected annoyingly.
Into this haven we crept, after feeding the horses,
and lay for an hour gathering energy for the eating
of lunch. We had brought the materials for a billy
of tea, and agreed that it was what we needed, but
there the matter hung. Finally we tossed up, and I,
who had suggested this solution in a spirit of fair-
ness, found myself condemned to walk out into the
broiling sun and endure the added warmth of a fire.

When a strip of shade came under the cliff we
moved over, horses and men, and hugged the rock
while we waited for the temperature to pass the
crisis. Even in the shade the breeze was scorching
and the sand so hot as to be uncomfortable to sit
upon. The horses stood with half-shut eyes and
panted as if broken-winded. To pass the time agree-
ably, Wellson told stories of various Mikes and Bills
who had preceded us into these cañons, and most of
whom, apparently, had concluded to remain.

In turn I related the following incident which had
been told me at Mecca by Johnny Thomas, one of
a number of prospectors who keep a sort of rookery
among the mesquits at the rear of the railway station.

"Summer of nineteen seven," said Johnny, taking
his favorite pose, squatting on his haunches, in
the shade of a screwbean, "I was camped over at
Cottonwood. I was working on my Blue Dick claim
then. Old Blue (that was my pack-burro) was a
renegade.[1] Old man Schneider bought him first from

[1] A burro that runs away at every opportunity. It is a common
fault, a mark of the depravity of the tribe.

the Indians at Martinez, but he could n't ever keep him. 'Most everybody in the valley owned him one time and another before I had him. Dick? why, he was my riding burro. Blue Dick, don't ye see?

"Well, one morning I wanted to go over and look at my Black Owl claim. It was only four miles away, so I walked, and left Blue and Dick and my other burro, a jenny, grazing in a little side cañon that was wired across. When I got back they were gone. That old devil had got away and took the others with him. It was too late to go after them that day, but next morning I took my small canteen and started to track them. I did n't reckon they'd gone very far, but I used up my water before I'd much more than got on their trail, so I came back again to the Springs.

"As it happened Aleck Cameron and Don Ferguson had just come in to Cottonwood that day. They'd been over to Placer Cañon in the Palens, but there was n't any water in the cañon and they came back. I borrowed one of their jacks and started out again next morning with a gallon of water and three or four biscuit. The burros had hit an old dim Indian trail that goes over to Piñon. It was a trail I did n't know about, but that old Blue devil savvied every trail and water-hole from Chuck Warren's to the river, durn him.

"I travelled all day, but the tracks went right on. When night came I had about a cupful of water left. I was only about three or four miles from Piñon, if I'd known, but I did n't know the country then, and the only water I knew about was behind. So I turned back. I left the jack tied in the brush, because I had to find my back tracks and I could n't do that unless I walked and sort of felt my way. It was n't what you'd call a trail, more like a jackrabbit run. I could n't eat because I was too dry to swallow without drinking, and I did n't dare to drink. It was August, long days and hotter 'n blazes. I durs n't use up that mite of water, so I'd take a mouthful, and hold it, and then spit it back in the canteen.

"It was the dark of the moon, but I had to travel, and I kept moving all night. I used up all my matches, looking for my tracks. When it got daylight my water was all used up. I was in bad shape, faint and awful thirsty, and I had n't made more than half the way back to the Springs. When it got hot I would travel say two hundred yards and then lie down in the shade of a rock or bit of brush. Gosh! I don't know how I kept going, except I knew I had to keep on or I'd die right there.

"When it came night again I took off my clothes, all except shoes, and carried them. It was a hot night, but the wind felt good on my skin. I don't know how I stayed in the trail; luck, I guess: and the only way I kept going was because I had to get to Cottonwood that night; I knew I'd never live through another day like I'd just put in. It was three in the morning when I got to Cottonwood. I went right to the water-trough and put my head in. I had sense enough left not to drink any at first. The boys were there, and they gave me some weak whiskey and then some coffee and other grub. I slept all that day, and next morning I walked the twenty-five miles in to Mecca. Frank Coffey came back with me to Cottonwood with two of his burros, and then I went back with three gallons of water and a loaf of bread. The jack was tied where I left him. He was pretty sick-looking and lying down. I went on and found my burros over at Piñon, and brought them all back to the Springs.

"That was about the closest call I've had. I did n't ought to have started with that little canteen, but gosh! us fellers are all fools, else we would n't stay with it. Well, after that I was through with old Blue: sold him to a rancher for eight dollars. Don't happen to have the makins, do you? Gracias."

We had agreed to start back at three o'clock, but when the hour came, our courage was wanting. However, Wellson handsomely offered to boil another billy, and when it had been despatched we braced up and moved off. On emerging from the cañon we took a direct line for home. It led us first over a plain of clay thinly covered with sand and pebbles, next into a region of dunes, discouraging to the tired horses, and then to the edge of a depression that was curiously broken up with fissures — a sort of miniature bad-land formation. From the tracks of wild-cats and coyotes that threaded the narrow gullies, it would appear that this is a kind of preserve of theirs, though what they live on, unless on one another, is a mystery. Tracks of sidewinders were here too, in great profusion; quite a nice populous neighborhood.

I was surprised to find fragments of pottery strewn about this hopeless region. In the cañon I saw none, but so far as I can learn there has never been any water discovered there, not even the natural tanks that almost all the desert ranges afford. It is hard to conjecture why Indians should ever have chosen to live in this locality, the most forbidding on the whole desert: one, moreover, that superstition prompts them to avoid. Perhaps the attraction was the fish they may have found here when this was the margin of the ancient sea.[1]

The sun did not miss the good shot we offered as we rode westward for hours, but at last he fired his final round for the day and sank behind friendly San Ysidro. I hung my hat on the saddle-horn, threw open my shirt, and basked in relative coolness. By nightfall we were back at our quarters. Our friends, stripped to the waist, were waiting supper for us. In the smoky lamplight the scene reminded me of a ship's forecastle. Afterwards it was the extreme of luxury to lie on a blanket and send up incense to the starry bands marching overhead, while the eternal talk went on of leads and lodes, veins and stringers, placers and pockets, till sleep brought silence.

[1] Lee Arenas tells me of a tradition of his people (the Cahuillas) that at one time all the fighting men of the tribe, numbering perhaps five hundred, went on the war-path against one of the Colorado River tribes, probably the Yumas. His story goes that the whole party, with the exception of a score or so, perished somewhere in these wastes. With such tales in mind, these potsherds scattered about the desert — what tragedies may they not imply? This is the only instance so far as I know of large bodies of Indians attempting the crossing.

CHAPTER XVII

A DESERT RIDE: "SAN FELIPE CITY" TO IMPERIAL VALLEY

WELLSON grumbled loudly when I roused him at five o'clock. We had agreed on a compromise between my four-thirty and his eight-thirty for our starting time, but he pretended that six-thirty was the hour for getting up instead of for leaving. He was comforted, though, when told that breakfast was under way, and punished the flapjacks with severity.

There was a long day's march ahead of us, but we took no water for the horses as Wellson knew of a water-hole that we could take in our route by going a little out of our way. Our mark was Coyote Wells, on the road between San Diego and the Imperial Valley, and of late also a point on the partly built railway which is to connect San Diego with Yuma and the East. There was no road or trail that would serve our purpose: we had simply to make as nearly due south as the nature of the country would allow.

The excitement of seeing any one off is rare at San Felipe, so the population assembled for the spectacle. Farewells were brief. Anything more than "Adios" or "So long" seems prolix to the Westerner. Turning in my saddle after five minutes I saw that our hosts still stood watching us, perhaps speculating how long it might be before they had more visitors to entertain.

Passing Fish Creek Mountain I had a better opportunity to note its metallic look. Patches of white, which my companion said were beds of gypsum, gave contrast to the purple-red of the rock. Cleft and cañon were marked by scorings of gray that shone in the morning light like waterfalls. If I had a fortune and an extra life to throw away I should be tempted to turn prospector and thoroughly explore Fish Creek Mountain. On the other side, Superstition Mountain showed now as total black. Ahead rose the cone of Signal Mountain, with the Cócopas, a wash of atmospheric pink, trailing off southward into Mexico.

A feature of desert travel whenever one is near mountains is the liability to come abruptly upon gullies ten or fifteen feet deep, with absolutely vertical walls. These are water-courses, carved, almost at a stroke, by the rush of water from the cañons. They are great consumers of time, often leading one far out of one's course before a crossing can be made. Their one good point is that a modicum of shade may be found there under the thorny tangle of a cat-claw or a smoke-tree — shade of the thinnest, yet a valuable relief. While we rested in one of these gullies, Wellson, recognizing the place, mentioned that a year or two ago a man whom he knew, one Walbridge, had come into this locality to look at a claim in Fish Creek Mountain. Wellson was to meet him on his return at Seeley, in the Imperial Valley. "I hung around a day or two, but he did n't show up, so I came out to see where he was. That's the gully where I found his tracks. I followed till I lost them up that cañon. — Find him? no, I did n't ever find him. He'd left his blankets in the livery barn down at Seeley, and he did n't ever call for them, so I reckon he's in there somewhere yet."

Between Fish Creek Mountain and Coyote Mountain is the cañon of Carrizo Creek, which we had left when we turned north at Agua Caliente. It is a wild, disorderly-looking piece of country. Hills and ridges of strangest shape and color seem to jostle for place. A low cone to our right appeared to be covered with black clay shards like those near Superstition Mountain. Another hill of vivid yellow was capped with the same material. Others were of entire red or purple. Over all, the opaque sky fitted like a china bowl, filling every notch and curve of the horizon with its stark, uncompromising blue. The crudity of the landscape here surpassed anything I had yet seen in this region of hard color effects.

Here we made an unpleasant discovery, that Wellson's pack-mare had cast a shoe and was already quite lame. Her spring-halt action had disguised the fact till the hoof was worn to the quick. It was a cruel necessity to keep the poor beast moving, but there was no alternative. This raised a question: whether to keep to the easier but longer route, or to strike over the shoulder of Coyote Mountain, which would save ten miles, but would bring us into rougher territory. I asked Wellson if he felt sure of finding his water-hole in case we took the shorter way, and as he had no doubts we chose it.

In the midst of the wide sandy channel of Carrizo Creek we crossed a faint track which marked the road to Warner's. To us it was of no value, for our way lay directly south. In winter, water might have been found here, the stream that gladdened Colonel Cooke in mid-January of 1847, when he arrived here after the perilous crossing of the desert with his ragged "Mormon Battalion." In three days and two nights they had covered the fifty-six miles from Alamo Mocho, without water for their animals, which were half starved, at that. Had it been summer a wholesale tragedy might easily have occurred.

Over a region of mesas of baked clay broken by gullies that forced us into tedious détours, we slowly made our way. If the gaunt and desolate has a degree of perfection, here surely it is reached. I do not see how Sahara, Gobi, or Arabia could improve on this for rigid nakedness and sterility. One here sees Mother Earth scalped, flayed, and stripped to the skeleton. Yet there is a strange beauty in it all. Perhaps the dormant savage in the breast, some strain of the paleozoic, wakes up in the presence of these chaotic, barbaric shapes. I felt a sort of excitement, a half sense of recognition, as if something nudged and whispered — "Your primal home. Come back."

The day was of the usual midsummer heat, and the horses were getting played out while we were yet many miles from the expected water. The mare was in great distress, but there was no help for it, we must go on. Coyote Mountain was near at hand, a sullen monster of brown. Every quarter-mile brought some novelty to sight. In crossing a bench of reddish clay I noticed numbers of bullets of some heavy metallic stuff, the size of marbles and perfectly round. Then came a tract covered with pebbles, various in color, but as even in shape and dimension as if carefully sorted. Again, plates of clear gypsum, as large as small window-panes and nearly an inch thick, projected from the sides of a gully. Next, stumbling over lumps of some brittle material, I found that they were compact clods of oyster shells (we were a few hundred feet above sea-level). It was a region to charm the geologist, though not the botanist. A few wretched creosotes and ocotillos alone held on to life, shrivelled, leafless, and half ossified.

Wellson now pointed out a red ridge, two miles ahead, which was the landmark for our water-hole. How to get to it, though, was a question. Before us stretched a tangle of gullies and washes, braided together like one's interlaced fingers. The two miles might turn to twenty, and nightfall find us as far from water as ever. We consulted, and resolved to make a direct dash for the place. Down we went into the maze, dragging the unwilling animals down impossible banks and hauling them up equal impossibilities on the other side, where we took our bearings afresh, and repeated.

Physical exhaustion comes quickly under these circumstances. For a few moments that afternoon I had a sharp realization of peril. A sudden faintness, the result of exertion in that extreme heat (it was nine hours since we had eaten), came over me, and with it the thought of danger, the hopeless danger that cannot be fought. Suppose something occurred to defeat us of the expected supply of water? Was it certain even that we had enough in our canteens to last till we got there? Something might go wrong — anything: what then? How long could I go without water, if by any chance I were left without it? In that fierce heat, and struggling with that terrible country, a few minutes was as long as one could go without drinking. In a flash I saw what would be my condition *in a single hour* — torture: two hours — delirium: after that raving madness, till agony passed into insensibility, and that into death.

Let not the reader think that I am overdrawing here. Those who travel the desert in the middle of summer, and *on foot* (*which makes all the difference*), know well enough that to be two or three hours without water brings a man within the grasp of death. In that terrific temperature one's bodily moisture must be constantly renewed, for moisture is as vital as air. One feels as if one were in the focus of a burning-glass. The throat parches and seems to be closing. The eye-balls burn as though facing a scorching fire. The tongue and lips grow thick, crack, and blacken. Every organ of the body is deranged, for the drought is not local, but runs through every vein. Life cannot endure for long when one of its elements is literally drained away. The brain's balance is overthrown and panic adds its terrors to the torment that gnaws each throbbing nerve. Then comes madness, and, whether mercifully soon or cruelly delayed, the end.

Meanwhile the sun shines on, showering down carelessly his death-dealing rays. Nature is merely the mathematician; her business is only to get the right answer. Given the season and latitude, the physical geography, and the constitution of the body, the result works out to a certainty.

At last we reached a wider gully leading in the right direction, and which Wellson thought he recognized. Here and there were what might be monuments, and we went on more hopefully. But the gully turned west, then north, and we knew we were on the wrong track. Wellson climbed a ridge to survey the country. It seemed we might have to go ten miles round after all, and our water was about exhausted. He was a long time away and I began to fear he was lost. I was on the point of signalling by firing my revolver when he reappeared and reported that if we could cross two more difficult gullies we should be in the cañon that led to water. There was nothing for it but to try, though I did not think the horses would ever do it, for they seemed not to have another effort in them. My poor Kaweah, I wager you remember that day.

Pushing, hauling, shouting, we somehow got them to scramble up a breakneck place that caved at every step. Then two hundred yards of baked clay, like bricks set obliquely on edge; then down into another ravine and across its piles of sliding rubbish, with another desperate wall to climb. Still one more headlong descent, and one more ladder-like cliff to surmount; next a narrow mesa littered with jagged rocks. And then, stumbling down a last crumbling, precipitous wall, we found ourselves in a cañon that evidently headed at our desired point.

It was a huge relief. Three hours had been spent over two miles of direct distance. I now once more had a mind that could appreciate the wild features of the region we were traversing. Cliffs, domes, and pillars of clay in strange and vivid colors — yellow, lilac, rose, green, dark red, ochre, light red, purple — are the commonplaces of this locality. On all sides something novel is constantly coming to sight. Great flakes of clear mineral like plate-glass are strewn among the gravel or jut from the sides of cañons, and black pottery-like fragments mingle with delicately tinted blocks of stratified rock that is veined and twisted into curios. The place is like a show. I hope some day to return there and look my fill, but I shall not go by the same route.

Following the narrowing cañon for a mile or more, we came into a little amphitheatre. Here was our water. A prospect shaft had been sunk by some unlucky miner and had yielded water instead of ore. The horses crowded up and thrice knocked the bucket over as they pushed their muzzles in simultaneously. Then we threw off packs and saddles and fed them the last of the barley. They ate a little, but were too dispirited to finish, and stood with drooping heads, a picture of equine collapse. Poor old Piledriver after a few minutes lay down and groaned. Every step of those long, rough miles must have been torture to her.

As for us, we lay in the shade for an hour before gaining energy to get the meal we badly needed, and waited for sunset before tackling the last ten miles of the day's march. There was no forage here and our barley was gone, so to camp for the night was impossible. A Government survey party, with base at Coyote Wells, had been working hereabout not long before, and had made a sort of road that we could follow, and luckily it was now all down grade.

With all my weariness, I do not think I have ever been so charmed as that evening by the sunset coloring. It brought real physical refreshment: one could not feel tired and stupid with that magic before one's eyes. It passed into the blood, and not only soothed the mind, but energized the body like an elixir. Before me stretched a golden plain: behind and on either hand, hills of gold and rose: far to the south, translucent in distance, the mountains of Mexico: yonder, like a billow of amethyst breaking on amber reefs, the Superstitions: overhead three cranes flew silently across a sky of violet on their way to the Salton. It was more than Nature, infinitely more than Æsthetics. Some words of the Psalter came to my mind — "Who deckest Thyself with light as it were with a garment." Yes, only that expressed it: it was the Vesture of God.

In dusk, then darkness, we marched on. The wind was not merely warm but hot; but the dim light gave a sensation of coolness. Our ten miles stretched out as the last miles of a long day will do; but it was pleasant enough to tramp in starlight down the long slope of the mountain (*falda*, skirt or apron, the Mexicans call it, with instinctive accuracy of phrase). Wellson was far ahead, hurrying to reach Coyote Wells before the populace should tire of the evening programme of loafing and go to bed. I hung the bridle over my arm and let Kaweah set the pace, which he fixed at a dejected shuffle.

The night silence of the desert is not like the silence of the day. That is terrifying in its vacuity, in its refusal of aid to the mind and its throwing of consciousness back upon itself. But in the desert night the stars, near and warm, give a sense of companionship and understanding. They are friendly guides, marching with you or passing with cheery salute. It is especially fascinating to watch them rise. Mounting one by one above the plain, they seem more significant than as we usually see them, mingled in bright disorder overhead. In their appearance at the level of the eye (seeming even lower than that in the vast desert perspective) there is something momentous, as if they were watch-fires kindled by some signaller who looked for our reply; and one follows their calm ascent with a kind of pleased curiosity, perhaps also a half recognition of an allegory hopeful to ourselves.

I was startled from my mood by a gleam of moving light to my right, then another on the left. For a moment I was puzzled, then knew they must be automobiles on the San Diego-Imperial road, which here runs parallel and close to the Mexican border, and also to the newly built railway. Half an hour later we limped into Coyote Wells. While I watered Kaweah a lounging, unseen Mexican proposed the regular trio of questions: *De donde viene? Adonde va?* and *Cuando sale?* Where are you from? Where are you going? and, When do you start? His reply to my own inquiry for the direction of Wellson's quarters was the eternal *Quien sabe?* which is their way of dodging unnecessary syllables.

I found Wellson at his camp beyond the railroad. A friend (or partner, as the word goes) of his had a sort of house, where Wellson kept a little stock of hay and barley. Our nags could now make up arrears. We were all pretty well used up by the day's work, about thirty-five miles in distance, but the equal of fifty in labor. Yet, though the hardest, it was also the best day of my desert travels thus far. We ate a cold meal and lay down too tired to unroll our blankets or even take off our boots. I don't think I changed posture till I awoke at daybreak.

By daylight Coyote Wells took its place as the dustiest, dismallest hamlet in my knowledge. The items of its total ugliness are half a score of board-and-canvas shacks and a cube of sheet-iron, the railway building. I returned from my tour feeling almost suicidal, and for relief ate my breakfast by a stack of sweet-smelling pine ties, the only thing of charm in the place. As a stopping-place on the old highway to San Diego it has long had a fame, not savory, of its own. To-day indignation was high among the Coyoteros over the arrest, the previous evening, of the local "blind pigger." It was felt that by this hard stroke all that made life worth living at Coyote Wells had been done away. I only partly shared this view, failing to see how even unlimited bad whiskey could make the place less of a purgatory.

I left my companion fitting the wincing Piledriver with a second-hand shoe. He was westwardbound for the mountains, after a day or two's rest, while my route led east. He urged me to join him, holding out the possibility of my becoming a prospector myself. But I doubted my qualifications. I always feared I was born under "a vile sixpenny planet," and with that belief how could one be a prospector?

I had now reached the southern limit of my journey, for in the conditions then ruling, Mexico was a country to be shunned. Coyote Wells lies at the extreme southwest corner of the Colorado Desert in the United States. My way now lay easterly, through that part of the Imperial Valley which borders on Mexico.

I must say I dislike these big-sounding names, which real-estate speculators think so irresistible. To me they savor of Martin Chuzzlewit's Eden, and give ever fresh point to the celebrated *mot* of the late Mr. Barnum. Of a piece with the brass band and the barbecue, these grandiloquent titles stamp the

West as still the land of Bunkum, Boom, and Brag, and call to mind the street faker with his shiny "topper" and cautionary gush of eloquence. In the heraldic quarterings of California the device of a megaphone should find a place.

I rode first toward Signal Mountain, just across the border. When last seen it had looked like a pale blue iceberg on the sea-like horizon of the plain: now, close at hand, it was a volcano-like cone of brown rising from a limitless gray of sand. To the southeast ran the line of the Cócopas, tailing off into the yellow murk of a sand-storm — type of poor Mexico's everlasting muddle. Superstition Mountain seemed from here a mere ridge of sand, but Coyote and Fish Creek Mountains rose high and rugged in tantalizing red and purple. I feel I have n't done with those fellows yet.

The country through which I was passing is one of intense dreariness, a plain of dust with a scattering of desert plants more than usually wretched and unkempt. A few ocotillos alone broke the torrid stillness with a skeleton dance on the quivering air. The sun was blasting, and my canteen of water soon became too hot for enjoyment, though I called on it incessantly for relief.

A straight white line marked on the desert proved to be a macadamized road which had lately been laid for the benefit of automobilists. This gave notice that I was approaching the settlements of Imperial. Two or three machines passed us, for there is a fair amount of traffic between San Diego and the new-born towns of the valley. In due time

I saw far ahead the buildings of the first of these, a hamlet named Dixieland, and about midday we arrived at a canal (or ditch, as they call it), the farthest one in this direction of the great irrigation system.

It was instructive to notice how the desert held out without palliation up to the very edge of the canal. On the other side began, equally abruptly, telephone poles, fields of cotton and alfalfa, pastures with cattle, horses, and hogs, green, rustling cottonwoods, and an unbroken succession of farms.

Dixieland I found to consist of a brick store, a small but ambitious-looking school, six or eight little houses, and a barn. Behind this I camped in a corner of the corral, but, for a change from my own cookery, persuaded a weary woman who lived in the barn to get me a meal. I regretted this when I faced the discs of tepid paste tendered as biscuits, and the bowl of yellow oil which passed for butter. However, honey, watermelon, and the kindly heart which overcame weariness and 122° Fahrenheit at the request of a stranger, made amends for all shortcomings, even the tablecloth.

I took my way next morning toward El Centro, the central point, as the name proudly announces, of the valley. A main crop of the locality is cotton, and a general Southern and cottony air prevailed, even to the colored brothers plying the hoe. Field beyond field of the pretty plants stretched away southward to the border, varied with blocks of milo-maize or squares of vivid alfalfa. Herds of cattle and bands of glossy horses were in evidence, and everywhere ditches of red, muddy water led off, branching, dividing, and subdividing into a veritable maze. As I sat under a eucalyptus to eat lunch, while Kaweah ripped away at juicy Bermuda grass, it seemed a miracle when I recalled the wanderings of the past weeks.

And indeed it is a miracle, the transforming, within a dozen years, of a tract of strict desert into a farming region of the highest fertility. The materials for the miracle were here, of course, from immemorial times — an alluvial plain and, contiguous to it, a great silt-laden river. Lower Egypt offers an exact analogy, and early Western explorers noted and reported the possibilities, which in fact are patent enough. It remained for speculators to undertake the work which Government might properly have shouldered, and for the public to grasp the idea that the word "desert" need not signify worthless for agriculture, so long as water, the lack of which is at the root of the condition, can be applied.

I shall have little to say, however, of economic matters, which are outside my purpose and also very largely outside my knowledge. I could compile a chapter of sensational facts and figures easily enough, but we Californians are not bashful about trumpeting our triumphs, and I feel that the sincerest contribution I can make will be by injecting, not a discordant, but a gently moderating tone into the blast. In a word, the Imperial Valley has been and is the scene of a remarkable agricultural success; but let it be realized that there are special drawbacks, in the nature of the case, and that it is not the business of persons with "interests" in the valley to advertise these.

In the two or three weeks that I spent in the farming localities I was unable to accommodate myself to the slipshod appearance of the farm buildings, both houses and outbuildings. While this is a weakness of the Western farmer in general, here it exceeded; though perhaps it is excusable in view of the trying climate that prevails for half the year. There is here, naturally, a larger percentage than usual of farmers who are unmarried, or whose womenkind do not live, at least continuously, on the farm: and without the woman the home can hardly be. Anyhow, the effect is discouraging, and suggests the idea, which is no doubt a true one in a great proportion of cases, that Imperial farmers as a whole are just "sticking it out," with a view to selling as soon as they can. Neither the chance visitor, nor, I would suggest, the prospective buyer, is likely to react happily to this impression.

We passed through one or two small settlements with stores, telephones, and post-offices, and with bales of cotton piled awaiting shipment. Automobiles were common, and soon became a nuisance with their obscene noises and the clouds of dust they gave in return for the right of way. When a true democracy arises one of its first jobs will be to abolish the automobile as an offensive chattel of privilege. By noon we were in El Centro, the county seat of Imperial County and the metropolis of the valley.

A sharp little earthquake had occurred in this locality some weeks before, and its work was plainly seen in wrecked or distorted houses, cracked walls, shattered windows, and piles of rubbish. The big new hotel, bearing, rather absurdly, the name of a recent "best seller" in local fiction, had hastily repaired its damages, but looked conscious of the concealment. The stores had a prosperous look, but many of the dwellings gave the same unpleasant impression that I had found in the farms. Some were quite sordid in their ugliness, even beyond the usual measure of these products of haste and incompetence. These ramshackle affairs, with their purlieus of bottles and boxes, cans and baling-wire, came as a rebuff. Almost before I had found a lodging I sighed for the desert again, where, if beauty be scant, at least squalor is absent. It is a truth of the widest bearing that "only man is *vile*."

In the bathroom of my lodging I learned that cold and hot are sometimes interchangeable terms, or, at least, taps. The cistern being set on the roof, by midday the "cold" water had reached a temperature higher than that from the boiler. It was only at early morning that one could get a tolerably refreshing tub. Another discovery was that El Centro in summer is practically a womanless community, the feminine half having betaken themselves "inside," as the phrase goes, for the hot term: and another, that Centrolians in summer are a coatless and waistcoatless race. A loose, blouse-like garment is the thing on street, in office, at restaurant, and I suppose at church and such social functions as may be attempted in the absence of womankind.

It was odd, too, to see beds set out on vacant lots

in the midst of the banks and mercantile places. Whether they were used by bank presidents and their kind, or by the common race, I never found out: nor whether the recent earthquake had any bearing on the matter. With their canopies of mosquito netting they had the look of palanquins or howdahs. The Oriental flavor was strengthened by the presence of many Hindoos. I fancied there was as much dislike as curiosity in the feelings of the Mexicans, who turned to stare at these silent, turbaned fellows, the latest interlopers on the pay-roll.

The most attractive town in the valley is Brawley, near the southern end of the Salton Sea. The first settlers had the good sense to plant trees freely along the streets, and the busy little place, embowered among cottonwoods and eucalyptus, has a much more finished and pleasing appearance than any of the other settlements.

Midway between El Centro and Brawley is the town of Imperial. This place formerly aspired to becoming the county seat, but in a sharp engagement of "interests" it was worsted by its southern neighbor. Imperial thereupon took to drink, and now exists mainly as a pestiferous nest of saloons, a resort, especially on Sundays, for beery parties from the surrounding country. As a place of genuine business it seems dead, a commentary on the often heard argument that the saloon is a necessity for any community that wishes to thrive.

A friend on whose farm I stayed a few days, revelling in unlimited dairy produce, drove me over one day to the twin towns of Calexico and Mexicali, lying on the Californian and Mexican sides of the line respectively. It was a drive of ten or twelve miles through good farming country of alfalfa, milomaize, cotton, and preëminently hogs. Here and there were lines of tall trees, seven or eight years old, but looking treble that age. Imperial Valley has a distinctive smell, a rather unpleasant acrid one, arising, I fancy, from the constant irrigation acting on some peculiarity of the soil. We passed through the little town of Heber, bare and blinking in sun and dust. Everywhere were canals of chocolate-colored water edged with vivid green of Bermuda grass, as to which I often heard the opinion expressed that "something's got to be done about that infernal Bermuda, or it'll take the whole valley." Already a serious pest, and disseminated everywhere by the canals, it is rapidly becoming a first-class problem.

Calexico is situated exactly at sea-level, the other valley settlements being all somewhat below. It is a town of dusty streets and ugly houses, apartment buildings, and stores. The main street runs close to and parallel with the international boundary. The earthquake had hit the place hard, and carpenters, bricklayers, and plasterers were busily gathering the dollars dropped by the ill-wind. A few people had been killed, for unfortunately the visitation was not confined to the gamblers of the neighboring town across the line. The channel of the New River runs close by, now perfectly dry. In the early summer of 1906, when the Salton Sea was filling, it was the terror of the inhabitants, who in spite of desperate work in the building of levees saw part of their town carried away by the flood that rushed along this perfidious water-way.[1]

Mexicali, across the border, is a mere rank of gambling-hell saloons, as offensive to the sight as they are disreputable in every other regard. A pimply youth with a megaphone was inviting the public to enter the widest of these numerous gates into the broad way to Destruction, and made me, as a stranger, the particular object of his attentions. "Wide open" is a literal as well as figurative description of the place, for the flimsy structure was fully open to the street. A dozen or so gambling-tables at which you lose your money at faro, monte, roulette, or what you please: a thriving bar: an incessant racket of "rag-time" from a quartette of tenth-rate musicians at the rear: three painted girls, or rather children, in dirty pink, who now and then ceased their crude blandishments of the men near them to shout the words of a ribald song (this was the vaudeville entertainment to which I had been bidden by Pimpleface): and a babel of shouts and cheerless, discordant laughter from a hundred or so loafers, mostly Americans, but with a sprinkling of Mexicans, Japanese, and I don't know what — that, six or eight times repeated, is Mexicali. If ground is ever sought for a declaration of war against Mexico,

[1] I have not learned how this stream got its name. Major-General Cooke, in the narrative of his expedition of 1846-47, notes that a few years after his crossing of this region, when the channel was dry, other travellers found a stream running in it. Probably some such party gave it its name.

I would suggest that the existence of this plague-hole on the border at once provides it.

A couple of burly brigands with huge pistols projecting from their hip-pockets, who were lounging over the barricade of another of the gambling-dens, proved to be *rurales*, members of that peculiar but efficient force that Mexico owes, along with much else that is questionable but necessary, to Porfirio Diaz. At the custom-house and post-office a trifling amount of business was being neglected, rather than transacted, by two irresponsible and highly unattractive clerks. Half an hour was enough of this. I managed a surreptitious photograph, to the mystification of a Cócopa "buck" with hair to his waist and fat squaw following, and recrossed to United States soil.

In the eastern part of the valley lies Holtville, a small but fairly lively place on the bank of the Álamo River, which flows, thick and sluggish, in a deep gorge with steep red walls and a trimming of rustling cottonwoods. Red and green, with overhead blue of sky, make the livery of the Imperial Valley.

One day while at my friend's ranch we were visited by a typical summer storm. The day was unusually humid, and we sat in collapse by the hour, existing on the momentary breezes from the Gulf. About mid-morning a brown wall suddenly grew up on the open desert to the east. It came rapidly nearer, growing higher every moment, and was soon revealed as a cloud of sand, so dense as to seem solid, and driven at wonderful speed. Its even line was very remarkable: it came on like a tidal wave, and not until it had approached to half a mile could I see the whirling of the sand on its crest. From the moment when it was at that distance until it struck the house cannot have been half a minute. With shriek and swoop it fell upon us in a blast of sand and fine gravel, with the momentum of terrific speed and semi-solidity. For five minutes it raged and howled in extremity of fury: then almost as suddenly the sand passed and there came a torrent of rain that lashed and swirled with equal violence. This lasted for half an hour or so, then came to an abrupt stop; and in a few minutes the sun was at work again, lapping up the moisture like a thirsty dog. The rest of the day and the succeeding night we were favored with a free-for-all Turkish bath.

This particular hurricane, born somewhere down in Sonora or possibly on the torrid waters of the Gulf of California, after sweeping the desert from southeast to northwest, jumped the mountains and landed among the orange groves of the coast, where it played havoc with the crop of late Valencias: then after wrecking the boats of the San Pedro fishermen, it finally worried itself into quiet amid the solitudes of the Pacific.

CHAPTER XVIII

A DESERT RIDE: IMPERIAL VALLEY TO YUMA

Night farming — A night ride — The sentiment of wonder — Wind, silence, and solitude — Camp at the Algodones — The desert's moods — New experience for Kaweah — Sand in action — A study in simplicity — Pilot Knob — Mirages — The Colorado River — Kaweah and the subconscious — Yuma, a frontier town — The river-steamers — Attractions of Yuma — Indian costumes — A wide view — A Bret Hartean specimen — Yuma types — The movies: "one touch of nature" — Farming country — Indian *vs.* Mexican taste — The Laguna Dam — Village of Potholes — — Mosquitoes — The saguaros — A fantastic region — The elf-owl.

THE "edge of cultivation" is as sharply marked on the east side of Imperial Valley as on the west. The farthest "ditch" draws the line between green and gray. Beyond it a long dry march lay before me, with Yuma, on the Arizona side of the Colorado River, for my objective. In view of the great heat, made doubly trying by a high degree of humidity, I resolved for Kaweah's sake to cover as much as possible of it by night.

Leaving Holtville in the afternoon I rode eastward a few miles to the farthest outpost of the canal system. The district (Number Seven as it is called, the valley being divided into numbered irrigation units) had a more attractive look than some localities I had seen, with better houses, bigger stacks of hay, and more frequent trees along the roads. To south and west ran the long line of the Cócopas, to-day showing that smoky-white hue that gives desert mountains their most weird appearance.

I came to the last canal about sundown and fed Kaweah at the haystack of a friendly rancher. His wife was away "inside," but I was made welcome at the supper-table where he and his two men exhibited their prowess at "baching." Supper over, he and one of the hands loaded their pipes, took each a bottle of coffee, and marched out to put in the night at irrigating, as it was their turn to use the water. The Imperial farmer knows not day or night: the water schedule is his rule of life, for no water, no crops.

I snatched a couple of hours' sleep, waiting for the moon to rise, which it did about eleven o'clock. Then I watered Kaweah and myself, filled my canteens, saddled up, and started. The half-moon gave a pleasant light, and though the night was sultry it was a great improvement over the travelling conditions by day. I needed no sombrero, and opening my shirt made the most of the faint airs that came wandering over the plain that ran unbroken to the Gulf, seventy miles away. In the uncertain light the dunes took the semblance of creeping shapes, their long shadows black as ink on the pallid gray of the earth. A scant growth of creosote bush blurred the view, and the vagueness added to the impression of space and monotony that is inherent in these great levels. The mountain outlines far ahead could hardly be seen against the dimness of the sky.

Only the stars and the climbing moon kept life and definition, and these held the mind with more than their wonted fascination. The sentiment of wonder, in its worthiest sense, finds little exercise in these days. Marvels of science and invention so crowd upon us that the faculty, kept at stretch, loses its elasticity. It is a pity, for along with wonder goes imagination, and even reverence. In this staling of the mind whole tracts of life are left untouched, with all their harvest of spiritual food. Novelty is a spice we cannot do without, but the great things are not novel. So night by night the motion-picture shows are crammed, while unless a comet comes along (and a big one too) the pageant of "this brave o'erhanging firmament, this majestical roof fretted with golden fire," is not thought worth a glance. As for "jocund day standing tiptoe on the misty mountain-top," who is going to get out of bed for that?

Hour after hour went silently by while Kaweah kept up his steady pace. Sometimes I checked him while I let the silence and solitude possess me. In the great indefinite space and under the full half-sphere of sky glittering with stars from zenith to horizon, I might have been the sole inhabitant of the planet. The faint, momentary breeze seemed to come from infinite distance; was born perhaps in Ceylon, and had ranged over starlit oceans and untrodden Asian peaks to pass me here, then roam on, and on, and die, maybe, among the snows of Spitzbergen. Geography took on a vital meaning. Ahead I seemed to look over the plains of Texas to the eastern seaboard, the Bermudas, the Canaries, Europe with its struggling, staggering nations. I felt the draw of my own land, the lodestone till death of every Briton. Behind was the vastness of the Pacific, the welter of awakening China. There lay the frozen tundra, and there, under friendly Polaris, the no longer defiant North Pole.

As it drew toward morning the breeze came cooler and more steady, growing to a low monotonous hum that seemed to intensify the silence. No hoot of owl or yelp of coyote told of life and Nature's interest in her children. But for the moon that now cast our shadows beneath us, or some meteor rushing to its fate, Kaweah and I seemed the only moving creatures in the universe. Once or twice I missed the track and had to dismount and search carefully for traces of travel, hardly visible on the pavement-like clay which we were crossing. The creosote grew sparser and seemed on the verge of death. The skinny arms waving in the breeze moved in ghostly rhythm, like spectres at a *danse macabre.*

At length smears of cloud showed in the eastern sky as the dawn whitened behind them. On the horizon a mountain line took form. The first dull color stole in, then quickly brightened; and soon the sun came rushing up, ploughing his way like a swimmer and sending beams to the zenith, as if bragging of his power. I went on for an hour in hope of sighting some sizable bush for shade; but only skimpy creosotes, half a dozen to the acre and almost leafless, kept on to infinity. I stopped and gave Kaweah his breakfast, crouching in his shadow while I ate my own.

We started on, to take advantage of the comparative coolness. Miles went by in alternate sand and clay, riding and leading, half awake and half asleep, until a ridge of dunes in front at last broke the interminable level. It was the great belt of sand-hills, known as the Algodones, that stretch for forty miles southeasterly, parallel with the Chocolate Mountains, ending at the boundary line a few miles west of Yuma. At the nearer base of these dunes a well had recently been sunk by the county, and here I hoped to find water.[1] I had ample for my own wants, but Kaweah was drooping already, for the heat was atrocious and the humidity killing. The wind had dropped and heavy clouds were climbing up from south and east. I looked anxiously for signs of the well, and reported the good news to Kaweah when a black speck appeared miles away with a white dot near it signifying a tent. It was an hour before we arrived, but then fortune smiled, for an employé of the county road department was camped there, and he had a little hay, of which, at sixty dollars a ton, I was free to use a feed or two.

We had travelled for fifteen hours with only one hour's stop, and I felt it was enough for the day. I off-saddled, threw Kaweah a dollar's worth of this princely forage, took a mouthful of chocolate, and fell asleep before I was ready for another. I awoke to find that a gale had sprung up and embedded me in sand like a fossil. At dusk I awoke again to a crash of thunder and at the same moment a torrent

[1] A few days ago, and a year after I crossed this tract, I read in a Los Angeles newspaper of a man who had just been rescued here-about. He was going from Yuma to the Imperial, had missed the way, and was found, crazed with thirst, and (as usual) naked, crawling on hands and knees about the sand-dunes. This is the third case of the kind that I have read of within the space of a month.

of rain. These are the moods of the desert in summer. I crept under a discarded piece of canvas, where I ate a cold supper: then watered Kaweah and turned in.

I was up at dawn and before sunrise we were on the march. The sand-hills, which form a barrier several miles wide, had lately been rendered passable by the laying of a rough plank roadway, which begins at this point. Kaweah is conservative and this was something new, so there was an argument with quirt and spur before he would set foot on it. The planks had warped and loosened, and he was kept on a continual dance of nervousness: still they were a great boon, for without them the five miles of shifting sand would have consumed as many hours.

The scene was interesting and in a strange way beautiful. The dunes rose in quarter-circle curves, broken sharply away to a face of two angles, one steep, perhaps 60°, the other low, not over 15°. Everywhere the same form was reproduced, the smooth arc, the sharp break at the edge, and the long slant at the foot. Along the faces and from the edges of fracture, a mist of sand was ever curling off and drifting in airy waves and feathers, following every contour of the dune. The whole mass of the sand was enveloped in this fairy-like veil, creeping like smoke, weaving in dainty frills and spirals. The vapor-like action was odd to see in a solid substance.

The color was wonderful in purity and sheer power of mass. The smooth, large outlines of pale yellow, the water-like transparency of cobalt shadow, and the soft brilliance of the early morning sky — that was all. But the scale on which these elements were drawn, the unity and rhythm of line and color, gave it the effect of a triumph of simplicity in art.

On reaching the eastern edge of the dunes I came in sight of my next landmark, Pilot Knob. This is an isolated peak five miles west of Yuma, and marks the junction of the river with the Mexican boundary. The usual route to Yuma here makes a circuit to the northeast, but I knew that the railway touched the river just east of this peak, and that a road from Mexico came in there also. I therefore struck directly southeast for Pilot Knob (or, as it was named by the Spanish explorers, the Cerro de San Pablo: the present name, no doubt, dates from the days of the fifties, when the river was navigated by flat-bottomed steamboats, carrying the traffic of the Arizona mines as far upstream as Ehrenberg).

There was now some variety of scenery. To the east was the southern end of the Chocolates, a red and purple wilderness of low but rugged mountains, and beyond them the higher ranges of Arizona, strongly picturesque. A few palo verde and mesquit trees grew at the margin of the dunes, but they soon gave way to the everlasting creosote, burro-weed, and ocotillo, with an occasional small ironwood. To my surprise, the ocotillos were in full leaf, the result of recent thunder-showers. To-day another storm was preparing, and seemed likely to catch us miles from shelter. Several times that morning I noted a mirage, the common one of a sheet of pale-blue water, with dark bushes showing here and there, the exact appearance of a flooded expanse of wooded country.

I stopped for an hour at noon under a bit of scrub that ironically offered shade. Betokening approach to the river, a butcher-bird appeared and vented his chronic ill-temper in screeches of abuse. Three sand-martins made better company. There is some spiritual quality in the happiness of all birds of the swallow tribe.

By this time Pilot Knob had become a threatening volcano under sulphurous-looking clouds, and I resigned myself to a thumping deluge. There was a chance that by hurrying we might escape, so we pushed on and were soon rounding the shoulder of the mountain. It was just twenty-five years since I had last passed this point, entering California for the first time. Under these circumstances the dark pyramid, like a quarter-century milestone, suggested serious reflections: but those clouds made it seem unwise to stand about moralizing, and again self-examination was successfully dodged.

Turning eastward I made toward the railway. Soon there appeared an expanse of bright green, the willow-covered flats of the Colorado River. A mile or two brought us to the railway, and, as I expected, to a road which took us to the river. Rain or not, I halted for half an hour to pay my homage to one of the great rivers of the North American continent, and the one perhaps most endowed with geological interest, by reason of that marvellous cañon which may be named the greatest natural wonder of the world.

The stream here takes a deep bend and the bank where I stood commanded a good view. It was not a specially imposing sight, I had to confess — a wide, shallow flood of chocolate-hued water, bordered by stretches of brilliant green, these rising to low red banks over which one looked in vain for any break in the monotony of the level. For seventy miles from this point southward to the head of the Gulf of California I doubt if there is anywhere an elevation of forty feet above the plain. Near by were the remains of an adobe building which was once a stamp-mill for grinding ore. A heron fished in the shallows with that air of magnificent calm which is so soothing to see, and a quarter of a mile away a torpid Indian moved about, doing something mysterious to the few stalks of corn in his little clearing.

But after all it *was* the Colorado River, and Kaweah, perhaps, caught a reflection of my own interest, for he stood long in meditative pose. I wondered if he felt stirrings of the subconscious in gazing at this stream, on whose headwaters his forebears may have roamed and practised those little arts which make the Western bronco so interesting and incomprehensible.

At this point the road from Lower California came in. I followed this for a couple of hours beside a levee, through thickets of willow and arrowweed, and by late afternoon came in sight of Yuma. The first feature to appear was the Indian school on the hill where the historic Fort Yuma once stood. Then the court-house came in view, attractive in its setting of green, the rest of the town, which lies lower, remaining unseen. That I was on the Reservation of the Yuma Indians was brought to notice by a wagon that met me, driven by a handsome fellow with hair hanging to his waist in the rope-like twists that mark the Yuma "buck," and with two squaws dressed apparently in counterpanes of green, purple, and yellow.

We crossed the river by the high iron bridge as the first raindrops plumped down; passed through a street or two of adobe or mud-and-pole houses, and got into a livery-stable just in time to escape a terrific downpour. Here I left Kaweah in good hands for a couple of days while I made up arrears of mail and looked about the old frontier town.

This place may be recognized by some of my readers in connection with certain well-worn jokes turning on warmth of climate. The popular belief that Yuma is separated from the nether regions only by a sheet of paper is probably an error, though not a serious one. The shade temperature did not go over 110° while I was in Yuma, but it was now September and the back of the summer was broken.

The town is on the Arizona side close to the junction of the Colorado and the Gila, and a few miles east of the point where California of the United States and Lower California of Mexico meet at the river. It is the Puerto de la Concepción of Padre Garcés,[1] and the site of the ill-fated Mission of La

_____
[1] The name of Fray Francisco Tomás Hermenegildo Garcés should be held in honor. He was a native of Aragon, and one of the most intrepid of those priest-explorers who early pushed their way into the Western deserts, planting the Cross far in advance of the flag. It was in 1771 (he was then thirty-three years old) that he first

Purísima Concepción, which was founded in 1780 and came to a tragic end in the following year along with the neighboring Mission of San Pablo and San Pedro, ten miles down the river. From earliest days this was a favorite place for fording the river, and from 1849 for many years there was a regular service by ferry. In 1850, following the war with Mexico, a fort, remains of which may be traced, was established on the hill where the Indian school now stands, and the place became known as Fort Yuma.

In 1852 the first of the river steamers, a sternwheeler, appeared at Fort Yuma, to the intense excitement of the Indians, who, having assembled at the report of the prodigy, beat a retreat on its approach, crying out that "the devil was coming up the river, blowing fire out of his nose and kicking up the water behind him with his feet." One of the old

crossed the Colorado River, but for several years before that he had been knocking about among the Yumas, Mojaves, Apaches, gaining their good-will by his geniality, tact, courage, and simplicity. It is said that he would eat Indian food and appear to enjoy it as much as his hosts — a stiff test for even the Franciscan "rule" and his native courtesy. His influence with Palma, the Yuma chief, smoothed the way for Anza's expedition in 1774, and he accompanied the gallant "Captain of Tubac" for the whole distance from Sonora to the coast, returning from San Gabriel alone.

It is sad to record that a few years later Padre Garcés fell a victim when the "bold and rebellious" Yumas rose against the whites. He, with three more priests and practically all the other white men at the two newly established Missions (including the military commander, Captain Don Fernando Rivera y Moncada, and many soldiers), fell in a general massacre in the summer of 1781. The bodies of Fray Francisco and a companion priest were found, the following year, where they had been buried by a kindly Indian woman in a little spot of grass and flowers in the midst of the burned area where the Mission had stood. The record says that among the flowers was the camomile — a pleasant touch of detail. I like the association of that modest little blossom with brave, simple Padre Garcés.

steamers rests to-day on its laurels beside the bank while another has been transformed into a bungalow by an ingenious citizen. The last of their skippers, Captain Isaac Polhamus, may still be met about the streets of Yuma, and has vivid scraps of history to recount, along with memories of soberer hue — for instance, of days and nights passed in getting free of one sand-bar only to immediately lodge upon another. Several days were often spent in making ten or fifteen miles.

The town is interesting to any one who cares for humble ways of life, though scorned by people devoted to progress. It reminded me of California's old capital, Monterey. Here as there one finds houses of all constructions and ages mixed: there is not yet a "choice residential section" or "Nob Hill" (charming name), but adobe, timber, brick, and "stick-in-the-mud" [1] are pleasantly jumbled together, with here and there a garden of old-fashioned flowers. Date-palms wave over the sidewalks, mingling with cottonwoods and even wildling mesquits. Half-naked Mexican children play in the dooryards of humble homes, and Indians use the main street as boldly as the banker, the mayor, or even the policeman. Altogether, Yuma comes near my idea of a model town.

Pictorially, the Indians are the making of it. The Yuma men are athletic-looking fellows, erect and well-featured, the finest, I think, among the Southwestern tribes; and they have ideas of dress that result in striking *ensembles*. One slim young man es-

[1] Structures of willow poles set upright and plastered with mud.

pecially took my fancy. He wore a close-fitting lilac tunic of knitted silk, closed at the throat with a scarlet ribbon; his hair hung in straight ropes to his waist and was tied with a cord of bright green; for sash he had an orange silk bandanna. Crude as this may sound, his lithe figure, open look, and general air of efficiency carried it off and made a really fine effect.

The women did not evoke my enthusiasm, though they did my attention. They are much inferior to the men in physique, though perhaps up to the average of our Western Indian women. Their features have none of the clean-cut look seen in the men, and as for dress, gaudy is the only word. Over the usual shapeless "wrapper," generally of blue-and-white check, the women without exception wear a square sheet of the strongest hues known to the dry-goods world — purple, grass-green, flame-color, scarlet, ultramarine, yellow. As a rule these have a two or three inch border of some violent contrast, such as purple on orange or green on blue. These startling draperies are fastened at the neck and left flowing to the breeze. The head is usually encircled with a *banda* of red, and the straight hair, which is seldom so long as that of the men, hangs in a shock on the shoulders. A group of Yuma women in a lively wind would give a futurist some valuable ideas.

A visit to the court-house revealed a rather depressing state of things: a fair exterior, but, within, a pervading carelessness and a general air of spittoons. However, I was repaid by two views that

I obtained — one from the room below the dome, a sort of dormitory furnished with a number of highly unattractive beds, provided, I suppose, for unfortunate jurymen. From here I could look out on all sides — to the green-bordered river winding in sinuous course toward the Gulf; or to range beyond range of mountains, of red, yellow, purple, or of mere haze; with an extraordinary peak, the Picacho,[1] standing up like an artificial obelisk twenty miles to the north, and more to the east the equally strange shape of Castle Dome, the Cabeza del Gigante, or Giant's Head: over all an evening sky where clouds sailed in majestic squadrons.

The other view was different but fully as impressive — a human being, in fact, but of a kind that I supposed had passed away. He entered the building as I was leaving it, and I turned back to have another look. I knew he was a judge before I saw him go into the court-room. Long, thin, goateed, shirt-sleeved, with cigar and wide-brimmed Stetson at free-and-easy angle — he was the devil-may-care, reprobate, Bret Hartean judiciary to the life, a sort of epic. Without doubt he had a gun in his pocket, perhaps another in the leg of his boot. I could hardly keep from taking his photograph. I reckon him to be the last of a species. Yuma must be careful with him, and when he dies he should be gently preserved under glass in some museum of American types. I have read of a person who was so gro-

---

[1] It was named by Garcés, *Peñon de la Campana*, or Great Bell-Tower Rock, a name quite expressive to one familiar with the isolated bell-tower of Spanish architecture.

tesquely ugly that he looked as if he were walking about doing it for fun. I had that kind of feeling about my Yuma judge.

One who thinks life dry without frequent thrills might find a summer evening in Yuma tedious: yet I look back on certain after-dinner hours there as among the most profitable of my trip. After leaning for an hour over the rail of the bridge, hoping that I was getting cool, I found it was a mistake and took my way up the street to share the general fate and lounge among the loungers. Mesmerized by the rhythmic thump of a mechanical piano I took a post opposite the Motion-Picture Theatre. The main street of Yuma makes something of a motion picture itself. Three Indians with headdresses of purple, green, and pink, sat inert on the curb in front of me, smoking countless cigarettes while they made hilarious comments on passers-by. Men on quick-pacing Indian ponies swung along, one now and then jerking up at the sidewalk to exchange a remark or borrow "the makings." Hard-featured men, and girls bearing the terrible stamp, passed and repassed: also Yuma's full complement of sales-ladies escorted by their fellows. A "For Rent" automobile drawn up close by showed several pairs of lightly clad legs and arms dangling over doors and seatbacks, apparently disconnected from invisible owners. A heavy-looking buck and his heavier-looking middle-aged squaw stopped to admire the colored posters of the play. In twos and threes the citizens slouched in to the show, clerks in the latest shirt-styles, with their girls, entering at the exclusive "two-bit" right, while the common ten-centers, mainly Mexicans and Indians, passed in on the left.

The rattle of the music roused in me an appetite (last satisfied years ago, I thought for ever) for movies, and when I saw the Indian and squaw come back down the street and enter, I walked over, paid my dime, and followed, taking the seat next behind them.

My attention was divided between the play and my front neighbors. The play, already well on its course, was the regulation kind of thing, and the acting of the regulation stagey sort, with full measure of the clenching of hands, smiting of brows, rolling of eyes, and heaving of chests that mark the authentic movie drama. The story does n't matter; there were stolen interviews, a secret marriage, a wealthy, cruel parent, reckless expenditure on cabs and telegrams, a baby girl, a death, the good old landlady with asides and risky buttons, realistic scenes of high-low-life in Rio or somewhere, a poodle, and so forth.

But it was the "one touch of nature" that caught us all. The baby, grown to a sunny-haired romp of five, came dancing downstairs and threw herself on grandpapa's neck with prattle, hugs, and kisses. It was then that our hearts gave way. The buck's right arm had been lying along the seat-rail behind his squaw's broad crimson back; the other hand was in his lap. At this point the free arm crept over and he clasped the hand of his woman, while the arm behind drew her closer. Would that I might have reached over and wrung those dark and dirty paws!

I don't know why I did n't, unless because I am English. Nor do I know why I should have thought it strange for two Yuma Indians to be at a level of sentiment that, as I was slightly ashamed to find, I had not left behind.

When the relentings, explanations, and reconciliations were done, and child, father, and grandfather had been seen locked in embraces (with great "business" by landlady and poodle), we lounged out and drifted down the street to the ice-cream and billiard parlor, where racial barriers fell again before a common passion for nickel ice-cream sodas. And so home to our respective beds.

That Goliath of the cacti, the saguaro, which is such a notable feature of the Arizona deserts, exists in small numbers at two or three points on the California side of the river, a few being found about fifteen miles above Yuma. As a rarity in California botany I thought it worth a side-trip to see and photograph them.

I took the road leading to the Laguna Dam, which was built a few years ago to bring a tract of land to the south of Yuma under cultivation. It was an interesting region that I passed through, considering what Nature had meant it to be. On either side of a willow-bordered road there stretched fields of corn and hay, and pastures stocked with horses and cattle. It seems to be also a stronghold of the turkey tribe, for large bands of gobblers and peepers were wading about in the tall alfalfa, a head coming to the surface here and there like a periscope. The houses here were more like homes and less like camps than those of Imperial Valley. Many of these had little orchards, a thing one hardly ever sees in the Imperial; and nurseries of date seedlings were a common feature.

Now and then a wagon passed us filled with Indians bound for town. There was no mistaking those tulip-like costumes at any distance. I caught glimpses of such *chic* arrangements as magenta with orange, and bottle-green with mauve. The Quakers will never stand a chance with these people. One rather pretty girl in flame-color and pea-green made a fine display of gold-filled incisors as she went by, I fancy for my benefit. The contrast of bare, dirty feet with this show of wealth struck me as unique, perhaps also symbolic. It is a far advance in taste that is shown by the Mexican woman, with her dark, plain colors and modest *rebosa*, or the Mexican girl's choice of pure and simple white. The Yuma men's favorite head-covering is a handkerchief of some bright color, twisted into a close-fitting turban; but often, and more pleasing, one sees the *banda*, a strip passing round the forehead and fastened above the long ropes of hair.

The dustiness of the road was mitigated by a green bordering of willows and alfalfa, highly approved by Kaweah. Everywhere were canals, large and small, the cement head-gates bearing the letters U. S. R. S. (United States Reclamation Service) which are coming to mean so much to many regions of the West. A dredge was lazily nosing with a scoop-shovel into the bank of damp red earth, enlarging one of the smaller canals. On all sides were tokens of improvement and, what is better, contentment; though one or two men I talked with had complaints to make on the score of their financial burdens under the Government irrigation plan.

Half a mile after meeting the main canal, which is forty or fifty feet in width, I came to the river and the head-works of the great Laguna Dam.[1] From the weir that stretched across the wide stream went up a roar of falling water. The massive head-gates bore again the mark U. S. R. S., like the symbol of a conqueror or the S. P. Q. R. of ancient Rome. Adjoining the dam on the California side is a Mexican village on the site of a former mining-camp of some note. It bears the pleasing name of Potholes, referring, I think, to the fact that the pay-dirt was found here to occur in "pots" or "pockets."

It was too late for me to hunt saguaros that day. I camped amid a confusion of old boilers and other débris of the construction time, using for sleeping-place the bed of a disused wagon, the only clean and level spot I could find. Mosquitoes kept me in misery, and I was glad when the rising of an arc of waning moon told that daylight and relief were at hand. At this spot, however, where a rocky bluff brings a break in the almost continuous thicket that borders the river, this pest was nothing in comparison with what I endured in other places. Whenever I entered the jungle of willow, cottonwood, and arrowweed, so delicious to the eye at a distance, I became the prey

[1] It is worthy of note that Captain Anza, in 1774, remarked upon the possibilities of a dam somewhere hereabouts. The old Spanish adventurers, both priests and soldiers, had a range of ideas much wider than their particular province.

of myriads of these demons. The hot dank air rings with their infernal pipings, and every moment is a misery. If equatorial Africa is worse than this, Livingstone and Stanley were heroes indeed.

A few miles to the north I found the outposts of the saguaros. Scarred and barren hills broke abruptly from levels strewn with fragments of rock of unusual hues, and the walls of every gully showed broken veins and ledges that made me again ponder turning prospector. There was no trouble in distinguishing the saguaros: they stood like tall posts among the stunted shrubs that sprinkled the mesa, varied only by small ironwoods, palo verdes, and mesquits where the shallow depression of a water-course collected the scanty rainfall. It was my first meeting with the saguaro and I was struck with its odd characteristics.

Its typical shape is a slender, straight column of equal diameter from top to bottom. From this a few stumpy arms may break out, and as these almost always turn upward, parallel to the main stem, a common effect is that of a gigantic candelabrum. Most of them, however, take original forms, each one a study in the weird. In close examination the plant is beautiful enough, the stem and branches glossy dark green and regularly fluted, and bearing in early summer white waxen blossoms which mature into edible crimson fruit. The tallest specimen I found was a solitary, old, ragged fellow, forty feet high, with a grotesque array of excrescences. An Alaskan Indian would have hailed it as a wondrous totem-pole.

Other features of the landscape gave the same effect of abnormality. The bare red plain was broken by distant hills of livid color and curious outline. To north and east, eccentric shapes gave the horizon a fantastic appearance. Of these Castle Dome was chief, the perpendicular mass of its central column looking as if the mountain were spouting up into the sky. Nearer at hand were these vegetable monstrosities, some straight and stark, others running to all sorts of bulbous curiosities. In color and shape every object was unexpected and unaccountable.

Almost all the saguaros I saw were bored with one or more round holes about four inches in diameter. My totem-pole saguaro must have had twenty of them. These are made originally by woodpeckers, but are mostly annexed by the little elf-owl (*Micropallas whitneyi*), who turns out the unlucky *carpintero* (as the Spaniards call the bird of chips), enlarges the hole, or perhaps bullies the other bird into doing it for him, and moves in, sometimes, no doubt, finding a young carpenter or two all ready for the house-warming. I searched a few of the holes in hope of getting a sight of this midget of his tribe, but if any were at home they had taken to the cellar.

CHAPTER XIX

A DESERT RIDE: YUMA TO BLYTHE

Autumn in the air — Northward now — Indian houses — Picacho Peak — A *tinaja* — Sunset splendor — The back of the Chocolates — Picacho Mine — Rock colors — Mineral country — Mexican hospitality — The Colorado River: its monotony: whirlpools: river of many names — Hoag's Landing — A taciturn hermit — A friendlier one — Frontier life — Riverside jungles — The fascination of repulsion — Mexicans preferred — Summer floods — Palo Verde — Infant prodigies — Water required — A boom "town" — Great expectations — "Home, Sweet Home" — Blythe: good points and bad — No Mexicans need apply — Pumped dry by mosquitoes — A bit of Arizona — Mojave Indians — Puzzle: find La Paz — Buried treasure — Country of the dead — Ehrenberg: population, 1 — The days of old — The missing citizens — Evening on the Rio Colorado.

IT was with a light-hearted feeling that I left Yuma. For one thing, cooler weather was at hand. People had told me that the middle of September would bring a break in the heat, and this was the 8th of the month. (The previous night, for the first time for months except when at Warner's in the mountains, I had found it comfortable to sleep under a thin blanket). For another, in leaving Yuma I was turning northward and in a general way homeward. Three months of travel in this desert country, nearly all of it alone, and with everlasting anxieties of water and forage, had brought a feeling that sometimes bordered on disgust.

Whether it was these considerations or some real difference in the air, somehow I felt as if autumn had come. I tried in vain to get at the source of the feeling. It might have been a bird sitting meditatively on a stalk of milo-maize; or a cow dreamily chewing; or a flock of blackbirds making jolly chorus in a willow; anyhow it was there, and even when birds and cows were left behind, and the desert again engulfed us, I felt the vague relief.

I chose the California bank of the river. There is a fairly good road, I am told, leading north on the Arizona side, while on the west side roads were problematical beyond Picacho, some twenty miles up. But I find untravelled ways most to my liking, and felt pretty sure I could get through, for water would be at hand if I kept near the river, and I heard of a ranch or two where forage might be found before I should reach the settlements of the Palo Verde Valley.

The first few miles led through the Indian Reservation, and at one or two of the *kans* (houses) the family was already breakfasting (mainly, it seemed, on watermelon) under the *ramada*, or brush-roofed shed, which is the general living-room during the hot months. The winter-quarters of most of the houses seemed snug enough, with good doors and windows, though these looked odd in walls of willow-poles caulked with mud. One young fellow dashed past me on a bicycle, with a shock of hair streaming behind him that for length, if not for texture, might be the envy of many a pale-face brunette.

Passing the last irrigation ditch we entered at once on a wide *mesa* with the ragged red hills of the Chocolate Range on all sides, except where, beyond the river, the mountains of Arizona were piled in solid masses of purple or aërial tones of blue. Ahead rose the Picacho pinnacle, like a dark pillar of thunder-cloud. It would be strange if the mines on the north flank of the mountain had escaped discovery. Any prospector or explorer coming within sight of that curious peak would be bound to go and see what it meant. I saw here an unusually good mirage, a sheet of pale blue water with slender towers like the minarets of mosques artistically grouped beyond. I used to wonder whether Kaweah saw these illusions. I cannot see why a horse should not, his eyes being at much the same level as a man's, but he never gave any token of noticing them. Are animals quicker than we to detect the unreality?

He had drunk little at starting and refused water at the ditch, but by early afternoon he was jaded. I searched each gully in hope of finding water left by the storm of a few days before, and by good luck came upon a *tinaja* of clear water. By lying down I could just make the canvas bucket reach it by using the forty-foot picket-rope. It was delicious water, cool and sweet, and we resolved on lunch. A chuckwalla that lived in a cranny of the gully amused me with reptilian antics while I ate. No doubt he thought my actions equally uncouth.

The country became rougher, with antediluvian looking hills coming in at every fresh view. Ocotillos were almost the only growth, and these, as brilliant as if dipped in vivid paint, made a striking show against the crude red of the rock. By late afternoon we rounded the flank of the Picacho, reaching the divide just before sunset. I shall never forget the sea of color that spread before me here. But why attempt to describe that which I felt it was hopeless to try to realize myself? It was superhuman. Words were below the trivial; even thoughts would hardly come.

In mere geography, it was the back of the Chocolates that I saw, a red ocean of ridges and pinnacles that if one could count them would run to hundreds, or more likely thousands. The level sun threw every detail into strongest relief, each point sharp and tense as if in action. Across this swept the splendor of an unearthly sunset.

The road here swung to the north of the Picacho, which had become a huge perpendicular cliff mysterious in shadow. Near by was another peak scarcely less original in outline. A mile brought us to the old mining-camp, a cluster of huts and sheds, all but one or two of them dismantled, with a larger central building occupied now by a caretaker. The property is involved in some legal difficulties and has long been unworked. This district has been noted for its rich placers since the early sixties, and it is said that when it was at its best ("in bonanza" as the phrase goes) any miner who failed to take out three hundred dollars per day was discharged as incompetent. Instead of the several hundred men who at one time made this a lively camp, I found only two or three Mexicans making a small living by working over the old placer-ground with dry-washers.

I persuaded the caretaker to spare Kaweah an armful of hay from his tiny store, and ate a cold supper rather than spend time over cooking while that wonderful afterglow filled the sky. The porch of a disused building where I spread my blanket proved to be the battlefield of the rats of Picacho and the camp cat, who charged across me from time to time.

We took our way in the morning down a picturesque cañon along which a light railroad used to run between the river and the mines. Rusty rails and machinery were strewn about, adding their quota of raggedness to piles of broken rock and old railway ties. The colors of the walls were extraordinary, splashed about in a way that suggested the upsetting of cauldrons of molten rock, pink, lavender, scarlet, green, and blue. The cool gray of smoke-trees made an excellent foil for these lively effects.

On the river-bank at the mouth of the cañon were the remains of the old town of Picacho, its population reduced to two or three families. This region for many miles up the river is a land of yesterday: of mines worked out, towns and settlements dead or dying. Yet it may revive, for mineral country can never be safely said to be dead. Any day the grizzled old man with pick and shovel, frying-pan and gold-pan, may strike a blow that will bring it to life literally as if by magic. Looking at that extent of mountains, all known or guessed to be mineralized, but in great part unprospected, one feels that bonanzas by scores might be hidden there.

The store, where I had counted on replenishing my saddle-bags, was closed, this not being one of the bi-weekly mail days. But at the adjoining house

I found a kindly Mexican family, and experienced again the courtesy of these often underrated people. While I drank my milk and talked with the *dueño* in the veranda where the family life went on, the phonograph was turned on for my pleasure. It was odd to hear the strains of "Pagliacci" by these lonely reaches of the Colorado. "Tipperary" did not sound so improbable.

I now turned northward along the river. The one difficulty I expected in making my way along the stream was the overflowed areas likely to be left by the yearly flooding which results from the melting of the snows on the headwaters. But fortunately this summer the rise had been less than normal and there should be little trouble, though I must expect détours and retracing of steps.

A hardly discernible track ran alternately along the river margin and the gravelly mesa that stretched from the bank to the belt of rugged hills. This gave variety to the march, sometimes through thickets of willow, again in open blaze of sun, while at intervals a ravine came down from the mountains, filled with ironwoods, palo verdes, smoke-trees, and the tedious but useful mesquit. At a little cove where firm ground allowed of Kaweah getting a drink I stopped for lunch and a congratulatory pipe, feeling not a little satisfaction in at last travelling along this famous stream, which had for years attracted my imagination.

The Colorado is not in its lower course a particularly striking river. That kind of feature it has in full measure farther up, where with roar of rapids or nobler quietude of motion it sweeps through the vast chasms of the Grand Cañon. Here it was a wide red flood, majestic in its expression of power, but with monotony for its prevailing note. This monotony, however, as I soon found, comes to be itself a feature of impressiveness. The union of silence with motion has also its peculiar charm, and the Colorado might well be named the Silent River. Its lack of sound might pass without notice if it were not brought to the attention by sudden swirls or whirlpools that now and again break the stillness with a rush of rapid water, followed again by the deathlike hush. These periodical suctions are a characteristic of this stream, and are caused by the continual shifting of the material of the bed. A phenomenal quantity of silt is carried by the Colorado, and its deposition results in constant changes of the bottom, a newly formed shoal at one place being balanced by a displacement at another. On the shores, also, every flood rebuilds and tears down the banks, which even at this time of low water I often noted to be rapidly caving at some point where I might be standing. This again causes changes of current in the channel, with the result of fresh alterations of the bed.

The river has had various names in the course of its history. We first hear of it in 1538 under the name Rio de las Balsas, river of the rafts, from the Franciscans, Fray Juan de la Asunción and Fray Pedro Nadal, who saw the Yumas cross the stream on rafts. Two years later one of Coronado's officers, Hernando de Alarçon, the first to discover its mouth and explore some distance above, named it the Rio de Buena Guía, or river of good guidance. In the same year Melchior Diaz called it the Rio del Tizón, river of the firebrand, because he found the savages carrying torches for warmth. Juan de Oñate in 1605 christened it the Rio Grande de Esperanza, river of hope, but in 1700 it received from Padre Eusebio Kino the ominous name of the Rio de los Martires, prophetic of the massacre, eighty years later, at the infant Missions near Yuma. But the name by which we know it, the Rio Colorado, the red river, is emphatically its own, stamped upon it by Nature. Red it is, both water and shores, approaching actual vermilion, and the hue is accentuated by the complementary green of the bordering vegetation.[1] I should like to view it again in late fall, when cottonwood and willow had changed to that tint of autumn gold which gives such depth and brilliance to the blue of the sky.

I whiled away an hour with the shades of the old padres and conquistadores, not forgetting the modern conqueror, Major John Wesley Powell, whose exploration in 1869 has lately been commemorated in a monument built on a point above the wonderful cañon. All the afternoon we moved slowly along, flanked ever by barren red mountains, these in California, those in Arizona. Reach after reach of the

[1] In an old map, printed in Paris in the sixteenth century, and showing California as an island, the Gulf is set down as Mar Bermejo, the Vermilion Sea, the name probably deriving from one of the "reports and narrations" from which the map was avowedly drawn, traceable to some early explorer, perhaps Alarçon, or Ulloa (one year earlier) who may have observed the discoloration of the Gulf water by that of the river, near its mouth.

river yielded little variety. Now and then a platoon of ducks flew up or down stream, or a heron or crane rose and flapped slowly off to a new fishing-ground, and often a covey of quail, caught unaware, scrambled with anxious chatter into the nearest thicket.

A smoke-stack, like a steamer's funnel, on the nearer bank, with nothing else of man's handiwork in sight, marked Hoag's Landing, where a ferry is supposed to ply, carrying an occasional passenger. I saw neither boat nor boatman, and wonder to this hour how long one might wait there for passage.

A mile or two farther on we came to a discouraged looking house and, after some search, a settler of similar mien who leaned on the rickety bars of a pasture that was occupied by a pair of burros. His niggardly words and lack-lustre eye were not engaging, and when I learned that there was another settler six miles above, I forebore to suggest our remaining for the night, and we pursued our way. Before we reached the other place sunset had come. It is surely by design of Providence that the refreshing color-flood comes over the earth just at the hour when otherwise man's spirit would tend to grovel. I reined up and gazed my fill over the solitary scene, now suddenly humanized by the magic of the evening light. The Colorado was no longer commonplace.

Just above where a rocky island, known as Lighthouse Rock, stood midway in the stream, I found the ranch and a hearty welcome from the rancher. He had lived in this isolated spot for many years, usually quite alone, only at long intervals visited by some wandering prospector. To my inquiry how often he got his mail, he replied "Oh, every few weeks," in a tone implying that this was not half bad.

My host had a small but substantial house, with plenty of good land and many of the makings of a comfortable home. On the river bank he had rigged up, single-handed, an engine and pump, which were all but ready to lift the water upon his fields. But the loneliness and the disheartening fight were too much for him, and he declared that he must quit unless he could find a partner. There are few people nowadays, I fear, who would be attracted by this frontier life, where one's own resources must provide almost every item that enters into success and comfort. If lumber is needed, you row up stream, fell and hew your timbers, and raft them down to your landing. If cement, or nails, your supply is forty miles away. If flour, or candles, or coffee, they are only to be had at the trouble of a day's journey. Society one must dispense with: and if you need a doctor — but one had better not get sick. Even the luxury of a diet of wild burro (which is the only fresh meat available) might not be thought to offset the other deprivations.

Kaweah met here an old acquaintance in the form of barley hay, which he munched with reminiscent air. After supper my host and I sat smoking and chatting for hours while he unburdened himself of hopes and fears, relieved with yarns of cougar and bighorn, treacherous river and waterless trail, while coyotes yelped and yelled in cheerful rivalry, California versus Arizona.

A long day's march was laid out for next day. I bade good-bye early to the friendly hermit, and we took our way again northward. At each approach to the river, bands of waterfowl flew quacking and clattering across the shining water. The track was dim, and was cut away in places by the summer flood, causing us many détours. The thickets became more jungle-like and difficult, and often the axe came into play. There were vistas in these willow woodlands where one might have thought himself in a wintry forest, every twig and leaf being coated with white wool from the seed vessels. Where the sun lighted these glades the resemblance to snow was exact, but the steamy heat and the mosquitoes forbade such delusion as to the time of year.

There was more of interest when the trail took to the *mesa*. Then the mountains were in view, and, forbidding as they were in their look of eternal drought and their uniformity of hue, their shapes were always stimulating. The mere geographical feeling, so to speak, that is excited by mountains is a luxury to any one fond of geography; and these desert ranges, with their look of geologic austerity, have a quality that amounts to fascination — the fascination of repulsion or something near that, a morbid and dangerous thing in general, but which somehow I find invigorating in a chain of blighted, bewitched mountains. One group of hills that I passed is named the Barren Mountains, as if in contrast with the other ranges hereabout, but it is hard to imagine what the difference can be.

On the Arizona side of the river about opposite to where I now was, a few settlers have taken up land. The locality is known as the Cibola Valley, taking the name from those Seven Cities that excited the old Spaniards so needlessly.

I recognized a relic of the mining era in the form of some cement vats on the bench above the river. No shaft or tunnel could be seen, so probably the pay-dirt was brought from a distance, this being the nearest water available for washing. In the bottom of one of the vats was a good-sized rattlesnake. I descended and did battle, Kaweah looking down like an old Roman watching a combat in the arena. He shares my dislike for these creatures, and gets as excited as I at the familiar rattle. As an instance of protective coloring, this specimen had taken on a dark red color that closely matched the ground.[1]

After a dozen miles or so we came to a clearing where Mexicans had cultivated their little patches of maize, *milpitas*, as they call them. The white settler who had lately ousted them was living in the stick-in-the-mud house. As it was noon I inquired of the wife whether I might purchase a meal and take it with them, which after some demur was granted. The man did not leave his reclining posture, on a dirty quilt in the shade of a *ramada*, during the hour and a half I stayed, except for a hurried visit to the table to gulp down his beans and coffee. With apologies to the kindly woman, I could not help wishing that the "damned greasers," as he termed the late

---

[1] I once, in grass country, killed a rattlesnake that was quite green in hue. Both the green and the red were regulation "diamond-backs."

occupiers, might have been my hosts. Anglo-Saxon superiority has sometimes to be taken for granted.

A wide wash, the Arroyo Seco, comes in here. There was no sign of recent rain having fallen hereabout, but the wash, dry as it now was, showed signs that a flood had swept down from the Chocolates within two or three weeks at most. I had seen the storm that I raced to Yuma, ten days before, breaking over this locality, and now congratulated myself that it had not overtaken me in the open, for fresh drift was lodged four or five feet high all over the wide channel. To be caught in one of these arroyos (which are tempting camping-places on account of firewood and shelter from wind), when a thunderstorm bursts on the mountains, would be much like being under a reservoir when the dam breaks.

Evening found us still far from Palo Verde, but a few hours' cool travelling was not a bad prospect. Before the young moon had set we had come into a well-marked road that comes up from Glamis, forty miles to the southwest, and along this we marched comfortably enjoying the grateful dusk. At length came fences, and then a light. We stumbled into a few sloughs that variegated the road, ran into a barbed-wire fence or two, and pulled up at an adobe store-building where a trio of teamsters were camping on the porch. Opposite was a corral and haystack, pleasing sights for Kaweah. The proprietor was routed out and we wound up a long day in very tolerable quarters.

Morning revealed Palo Verde as a hamlet — I choose the smallest term, but it is too much — con-

sisting of a store and half a dozen scattered buildings, mostly old or of the modern kind that does not
need years to make them disreputable. The population might number a score when all should have returned from "inside." A backwater of the Colorado
gives the place some attraction, and it appeared to
be well stocked with fish and waterfowl. Not only
the youth but the infants of Palo Verde find their
pleasure in this lagoon. A proud father pointed out
to me his boy, aged three, who he assured me was an
expert swimmer, while his next younger, a baby-
girl, was in training and showing promise.

As for farming, the district seemed not to have
made a beginning. A few untidy fields could be seen,
but not one instance of thrifty cultivation came to
my notice. This settlement lies at the southern end
of the Palo Verde Valley, the upper part of which, as
the next day's travel proved, tells a very different
tale. No doubt the tide of prosperity, which means
the flow of water in the irrigation canals, is on its
way and will break on Palo Verde itself in due time.

Through a pale, unpleasant land we took our way
again northward. There was not now much comfort
to be had from the mountains, for they were farther
away and almost lost in summer haze; and the river
had dropped out of sight. The vegetation was of the
dismal kind usual on these silt levels, hummocks of
atriplex varied with an occasional mesquit. The
ground was cracked and gaping with heat, and the
so-called ranches added the last touch of depression
with their gunny-sacking and baling-wire make-
shifts. Here and there an attempt at cultivation had

been made, but abandoned. The bitter dust rose listlessly from the road and hung about like an annoying companion. A team crept along half hidden in its own gray cloud. As we passed I noticed that the load was burlap, for baling the cotton-crop of the northern end of the valley.

A new, vacant store-building with one house adjoining proved to be a "town" named Rannells. The law of supply and demand cannot be the simple thing many of us suppose, for here was a man who thought, apparently, that a store automatically produces customers. But the mind of the land-boomer is one of the last puzzles that philosophy will solve. Meanwhile one shakes the head and passes by.

Gradually the look of things improved. The patches of cotton seemed less hopelessly starved, and here and there a decent house appeared. At a little homestead I noticed half a dozen thrifty young date-palms bearing a good crop. As I stood admiring, an old woman smoking a clay pipe came out of the shack and invited me to inspect her treasures at close range. Did I ever see such dates as them? No, she'd bet half a dollar I never did. Them was reel Deglets and raised by hand. Laws, I would n't believe the water they took, them six! and did I notice them offshoots, five of 'em? That would make near double the number when she set 'em out; and in three or four years they 'd double again, and keep a-doin' it till, laws! in like no time she and her old man would have a date place folks 'd come from Los Angeles in their autos to look at.

And so on, puffing and chatting away, friendly, garrulous, admirably hopeful.

At the next settlement, called Neighbors, really good farms began, with cheerful horses and men, big haystacks, and a general air of something going on. The well-fenced fields showed excellent crops of alfalfa, cotton, and milo-maize. The difference between this locality and the one I had just left turns wholly on the question of water, the very blood of life to desert soil. Teams became more numerous, then occasional buggies with women and children. Passing a prosperous looking ranch I caught the sound of a harmonium. Some one was playing "Home, Sweet Home."

We were soon entering the town of Blythe, which I found to consist of a dozen good stores, a neat little bank, hotel, moving-picture theatre, and so forth, and a few score of modest dwellings. But again I rebelled at the slovenliness that makes our new Western cities so deplorable. One picks out the redeeming features eagerly enough, every tasteful building, every bit of lawn, every decent job of fencing: but these only give contrast to the general vileness. One would think effort had been made, real ingenuity called in, to achieve this hideous result.

Blythe has no livery-stable, but I found makeshift quarters for Kaweah at a corral surrounded by dirty tents and mud-and-pole hovels, and put up for a day or two while I attended to matters of business. The opening of a new pool-room was to be celebrated that night and the next, with a dance given on the first night by the Mexicans, who are a strong element in the town, and on the second by the Americans. As I stood at dusk talking with the saddler and watching the Mexicans trooping to the *baile* in chattering family groups, all the femininity in snowiest array, I noticed a few American youths and girls passing in with them, and remarked that it was good to see the two elements so friendly. "Huh!" said my companion, "those store-clerks would go anywhere there's a show for a dance." "But," I said, "don't the Mexicans invite them?" "Sure." "And then of course the Mexicans are invited when you get up a dance." "What! invite the greasers! Well, I just reckon we don't."

A map published in 1915 by some California concern for the benefit of autoists shows the towns of Ehrenberg and La Paz, on the Arizona side of the river almost opposite Blythe. They were noted places in their time and should be worth a visit even in decline. I took the road eastward, at first among farms, then through the jungle of the bottom-land. A few autumnal lavender asters had already appeared, a hundred-fold delightful after the long absence of such charmers of the way. Wild hemp (*Sesbania macrocarpa*) was plentiful in places and still in blossom, but its spindling growth and formal leaves had made it tedious from first acquaintance.

It would have been a pleasant woodland lane through the willows but for mosquitoes, which here were at their worst. Kaweah stopped once or twice and looked round at me with a questioning eye, but I was no better off than he except for my smaller area. I tried tobacco, but this they seemed to find an interesting novelty. When I put Kaweah to a gallop I only got more bites in less time and barked my shins against the close-growing trees. The mosquitoes here were of the large mottled kind that leave a mark like an old-fashioned legal wafer.

A cable ferry plies at this point, which in the early days of the West was a main crossing place for California travel. In answer to my hail a grizzled old fellow came out of a cabin on the farther side, and in the leisurely manner of ferrymen the world over, brought his boat across. This was a new experience for Kaweah, and I expected him to balk when I rode him on board; but the Egyptians were behind, and the river, he knew, was our Red Sea of safety. When I asked the ferryman how he endured the mosquitoes, "Why," he replied, "there's no more blood in me, you see. They got the last out of me about nineteen ten, so they've quit coming around."

I found a road following the stream, and turned northward over a clay mesa bearing the usual assortment of plants but with a few saguaros added to give the characteristic of Arizona. A mile or two along I found a house of the familiar stick-in-the-mud type, where a young rancher had taken up an abandoned piece of bottom-land. He was no exception to the rule of friendliness, and indeed urged me to stop with him more or less indefinitely. The house had been built by Mojave Indians, whose tribal territory begins hereabout, and it still bore marks of their régime such as *ollas* and *metates*, and on the walls crude drawings of trains, city buildings, and so forth. Probably some much-travelled Mojave buck had been illustrating to his household circle the wondrous things he had seen on a visit to Needles, perchance even to Phœnix, the State capital.

A few other houses of the same kind were passed, but all were deserted. In the rear of one, which appeared to have been a store, there were the remains of an *arrastra*, the primitive contrivance for grinding ore by crushing it with rocks in a circular pit by means of a capstan operated by horse, burro, or ox power. One is constantly meeting these reminders of "the days of old, the days of gold," in all sorts of unlikely corners about the desert, and comes to have the feeling of being in a region of the dead.

The young rancher had warned me that La Paz was not now much of a place, but had told me how to find it. Five miles farther on I glimpsed his landmark, a cone-shaped cement monument visible from the road on the right. On making my way to it I understood the point of his remark that I must be careful or I might miss the place. The monument, he told me, stood at the head of the principal street. I gazed all around. I was in a waste of mesquit scrub and arrowweed: perhaps the houses were hidden by the brush. I searched for houses, then for any token showing where houses had stood. There was nothing, not so much as a scrap of foundation, or adobe wall, or of lumber, or even débris. Apart from the monument and a few mud bricks close thereby not a sign remained of the city of La Paz, which forty or fifty years ago was a place of five thousand or more people, the county seat, and hopeful of becoming the capital city of the Territory. Some one has recently written about these defunct mining towns, which he calls the ghost cities of the West. La Paz is not even a ghost, merely a legend.

The top of the monument had been knocked off and a hole broken in the side. I was told later that it marked the grave of the wife of an Italian citizen, saloon-keeper, merchant, and man of wealth of old La Paz. He had lavished diamonds on his lady in her lifetime, and rumor said that the jewels had been buried with her. Some ghoul felt that he must put that to the proof, and did so with crowbar or dynamite. Whether they discovered diamonds, or only proved that rumor had lied once more, I could not learn.

East of the town there is a spot once known as Friar's or Fryer's Gulch, from which, it is said, millions were taken out. Fifteen feet square was allowed to each man, and fights to the death no doubt took place over these narrow boundaries. Ghosts there well might be about the old cemetery of La Paz, if ghosts could find it, which is more than I could do.

I climbed the bluff to see if from higher ground any indication of the former town could be traced. The wider outlook did but emphasize the vacancy and desolation, to which the ruined grave gave a touch of the definitely uncanny. Opposite, across the silent river, rose the brick-hued Maria Mountains, with range behind range in paling distance beyond. In all directions it was the same: everything spoke of the dreary or savage, and over all was an eternal note of weariness, as of a land long since drained of life, and left wan, blasted, and forsaken.

It was near sundown when we returned to the ferry. Hard by is the old town of Ehrenberg, whose founder one might fancy to have foretold by his lonely and tragic death the fate of the place that took his name. Here, however, there was at least a skeleton left — a dozen or so adobe houses, all but one or two wrecked and deserted, gaping open to the sky. In the largest habitable building Ehrenberg's one and only citizen solemnly keeps store all by himself. Until a year or so ago, two saloon-keepers competed with him for the business of the place, or rather, of the rare passing traveller and the festal topers of Blythe who were driven by county prohibition laws to cross the river for their harmless little lagers and cocktails. Then the incredible happened: Arizona itself "went dry," and the priests of the flowing bowl and dirty apron sadly closed their temples and fared forth into a world suddenly become virtuous and unprofitable.

Ehrenberg is probably the only case extant of a town with but a single inhabitant; almost certainly the only instance of such a place keeping a store going. We have read of that doubtful island where the people "eked out a precarious livelihood by taking in one another's washing." Here, though, is an authentic case of a person making a living off himself. This I judge to be unique, and would suggest that some political economist go and interview him and find out how it is done.

I would have done this myself, but at the moment

I arrived he was just closing up town to go over to Blythe for the evening. Thus the twilight hour was my own, to wander and muse. I wish I had skill to do justice to this Deserted Village of the West. Bret Harte would have drawn it to the life. As I prowled, an owl flapped from the gate-post of the old corral, and a bevy of quail, in the act of going to roost in the mesquits that had invaded the main street, scurried back with reproachful murmurs into the arrowweed thicket by the river. One handsome date-palm waved in melancholy grace over a little enclosure rank with weeds. The schoolhouse, to be known by a fragment of blackboard on the wall of its single room, is said to have housed the second school established in the old Territory. The confessions of early passion which certain young Felipes and Josefas, Enriques and Marías, were impelled to publish on the walls of their Alma Mater are still in evidence against them.

In days when flat-bottomed steamers came up from Yuma with freight for the hustling frontier towns and mining-camps of Arizona, Ehrenberg was a port of size. The rate for hauling goods from here to Prescott is said to have been eight cents per pound, or in the case of breakable or perishable stuff, twenty-five cents per pound. A small army of freighters and an imposing one of mules were continually on the road to and from the camps of the Harquahalas, the Hualpais, and the Agua Fria. One man alone owned fifteen teams, of eighteen mules to the team. Those were spacious days in the West, when no smaller coin passed than the contemptible "two-bits" ("do' reales"), a sum so mean that the very term became a reproach, and so remains even in these penurious times.

I found a number of Ehrenberg's missing citizens up on the mesa, a quarter mile out of town. Here, in the most thoroughly dismal cemetery I ever beheld, were some sixty or seventy graves, mere shapeless piles of gravel and boulders, with one, more ambitious, a yellow hump of adobe. There was no sign of its ever having been fenced: it lay open to coyotes, cattle, and burros, whose tracks went in and out everywhere. I suppose shallow graves were dug, but it looks more as if bodies had been dropped uncoffined on any vacant space and stones and gravel thrown hastily upon them. Each grave was a burrow of ground-squirrels. Few had any pretence of cross or mark of identification, and on still fewer could one make out a date or name. The place seemed to put a stamp on the record of bygone Ehrenberg as a community unlovely in life, brutal in death. Yet, Heaven forgive me for saying so, when many, or most, of these dreary mounds may mark the end of a life which, though cast in harsher setting, may have held more of usefulness, kindliness, and genuine worth than ours who gather easy "impressions," and write books, or sell stocks, or sugar, and are marked in Evergreen Cemetery with tasteful marbles and non-committal texts.

The Colorado looked poetic enough as I rode down to the ferry. I was not sorry when in answer to my call the ferryman shouted from his cabin door that he was "a-cookin' supper right now" and I must wait. The sun had long set, but a carmine stain still lingered, merging into clear beryl green, and that shading to tender purple in which a half moon stood vertical and the stars were taking station. Three cranes rose with sudden clatter and flew slowly down stream, their shadows flickering on the calm water which swept past in a broad sheet of palest green streaked with crimson. I was glad to have time for this to stamp itself upon my mind as my parting impression of the Rio Colorado.

The odors of bean-frying and biscuit-baking that came with our ferryman were well calculated to replace sentimentality with thoughts of supper. We crossed, I waved adieu to Arizona, and watched the boat slip mystically away into the gloom. A five-mile gallop through moonlight and mosquitoes brought us again to Blythe, which had suddenly burst into bunting in readiness for Mexico's Independence Day on the morrow.

CHAPTER XX

A DESERT RIDE: BLYTHE TO COACHELLA VALLEY

Viva Mexico! — Homeward bound — A hard choice — A dirty trick — A sunrise vision — The Ironwood Mountains — Desert pavement — Palens and Cockscombs — Lack of the humane element — Entering the Chuckwallas — Trail troubles — Moonlight and mystery — Corn Springs — Picture-writings — Hotel de Corn Springs — More trail problems — The heart of the Chuckwallas — The desert and music — Quite at sea — Lost: The Red Cloud Mine — More guessing — At last a road — A long night march — — Kaweah discouraged but game — Night company — Faint yet pursuing — Eureka! a sign-post — Dawn: peace and war — Shafer's Well: rest and water — Mecca and civilization — The desert in review — Still the Sphinx — The riddle unread.

IN reaching Blythe three sides of my proposed circuit had been completed, and I now turned westward toward the Coachella Valley where it began. There was no difficulty about waking early, this sixteenth of September, for the Mexican half of Blythe was up at dawn and making no secret of its patriotic fervor. However, we had only a short march before us for the day, so made a late start, spending the morning in a round of gaiety and gunpowder, and joining whole-heartedly in the shouts of *Viva Mexico!* that all but drowned the strains of the Mexican National Hymn — a fine stirring air even when screeched on a broken-winded phonograph.

A very few miles took us beyond the limit of the cultivated land: then at a slight rise we were again on the characteristic wide mesa broken by isolated mountain ranges. Far in the south the pinnacles of

El Picacho were unmistakable, though mere ghosts of hazy blue. Near at hand to the north rose the purple ridge of the Marias, shading into the dimmer Ironwoods, and those into the long wavering chain of the Chuckwallas, around or through which I was to find a way. A glance behind showed a wilderness of uneasy outlines that stood for Arizona.

Ten miles out I found the ranch of a solitary settler who had sunk a well and obtained a flow of water, small indeed, but enough to make a promising experiment with dates, spineless cactus, and other likely novelties. Here I put up for the night, but gained the unwelcome news that water was not to be had at Ford's Well, some twenty miles out, where I had meant to make my next camp. This threw me on a waterless stretch of about forty miles, either to Gruendike's Well or Corn Springs. As an alternative, I could strike across to Wiley's Well, and then by an old road along the southern base of the Chuckwallas. The latter plan involved two thirty-mile stretches between water, but seemed preferable on Kaweah's account. I resolved on the shorter spans.

As I was saddling up next morning a prospector chanced along. He was driving a buckboard with two small mules, and was bound for Blythe, having come by way of Wiley's Well. Was I going that way? he asked. I told him, Yes. "How long rope have you got?" he inquired. "Forty feet," I said, indicating Kaweah's picket-rope. "That won't do you no good," he remarked. "It's sixty foot down to water. If I had n't had them two long tie-ropes I'd have starved when I got there yesterday. Some ——

—— son of (et cætera) has stolen the rope off the windlass. I hope he'll die raving mad for a drop of water right where he can see it, like I might have done. Roping up's too good for that kind of dirt."

Perfectly true, for a more scoundrelly trick can hardly be imagined, as cold-blooded as if a sailor should cut the life-line that has just been his salvation. It illustrates the chances that lie in wait for the desert traveller, and keep him anxious from the time he leaves one water-hole till he reaches the next. So far as we were concerned, we could have returned to this ranch; but in the case of a man arriving at that well in bad straits for water, perhaps having used his last supply freely in expectation of surely renewing it here, death would be a not unlikely outcome.

I changed my plan perforce, but stayed over for the day so as to make an earlier start the next morning. My accommodating rancher had a fair store of hay, purchasable at a price, and I had brought a few feeds of barley from Blythe, so Kaweah passed the time profitably, while I indulged myself with such ancient magazine literature as the house afforded.

By daybreak we were on the march. The air was cool and Kaweah seemed to know that he was headed for home, though home was well over a hundred miles away. We had knocked off a few miles before the sun came up, and when it rose I wheeled and sat enjoying, as I don't often find possible, the magnificence of the desert sunrise. I felt I could afford to do Sol justice now that a few days would bring the end of my journey. Moreover, the equinox was at hand and I could almost pity the bully now that his power was waning.

So it was fine to watch each rift or ridge of mountain flush to full life as it was overtaken by the tide of light: to note the kindling of beacon beyond beacon, and, in fancy, to see it carried on from Cockscombs to Cottonwoods, then to Santa Rosa, San Jacinto, and San Gorgonio, and thence along the great Sierra wall where snowfield, glacier, and many an icy lake I knew would start to a sudden glory of rose or sapphire. I saw the forests stir in the wind of dawn, the deer go down to the brook, the cyclamens and gentle lavender daisies awake and smile as when we awoke and smiled together. Suddenly I asked myself, Why, what am I doing here, raking among the bones of the earth? I have wasted a precious summer, and, what is worse, gone back on my friends. A bad, bad mistake. . . . Well, at least I know one more corner of my inheritance.

Rounding a spur of the Ironwood Mountains (sometimes called the McCoys, after one out of several worthies of that name who figure in the epic of the West) we travelled for some miles through what might be termed, for the desert, a forest of ironwoods. Many of the trees were twenty feet high and some of them nearly two feet in diameter of trunk. Kaweah had a fancy for the young twigs, so I gave him ten minutes to browse as there was no prospect of hay until we reached Mecca.

Wide spaces of this mesa were covered with the black pebbles I had noted in other localities. They formed a sort of pavement, and had the look of actually being burned black by the sun. On breaking some of the pieces the inside color was always light red. These stretches are one of the peculiar features of desert geology, by reason of the uniformity of the fragments in size and color, and the impression they give of having been rolled into place. Their polish also suggests friction under enormous weight, as if red clay had been vitrified to a kind of flint by heat due to compression.

Long before the Ironwoods were left behind, the sun had warmed to his work and taken his old place in my regard. Next the Palen Range slowly came into view. The travelling became bad, then worse, finally heartbreaking. Each wash outdid the last in muscle-demand, and Kaweah parted early with his morning gaiety. A few miles of this sort of thing has greater effectiveness in reducing mental excitement than any medical sedative I know. At last the Cockscombs opened up in the northwest, their serrated crags remarkable as ever though robbed of their realistic red by the haze of heat and distance. Our objective, the Chuckwallas, flickered in long forbidding rank on the southern horizon, seemingly unapproachable. Hours of laborious travel wrought no visible change in their obstinate contours.

Half an hour was all I could allow at noon for rest and lunch. The trees had long been passed, and without a square foot of shade there was no inducement to lose time. I found languid interest in watching the play of light on distant ranges, and in wondering what legend might have been framed by the old Greeks that could give glamour to this profound monotony. When at last deeper tones of color began to outline the cañons, imagination came feebly to life, but I felt, as ever, that the sole human attribute suggested by the desert is hopeless, prosaic endurance, never anything of the dramatic or stimulating. All is tedious, explicit, bald. A poet here would soon be gasping for want of air.

All the afternoon we marched steadily, and at sundown came to a point where a track branched southwesterly toward the Chuckwallas.[1] Before turning into it I let Kaweah graze a few minutes on such scanty galleta grass as he might find, while I lay motionless hoping to radiate off a little of the heat I had been absorbing, particularly the last two hours, when I had offered a frontal mark to the sun. Although there is little slackening of the heat until the moment of sunset, thereafter the air cools rapidly, so by the time we were ready to move there was a decent temperature; while the mingled twilight and moonlight made a kind of bath of dusk, in which my jaded frame was gently massaged with soothing psychologic touches.

The track dwindled fainter and fainter. Some storm had lately broken over the Chuckwallas and spread a sheet of sand and gravel over the whole northern slope of the mountain. Before long we were wandering in a chaos of washes. I dismounted and led Kaweah, picking every foot of the way with utmost care, yet often going far astray. Luckily there

[1] The name comes from a species of lizard, *Sauromalus ater*, common in many parts of the desert but especially in this range. It is harmless, but ugly, with much the look of a miniature alligator.

was a bright moon, in its second quarter, but at best it was guesswork half the time. Often I tied Kaweah and prospected far ahead before I could pick up the trail.

So much time was being lost in this fashion that I determined to cut loose and trust to luck. The mountain wall loomed shadowy, the cañons uncertainly marked by darker massing of gloom. The route I had in mind followed a cañon that led straight through the mountains, crossing by a pass at the head of which is a water-hole known as Corn Springs. Scanning the dark wall before me I made out a black slash that by its bearings should be the cañon I wanted. It was doubtful, yet probable, and I resolved to take the chance.

Where we spent the next hour or two I am not clear, except that in a general way we were on the flanks of the Chuckwallas. Occasionally I got sight anew of my landmark, which I identified by a notch on the skyline: otherwise I guided by the stars. We pulled up at last in the bottom of a deep gully choked with a thicket of smoke-trees. Out of this there was no way, except by going back, unless I could get Kaweah up a thirty foot cliff. I felt sure that once on the farther side we should have easy going, though it was still doubtful whether the cañon we were heading for was the right one.

Kaweah was dead tired, but game. Picking out the best looking place I threw the bridle over the horn and led by the picket-rope. The bank was loose gravel and much too steep for any chance of stopping midway. It must be made in one rush or not at all, and failure meant a bad, perhaps serious, fall for the horse. I clambered a little way up, gave him plenty of rope, and then shouted to him, at the same time scrambling ahead. The good little fellow came up with a run as if hand over hand, sending an avalanche of stuff to the bottom. I kept cheering and hauling him on, and in a few moments we were on the top. There, almost at the edge, was a well-marked track, heading for the cañon. (I take it to be a crosscut between Corn Springs and Gruendike's Well.)

I now had leisure for the scenic features of my surroundings, which indeed were sufficiently weird. To the right was a mesa of the curious mosaic-like character that I have described elsewhere: to the left was the deep *barranca* on the brink of which ran the track. The moon shone clearly down on the gleaming black floor, which might have been the pavement of some ruined city of antiquity. At intervals stood great ocotillos whose gaunt arms waved aloft in sinister contortions, while here and there a dead one lay bleached to the hue of bone. Looking down into the ravine I could make out dark forms of palo verde and ironwood, or gray smoke-trees, like ghosts, outlined on the pallid sand of the bottom. The only sound was that of Kaweah's hoofs hoarsely rattling the gravel of the track. Close ahead rose the black wall of the Chuckwallas, with here and there some bolt of rock taking questionable shape under the eerie touches of the moon. The total impression was freakish and unearthly: it was

"A place nor uninformed with phantasy
And looks that threaten the profane."

At last we passed into the cañon, and black cliffs rose high on either hand. The ground was again of sand, and in the moonlight every track of bird, snake, coyote, or bighorn showed sharp and clear. Small trees leaned out from crannies to which they clung by knotty roots, and from a cave came a stream of shadowy bats with click of tiny teeth and soundless flicker of wing.

Somewhere near the mouth of the cañon is a *tinaja* known as Granite Tanks, but it was unlikely that I could find it without daylight. We kept on therefore for two or three miles, coming an hour before midnight to a group of small palms and mesquits which gave notice of water. Among them was an old cabin, and near by it a spring. We both drank deeply. It was eighteen hours since Kaweah had had water, and the day had been hot, with unusually heavy travelling. I dealt him a good feed of barley and picketed him on the half-dry grass: then ate a few cold mouthfuls, threw down my blankets, and almost literally *fell* asleep.

Next day being Sunday, and forage sufficing, we took it easy in camp, revelling in shade of palm and willow and the proximity of plentiful water. In a walk down the cañon I noticed near the spring a fine exhibition of Indian picture-writings. The figures were scratched in firm outline on the faces of smooth slabs of rock, and stood out white against the red of the granite as clearly as if done but a year or two ago. The cañon by daylight was picturesque, the high walls enclosing a gully-like passageway in which grew the usual assortment of mountain plants. Unlovely as these mainly are, one finds them interesting in proportion to their rarity, and stops to enjoy a twelve-foot smoke-tree or some weak outbreak of originality in an ocotillo as if they were the gnarly heroes of a forest.

The presence of the house was explained by my coming upon an abandoned mine. The place has evidently long been the haunt of prospectors. On the door was roughly painted the invitation: "Come in and Camp: Wood and Water Free": and above the fireplace was a square of pasteboard with "Hotel de Corn Springs" set out in an attempt at the sign-painter's art, with further flights of fancy scrawled by departed guests. One wall did duty as a register, showing the names of visitors for several years past. It appeared that the patronage of this select hostelry runs to a score or two per annum, though this is only through the frequent recurrence of one or two regulars on whose prospecting beat it lies.

I was in no hurry to start next morning, as I intended to make only a dozen miles or so, to the Red Cloud Mine, at the other base of the mountains. We left about eight o'clock, finding a doubtful looking track leading west. A mile brought us to the divide, and to the end of anything that could be called a trail. Looking across to the south I could see what seemed to be a well-marked road climbing the mountain-side. Here was another of those conundrums that plague the traveller in unmapped and little-known country. Was it a new route to Dos Palmas, the point I was making for, or did it merely lead to some mine of which I had not heard? I had been

told that my trail followed the main cañon, yet there
was no sign of travel that way. This business of
guessing, when a mistake may spell disaster, gradually gets on one's nerves, knocks out the fun, and
finally puts one out of humor with desert travel.

I tied Kaweah and prospected ahead, picking up
at last what seemed to be a continuation of the trail,
though so broken and casual that it could only be
followed by using extreme care. The storm that
had washed over the northern slope of the mountains had obliterated the track here also. Another
mile, and the trail, such as it was, turned into a side
cañon toward the south. Disgusted, I resolved to
trust my sense of direction and keep on westward.
At the worst I could return to Corn Springs, and
to-morrow try the other route.

One has little mind for scenery under these circumstances, yet I could not fail to be struck by the
intense desolation of the country we were traversing. I was in the heart of one of those scorched and
scarified ranges that even viewed through the ameli-
orating veil of distance seem the last word of the
gaunt and hopeless in physical Nature. Rock,
gravel, sand, and sky, all alike repressive and repellent, make up the total, but for a few lean
shrubs that clutch the blistering slabs of the mountain wall, and the cacti that crouch among the boulders and reward every careless step with torture.
For all of sentient life a raven flies heavily by, or
some snake glides away or waits coiled and threatening in your path; and if you overturn a scrap
of stone, centipede or scorpion will resent your

violation of its solitude with instant menace of poison.

I sometimes wonder what kind of interpretation music might give of these landscapes. No doubt something unique might be achieved by the modernists, some crude depiction of the obvious and sensational: but what I mean is, the impression that the desert would make on the mind of a master. What the expression would be we are not likely to know; for music seems to have lost self-control, and cannot wait to comprehend its theme before it is ready with some noisy but futile demonstration.

After awhile my fading hope that we were on the right track was strengthened by coming on marks of another old mine. There was a puddle of water at the bottom of a prospect hole, but it was foul with decaying rats and lizards, and quite unusable. We made our slow way down the gradually widening cañon, now and then on a sort of phantom trail but usually picking a trackless way by guesswork and probabilities. It was the most worrying job of its kind that I met on the whole journey, and the water problem kept nudging at me like a pestering fiend.

Noon came, and we should be nearing the Red Cloud Mine. There we should find water, and probably a caretaker, though the mine was not being worked. The cañon had opened into a delta of interlacing gullies, all rocky, choked with boulders, and crossed at short intervals by abrupt, slippery ledges which bothered Kaweah considerably. My fear was that we might come to some impassable place and be obliged to turn back. I had noted the landmarks carefully, but felt no certainty of being able to find the way through this wilderness to our last camp.

Suddenly I spotted two tents in a side gully. We made for them hopefully, but there was no sign of recent habitation, nor any indication of water. It was the camp of some prospector who came once or twice a year, at times when the tanks would yield a supply. A trail led up the mountain-side at the rear of the tents. This looked inviting, and we followed it cheerfully for two steep miles. Then it turned directly north and I saw it was useless to go on, so with the loss of an hour of valuable daylight we turned to our problem.

Evening was coming on. I climbed a ridge and scanned the country. There was plenty of it, and all alike. The mine was no doubt somewhere within the scope of view, but I could not guess even whether it lay to north or south. To hunt for it in twenty square miles of wash and gully offered slight chance of success.

I sat down and figured things over. We were now clear of the Chuckwallas. To the south was a ridge of hills that, as I reckoned, shut me off from sight of the Salton Sea. Ahead a wide valley opened, running due west for many miles. If I could make southwest across country I ought to come out into the Dos Palmas road; but it was nearly dark, the country was a labyrinth of *barrancas* — the worst of all country to get lost in — the last traces of any trail had been left behind hours ago, and the spectre of thirst was keeping me ever closer company. Even if I could find Corn Springs again my problem would not be finally solved. On the whole, the open valley ahead was the best prospect. It led in the Cottonwood Springs direction and ought to bring me into the road by which, two months before, I had come from Dale. We would go ahead and see what happened.

We had not eaten for twelve hours, for I had been too much preoccupied to think of food. Kaweah had not drunk either, but I relied on the coolness of the night to refresh him. I gave him the last feed of barley, ate a scratch meal myself, and with an encouraging word to my anxious companion we started on.

Daylight had gone but the moon was well up and afforded aid and comfort. Except for the discomfort of doubt I could have revelled in the charm of the scene. The uncouth Chuckwallas rose dark behind and to my right. Moonlight whitened here and there the angle of some buttress, touching with charm of fancy the leagues of shadowy mountain. Our shadows marched before us, mingling with filmy pattern of creosote or skeleton of cactus or ocotillo. To the left the horizon line was a procession of dusky shapes, shifting and vanishing like monsters seen in a nightmare.

We had gone for a few miles in a sort of dogged muddle, when wagon tracks appeared without warning, crosswise of our line of march. Whither they might lead in either direction I had no idea, but they came as a vast relief. I made a rapid guess and chose the right-hand track. Another mile and we ran into an unmistakable road and were heading westerly into the long valley. It was now only a question of Kaweah's holding out. He was certainly very tired and necessarily very thirsty, while by my reckoning we were about twenty-five miles from water, whether we reached it at Cottonwood Springs or Shafer's Well. But the coolness of night would help us out, and Kaweah, blessings on his tough little carcass, is pure Indian and would go till he dropped. As for myself, though I was muscle-weary to the limit (for I had been on foot all day) I felt I could travel forever in that refreshing temperature, and I still had a quart or so of water.

All night we toiled along. Played out as Kaweah was, whenever I stopped him he was anxious to go on, though with dragging step and muzzle almost touching his knees. I tried to buck him up with promises of the bully times we would have the coming winter — We'll chuck this everlasting clutter of saddle-bags, blankets, and canteens, and just knock about and enjoy ourselves, eh, pony boy? And it was clear how all-in he was when he failed to respond to my fraternal slap with humorous show of ill-temper such as flattened ears or playful pretence of a bite. Stars rose, stars set: the moon overtook, passed us, and sailed ahead as if rallying us on our despicable pace. I was drowsy, but well content so long as the track kept on westward, for I knew it must bring us into some road that ran down to Mecca. So I whistled, dozed, and plodded on, cheering my plucky little nag, and counting off the miles by the hours we travelled. Rabbits played about in the road, careless of our approach until we almost kicked them away. Now and again a sentimental coyote, maudlin with moonlight, vented his blighted affections in hysterical yawpings, and once half-a-dozen wild cattle rose suddenly out of the brush and gathered in a knot as if to stampede us. The sight of a man on foot is so strange to these roamers of the ranges that they are apt to be dangerous to such a person. The cowboy who looks them up twice or thrice a year must be thought a kind of centaur, while a pedestrian must seem a fragment or monstrosity.

Slowly we neared the western opening, and new shapes appeared on the skyline. I tried to recall their outlines; were those the Eagles? those the Pintos? those the Cottonwoods? Could I have been mistaken in my impression of the lay of the land, and would the road after all turn north and lead us into some new pickle? [1]

One o'clock; two o'clock. By my reckoning we should be nearing the cross-road. The moon was nearly down. Poor Kaweah plodded along, "faint yet pursuing," his spirit as flat as his ears. Three o'clock, and no hopeful sign. Then at last something showed ahead beside the road. Could it be a sign-post? It could, and it was, one of those enduring metal posts that the good county of Riverside has placed at some of these main cross-roads, and that every county whose territory runs into the desert should be compelled to provide on all routes of

[1] I learned afterwards that during the night I had passed, without knowing it, close to one place where I could have got water. This is a spot humorously known as the Hayfields, where a thin growth of grass is used by cattle-men for pasturage, and water has been piped to a trough.

desert travel. I struck a match and eagerly examined the sign. Good luck! I had figured rightly. Five miles to the southwest was Shafer's Well.

Before turning the shoulder of the mountain I stopped and looked back to the east. Down a long gallery whose walls rose dark and high on either hand, a splendid planet, Jupiter himself

" . . . with new-spangled ore
Flamed in the forehead of the morning sky."

The firmament about him was silvering to the dawn. Toward me stretched a purple ribbon of sky glittering with a myriad points of gold. The dawn wind came as cool and pure as if it were the first breath of Creation. The stillness was superb, the silence so absolute as to be startling. Could the central calm of the universe be holier, more inviolable, than this? The thought of war, with its ruin, chaos, and fury, was an impossibility, one could not realize so vile a blasphemy against the vast peace of Nature. But the wild forms of the mountains showed that here too war had been waged against the old forces of repression, forever too stupid to know that to oppose freedom is to be blown sky-high.

As I turned to move on, the moon was sinking behind the western mountain. I watched the soft light leave the plain, then pass up the shadowy wall like the rising of a silver mist. In these great silent actions of Nature, never so impressive as in desert solitude, one feels both the majesty and the beneficence of natural law, and realizes by such tranquillity how trustworthy the universe must be.

It was yet five miles to water, but the knowledge that it was at hand made them short. Kaweah recognized his surroundings, and livened up so much that I suddenly found myself desperately footsore, so got into the saddle and rode. Daylight came, the stars one by one went out, and cactus and ocotillo lost their wizard look and became again objects of commonplace dislike or cool botanical interest. A coyote, hailing us from across the valley, sounded like a friendly halloo. By the time we reached the entrance to the cañon its white cliffs were cheerfully trimmed with rose, and before the sun was up we were at Shafer's Well.

I seized the pump-handle and worked it up and down affectionately. I think I never shook hands with such hearty feelings for any one as I felt for Shafer. As for Kaweah, it would have been happiness to pump for him for hours, as indeed it seemed to me I did. Then I threw off saddle-bags and saddle, washed him down, and began a hunt for forage. By the best of fortune some freighter had lately fed his team and had left enough hay on the ground to make a very fair meal for a thrifty Indian pony. My companion fell to work at this, while I threw down my blanket roll, followed it myself, and fell asleep in the action. It was twenty-one hours since we left Corn Springs, and we had travelled practically without a stop.

In the afternoon we made the remaining twelve miles down to Mecca. It seemed a foretaste of Elysium to get among artesian wells and patches of emerald alfalfa. To make water run by turning a tap was a miracle; not less so the watermelon I captured at the store. Dates in massive clusters of crimson and yellow were ripening to super-Arabian excellence at the Government Experiment Station, and ranchers' wives who had been "inside" to escape the heat were drifting back to spend the glorious winter of the desert in darning their men's summer arrears of hose.

We took our way leisurely up the valley, culling here a lettuce, there cucumber or tomato, and everywhere the juiciest of the Coachella's alfalfa. It was the last day of September when we reached Palm Springs, which we had left at the beginning of June. The four months of heat and dryness had left a psychological drouth in my bones that I feared might be permanent and drive me into regrettable courses. Like Teufelsdröckh, "after so much roasting I was what you might name calcined." However, the desert itself had the remedy up its sleeve, and produced it a few weeks later, when I found myself flooded out of winter camp and subjected to a monumental sousing that brought me within measurable distance of drowning.

A normal balance of constitution being thus restored, I could review fairly the summer's experience. Unpleasant details, once in the rear, soon became only amusing incidents in the general impression: and these, after all, even while in prospect, had made a part of the attraction. There remained the satisfaction of having accomplished an old persistent project; yet the satisfaction was not unqualified. I had wished to see the desert. Well, I had seen it. But my ambition had not been merely to view it as a new and interesting tract of geography. I wanted to know it more intrinsically than that: I hoped, by living with it night and day, to learn something (though it could be little at best) of its lonely heart, its subtle, uncomprehended spirit, its repellent yet enthralling beauty, its agelessness, changelessness, and weariness, its implacability, solemnity, and terror.

The objective part of my plan I felt to be fairly accomplished. Not so the deeper side, however: the subjectivity of the desert is of too rare a sort, its effect upon the mind is too strange and complex, to take form in any clear conception. Yet, since inevitably one strives to realize one's experiences, I ask myself again, into what single impression does the desert render itself? What one sensation remains most strongly on the mind? The mountains, the sea, even the vast and changeful sky, have each some predominant genius for those who love the fair features of our earth. What sentiment does the desert yield by which it may be linked with human emotions? What analogy exists by which we may come into touch with it?

The answer must be, There is none. At every point the desert meets us with a negative. Like the Sphinx, there is no answer to its riddle. It is in the fascination of the unknowable, in the challenge of some old unbroken secret, that the charm of the desert consists. And the charm is undying, for the secret is — Secrecy.

APPENDIX A

HINTS ON DESERT TRAVELLING

(Extracts from Water-Supply Paper 224 of the United States Geological Survey, entitled "Some Desert Watering-Places in Southeastern California and Southwestern Nevada," by Walter C. Mendenhall; reprinted here by kind permission of the Survey.)

[*Author's Note:* Some of the suggestions that follow may carry less weight now than when they were compiled (1909), through the recent improvement of the main desert roads, with, as consequences, the advent of the automobile and an increased amount of travel, and through the beginning that has lately been made at bettering water facilities and installing direction-posts. Nevertheless, the characteristics of the desert remain, prudence is never obsolete, and these hints may prove to well repay some traveller's attention.]

WHERE teams are used, animals accustomed to the desert should be procured, if possible, for horses or mules that are unused to desert conditions fret on the sandy roads and rapidly weaken from drinking the saline waters. They are also in danger of pneumonia from the cold of winter nights and the wide extremes of temperature. During winter journeys blankets should be provided to protect the animals at night.

Travel in the desert far from the railroads and from food-supplies is, of course, more expensive than in other regions. A party leaving a supply station to go one hundred miles or more into an uninhabited part of the desert must take along everything needed, even to the most minute detail. This means that if the trip is to last for two weeks, enough hay and grain for each animal and enough provisions to last each man that length of time must be taken. For four horses, drawing a wagon that carries four persons and their bedding, provisions, and tools, another team of four horses must also be taken to haul sufficient hay and grain to feed the eight horses for two weeks. There are but few places in the desert, away from the railroads, where hay or grain of any kind can be procured. As the teams are rarely able to travel faster than a walk, heavy horses that are good walkers should be selected. The tires should be as wide as can be procured. Desirable widths of tires for freight wagons are six to nine inches; for light wagons, three inches.

§

Travellers will often find springs choked by débris washed in by rain-storms, or contaminated by the bodies of desert animals that have fallen in and drowned. It is therefore necessary to provide a pick, shovel, bucket, and rope for cleaning the wells.

At all times except in midsummer — when the desert should be avoided — the traveller must be provided with clothing suitable for both extreme heat and extreme cold. His route over a part of the journey may extend through heated valleys that lie near sea-level, or he may have to camp in the mountains, at elevations of three thousand to six thousand feet, where the temperature may fall nearly to the freezing-point before morning. For protection during the early morning hours he must therefore have warm, heavy blankets, and a heavy overcoat or its equivalent. Many cases of pneumonia and "mountain fever" have been caused by extremes of temperature for which no adequate provision had been made. In winter the temperature in this region may reach 85° or 95° during the day and fall to the freezing-point before midnight. The traveller should be provided with a canvas sheet that is long enough to lay under his bedding and fold back over it, as well as to cover his head in case of sand-storms.

The outer clothing should be of a color that will reflect as much heat as possible — that is, white, gray, or yellow

— and the underclothing should be of wool. The hat should have a wide brim and be thick enough to exclude all rays of the sun. The proper headgear is a broad-brimmed gray felt, or, for summer wear, a big opaque helmet of white or khaki color, the bigger the better. The hair should not be cut very short, as it is a natural means of protection.

Travellers with their own outfits and a minimum means of transportation will find that they must walk much of the time, for teams with heavy loads can crawl through the sands at the rate of only two to three miles an hour. Sand and sharp flints will wear out the soles of shoes and boots very rapidly. Hence stout, hobnailed footwear should be worn.

§

Owing to the intense heat of the desert there is a rapid and abundant growth of minute forms of animal and vegetable life in waters that are not too saline. All water should therefore be boiled before drinking. Filters form a part of the more elaborate outfits. There are now on the market several small, compact filters from which the traveller may select such as he may think desirable. It is not practicable to distil water except for mining camps or for large parties.

It is advisable to drink heartily in the morning and at night and as little as possible during the day. The practice of drinking water in excess of the amount necessary to relieve thirst may easily become a habit and should be avoided. At best it places an unnecessary tax on the system, and, when alkaline waters are used, may easily result in illness that could have been prevented by the exercise of greater foresight and self-control. It has been recommended that raw oatmeal be placed in the canteens, and some travellers even add to this a small quantity of chocolate and sugar. Condensed cream counteracts in great measure the irritation produced in the digestive tract by the alkaline desert waters, and is therefore especially desirable. When the water becomes tepid, additions of this kind make it more palatable to some, and there is less temptation to drink too much. It is well, also, during periods of extreme heat to wrap a wet cloth around the wrists and to put a water-soaked handkerchief in the hat. These are old-fashioned but effective devices. Each person in a party should be supplied with a large canteen, and extra ones should be taken along in the wagons to provide for leaks and accidents. An ample supply of water barrels and kegs should also be carried for use at dry camps and during prospecting trips, the number depending on the amount of stock taken and the route followed.

"Poison springs," said to contain arsenic, have been reported from many parts of the desert. The writer has examined the water from several of these, but has failed to find any arsenic or similar poison, though he has found large quantities of sulphate of soda (Glaubers salt) and some sulphate of magnesia (Epsom salts). Salt Spring, in South Death Valley, is of this character, and prospectors are known to have perished there, so that the spring is called "poison" by many, but it contains only sodium and magnesium salts, and no arsenic or copper.

The intense heat of the summer, the exhausted condition of the famished prospector, and the abundance of these harmful salts in the waters are sufficient explanation of the deaths that have occurred. Such waters are dangerous to a hearty, healthy man who uses them with the greatest moderation, and they may be quickly fatal to the thirst-tormented sufferer who drinks them without restraint.

§

The traveller who is unacquainted with the route over which he is journeying should stop at places where the ground has been cleared of brush and where there is other ample evidence of the presence of many visitors, and satisfy himself as to the nature of the camp. It may be a "dry camp," such as are made on long stretches between springs, or there may be a spring or well in the vicinity, which is covered over to keep out animals, and is hidden by drifting sand. Experienced men will have no difficulty in quickly determining the nature of the camp. An inexperienced traveller should not enter the desert alone. If he cannot find an experienced companion, he should proceed with the greatest caution, gathering all possible information about his route in advance, keeping himself abundantly supplied with water and food, and never leaving one water station without a definite idea as to the location of the next.

A traveller can rarely see exactly where water is to be found, except by going over the camp-ground and looking carefully for wells. Many of the wells are mere shafts, twenty to forty feet deep, rectangular in shape and covered with a few boards, which may in turn be covered by drifting sand. Only a few wells are equipped with a windlass or pump. These conveniences, even if originally supplied, quickly disappear as fuel for some traveller in need on a cold winter night. He uses them to maintain his camp-fire, justifying himself in the belief that self-preservation is the first law.

Fuel is scarce on the desert, especially in the vicinity of the better-known springs, where it has been entirely cleared away. The traveller, therefore, usually finds it necessary to begin gathering brush and mesquit roots long before he reaches the spring, so as to provide fuel for cooking. Camp-fires are luxuries that can be indulged in only among heavy mesquit and cottonwood timber, or off the beaten lines of travel.

§

One unacquainted with the desert should accustom himself to its clear air and the resulting exaggerated detail, which makes distant objects look near. No walks without water or provisions to what appears to be a nearby hill should be undertaken without definite knowledge of its distance. Landmarks should be studied, so that they will be recognized from any point of view, that they may be known when they are reached again. Before he begins a journey that does not follow a beaten and unmistakable track, the traveller should determine his general direction by compass or map or inquiry, and should adhere to that direction. The inexperienced traveller often gets at once into a panic on losing his way, and wastes his remaining energy in frantic rushes in one direction and another. This tendency to become panic-stricken should be controlled, if possible. Sit down, get out your map and compass — if you are provided with them, as you should be — and study the situation carefully before acting. At least, rest a little and think it over. If it is hot and you are far from camp, get your head into the shade of a bush or rock, and wait till night. Thirst will be less intolerable then and endurance greater. If you have camp companions who are likely to look for you, start a signal fire by night or a smoke by day from some little eminence, and then stay by it until help comes. If you must depend upon your own exertions, think carefully over all the possibilities and adopt a plan of action and adhere to it. Remember the proneness of the lost person to exaggerate the distance he has travelled. It is well to count paces and to remember that about two thousand make a mile. You will thus have a good check on the distance that you go, and at the same time will keep your mind occupied. Keep your direction true by travelling toward or from some selected landmark, or by the sun during the day or a star at night, or by keeping with or against or in some fixed direction in relation to the wind. If you think these things out and have studied the country beforehand, so that you know the relation of a road, or a ranch, or a spring, or a river to a given landmark or to the points of the compass, you should have no difficulty in finding your way again. With some persons, however, the faculty of getting lost amounts to genius. They are able to accomplish it wherever they are. The only suitable advice for them is to keep out of the desert. There are safer places in which to exercise their talent. Still others have a geographic instinct and a power of geographic observation which defies time and place. They cannot be lost anywhere. For such these lines are not written.

APPENDIX B

NOTICEABLE PLANTS OF THE DESERT

BOTANISTS must kindly overlook the lack of exactitude in these descriptions, which are necessarily brief and in which technical terms have purposely been wholly avoided.

It should be borne in mind that a number of plants may be met on the desert, especially about settlements or cultivated areas, that are not native there. A few of these, such as are most likely to come under observation, are included below. If there seem to be omissions in the following list, the explanation may be that the plants in question do not properly come under desert classification.

Abronia aurita. Sand Verbena (not really a verbena, but somewhat like that plant in its flowering). A low, trailing, sticky, soft-stemmed plant, bearing close clusters of fragrant, rosy-purple flowers. Blooms in mid-spring.

Acacia greggii. Cat-claw: Span., Uña de Gato. A bush up to 10 feet high, crowded with small sharp thorns, common in cañons and on hillsides; often mistaken for a small mesquit, the leaves being like those of that tree but smaller. Flower a yellowish "spike" (resembling a pussy-willow catkin); fruit a pod, often curiously twisted. Blooms in early summer.

Adenostoma sparsifolium. Red-shank, Bastard cedar: Span., Chamiso, Yerba del pasmo. A tall, fragrant bush with red, shreddy bark and fine, stringy foliage. Found in the mountains bordering the desert, not widely distributed. Flowers small, white, profuse. Blooms in late spring.

Agave deserti. Wild Century-plant: Span., Maguey, Mescal. Leaves blue-gray, very large, succulent, with strong prickles on edges and a thorn at apex, starting from the ground. Flower-stalk 8 or 10 feet high, bearing many sets of clustered, yellow, bell-shaped flowers. Common in parts of the desert mountains. Blooms in mid-spring.

Amsinckia spectabilis. Fiddle-head: Span., Zacate gordo. A very common, small, hairy, slender-stemmed plant, with narrow leaves and small orange flowers on stalks that curl at the tip. Blooms in early and mid-spring.

Anemopsis californica. Span., Yerba mansa. A low, rank-growing plant found only in damp places. Leaves large and coarse: flowers large, white, with protruding conical centre. Blooms in mid-spring.

Aphyllon cooperi. Cancer-root. A low, succulent plant, somewhat like a stalk of asparagus, bearing a number of small, purplish flowers. The plant is a parasite, growing on the roots of other plants. Not common. Blooms in late summer.

Argemone hispida. Thistle poppy: Span., Cardo, Chicalote. A prickly, gray or bluish leafed, thistly looking plant, 1 or 2 feet high, with large, fragile flowers, white with yellow centre. Blooms in mid- and late summer.

Aster orcuttii. A hardy looking plant of the driest desert cañons, 1 to 2 feet high; rather rare. Leaves stiff and paper-like, with prickly-toothed edges: flowers large and handsome, of lavender rays with yellow centre. Blooms in early summer.

Astragalus coccineus. A low plant with almost white stem and leaves and handsome cardinal-red flowers. Found in the desert mountains, but rare. Blooms in mid-spring.

Atriplex canescens. Salt-bush, Shad-scale. A good-sized roundish bush with small, grayish leaves, inconspicuous flowers, and tassels of striking, bright green seed-vessels. Blooms in early summer.

Atriplex hymenelytra. Desert holly. A stiff, shrubby plant 1 or 2 feet high, with whitish, holly-like leaves and inconspicuous flowers. Found in alkaline soil in dry cañons or on open desert. Blooms in mid-spring.

Atriplex lentiformis. Quail-bush. A large gray bush very common on silt or alkaline soil, up to 15 feet high, and usually of smooth, dome-shaped outline. Flowers inconspicuous. Blooms in mid-spring.

Baileya pauciradiata. Cotton-plant. A small, loosely growing plant with pale gray-green stems, narrow woolly leaves, and small, lemon-yellow flowers. Blooms in mid- and late summer.

Bebbia juncea. A roundish, dark green bush a foot or two high, with many slender, almost leafless stems and numerous small, yellow, fragrant flowers. Blooms throughout summer.

Beloperone californica. Span., Chuparosa. A good-sized bush, almost leafless, with purplish green, downy stems and handsome, dark red, tubular flowers. One of the earliest blooming desert plants, continuing all spring.

CACTI —

Cereus engelmanni. Hedgehog cactus. A cluster of spiny short stems about the size and shape of cucumbers. Flowers very handsome, large, cup-shaped, bright rose-purple with plumy green stigma. Blooms in mid-spring.

Cereus giganteus. Span., Saguaro, Pitahaya. The giant cactus, common on the Arizona desert hills and found sparingly in California adjacent to the Colorado River. It is usually a tall, fluted column up to 60 feet high, with similar vertical offsets for branches. Flowers large, white: fruit crimson, edible. Blooms in mid-spring.

Echinocactus cylindraceus. Barrel cactus, Nigger-head: Span., Biznaga (or Viznaga). A large, cylindrical, ribbed cactus up to 6 feet high (globular when young) covered with long curving spines. Flowers greenish yellow, cup-shaped, in a circle on the top. Blooms in mid-spring.

Mamillaria tetrancistrus. Pincushion, Strawberry, or Fishhook cactus: Span., Chilito. A small, round cactus, usually 1 or 2 inches in height and diameter, with a fuzz of fine white spines and a longer sharply hooked black one in the centre of each tuft. Flowers fleshy, lily-like, of rich claret color: fruit scarlet, finger-shaped, edible. Blooms in late spring.

Mamillaria sp. Like a larger growth of the foregoing, but somewhat irregular in shape and with waxy-white flowers. Blooms in late spring.

Opuntia basilaris. A flat-lobed, grayish cactus, velvety-looking, without noticeable spines but set with myriads of minute prickles. Flowers very handsome, large, cup-shaped, cerise, set in a row on edge of lobe. Blooms in mid-spring.

Opuntia bigelovii. Span., Cholla. A plant up to 6 feet tall, branching in stumpy arms, the whole plant densely clad with greenish white spines. The older parts turn almost black. The joints detach very easily and litter the ground. Flowers greenish white. Blooms in mid- and late spring.

Opuntia chlorotica. Prickly pear, Indian fig: Span., Nopal.

The common flat-lobed cactus of the coast, found also on the desert mountains. Flowers pale yellow, sometimes with reddish tinge, set in a row on edge of lobe: fruit dark red, edible, but covered with fine prickles. Blooms in mid-spring.

Opuntia echinocarpa. Deer-horn cactus. A very branching cactus up to 5 feet high, the joints pale green, very spiny though less so than O. bigelovii. Flowers greenish with bronzed look outside. Blooms in mid-spring.

Opuntia ramosissima. Similar in habit to O. echinocarpa, but with much slenderer stems and fewer but stronger spines. Flowers small, brown. Blooms in late spring.

Cassia armata. A low bushy plant with handsome yellow flowers, found in the desert mountains, but rare. Blooms in mid-spring.

Centaurea melitensis. Star thistle: Span., Jocalote. A small, usually single-stemmed plant a foot or so high, with narrow gray-green leaves. Flowers small, yellow: flower-heads very prickly. Blooms in mid-spring and summer.

Cercidium torreyanum. Span., Palo verde, Lluvia de oro. A tree up to 30 feet high, noticeable for the smooth green bark of the entire tree. Foliage small, scanty, and short-lived, so that the tree is usually bare: the twigs bear short thorns. Flowers profuse, bright yellow: fruit a pod. Blooms in mid-spring.

Chilopsis linearis. Desert willow (not properly a willow, but belonging to the Bignonia family). A small, willow-like tree, up to 20 feet high, usually found in washes. Leaves narrow: flowers handsome and plentiful, white marked with lilac and yellow, fragrant: fruit a pod, very long and narrow, remaining on the tree after the seeds have fallen. Blooms from mid-spring to autumn.

Chorizanthe brevicornu. A small, leafless, yellow-green plant, resembling the dry yellow moss sometimes found on pine trees. Flowers inconspicuous.

Coldenia plicata. A hardy looking, mat-like plant with small, deeply-veined, dark-green leaves and tiny white flowers. Blooms in mid-spring.

Croton californica. One of the commonest desert plants. A thin bush 2 or 3 feet high, with many slender straight stems and few light-gray oval leaves. The plant gathers into a goblet-shaped tuft as it dries. Flowers small, yellowish. Blooms from late spring to late summer.

Dalea: — the genus has been re-named Parosela, q. v.

Datura meteloides. Jimson weed: Span., Tolguache (or Tolu-ache). A rank-growing plant 2 or 3 feet high, common on both coast and desert, with large, coarse, dark-green leaves and very large, white or pale lilac, trumpet-shaped flowers that open in the evening. Blooms from spring to autumn.

Dithyrea californica. A small coarse-leafed plant found in sandy soil usually about bushes. Flowers small, fragrant, of four white petals. Blooms in early spring.

Encelia californica. A stiff, bushy plant with dark-green leaves and brittle, woody stems, common on and near the base of desert mountains. Flowers bright yellow, on straight stalks that project well above the rest of the plant. Blooms in mid-spring.

Encelia farinosa. Incense bush, White brittle bush: Span., Yerba de incienso. One of the commonest of desert plants in the neighborhood of mountains, in form a compact rounded bush 2 to 3 feet high. Leaves silver-gray, firm in texture: flowers like those of E. californica. The plant exudes drops of amber-colored gum. Blooms in mid-spring.

Ephedra californica. Desert tea: Span., Canutillo. A shrub 2 to 3 feet high, entirely composed of straight, smooth, dark-green stems without leaves. Flowers inconspicuous.

Eremiastrum bellioides. Desert star. A small prostrate plant, hardly noticeable except for its pretty, daisy-like flowers, borne on radiating horizontal stems. Blooms in mid-spring.

Eremocarya micrantha. A small, slender herb with small linear leaves and tiny white flowers. It dries to a whitish, woolly-looking little plant that is greedily eaten by horses. The root yields a bright madder stain. Blooms in early spring.

Eriodictyon tomentosum. Span., Yerba santa. A bush 5 or 6 feet high, found in cañons, with narrowish, gray-green, woolly leaves and clusters of lavender funnel-shaped flowers. (It is the coast species, E. glutinosum, or E. californicum, with smooth, dark-green, sticky leaves, that was so highly valued for its medicinal properties by the Spanish Californians.) Blooms in late spring.

Eriogonum inflatum. Bottle plant, Desert trumpet. A plant up to 3 feet high, with a few slender, straight, straggling stems that end in elongated swellings. Leaves heart-shaped, growing only at base: flowers small, yellowish. Blooms in mid-spring.

Eulobus californicus. A slender, straight, spindling plant, a foot

or so high, with small yellow flowers and very narrow straight
seed-vessels. Blooms in late spring.

Euphorbia polycarpa. Rattlesnake weed: Span., Golondrina. A
flat-growing, mat-like plant with radiating reddish stems and
small, roundish, bronze-green, white-edged leaves. Flowers
very small, white or pinkish. Blooms in late spring.

Fagonia californica. A low, open-growing plant found on rocky
desert hillsides, with hardly noticeable leaves but many pretty,
star-shaped, pale magenta flowers. Blooms in mid-spring.

FERNS: These are naturally rare in desert regions, and are found
only along the bases of the mountains, where falls the greater
part of the little rain that occurs in this arid territory. Besides those named there are a few others which are very
rarely found.

Cheilanthes viscida. Lip fern. Fronds elongated, dark green,
very much dissected, and covered with a sticky secretion.
Found usually in crevices of the rocks in cañons.

Notholæna cretacea. Cloak fern. Fronds triangular in outline,
moderately divided, and thickly coated with a white powder. When dry they roll up into brittle balls, but when rain
comes they unroll and resume life. This and the species next
named usually grow under the edges of rocks and boulders on
hillsides, or on the sides of cañons.

Notholæna parryi. Cloak fern. Fronds elongated, rather narrow, pinnately divided, the upper surface densely clothed
with whitish hairs, the lower brown and woolly.

Fouquieria splendens. Candle-wood: Span., Ocotillo. A unique
plant composed of a number of long gray thorny canes diverging at the ground: usually 6 or 8 feet high but sometimes double as much or over. Leaves small, dark green, and short-lived:
flowers scarlet, tubular, in a long spike at ends of canes. Blooms
in early spring, or at any time when sufficient rain has fallen.

Franseria dumosa. Burro-weed. A stiff, brittle, rounded, gray
bush, common on and near the base of desert mountains.
Leaves small, gray-green: flowers yellowish, in close spikes.
The plant has a strong, somewhat turpentiny smell. Blooms in
mid-spring.

GRASSES —

Cynodon dactylon. Bermuda grass. Not properly a desert
grass, but has become established in the irrigated areas,

where it is now a pest, being almost impossible to eradicate wherever it gains foothold. It is bright green and close-growing, with small, pointed leaves. It makes good emergency forage.

Distichlis spicata. Salt grass. A low-growing, pale green or gray grass, the leaves arranged in double rank, herring-bone style. It is very common, forming a close sod on moist, and especially on alkaline, soils. Its forage-value is low, but animals will eat it when hard pressed.

Epicampes rigens. Basket grass: Span., Zacaton. A tall, rigid, slender-stemmed, pale green grass forming large tussocks from 2 to 4 feet high. It grows among rocks near streams, and on dry hills, and though of little use as fodder it is much valued by Indian women for basketry purposes.

Oryzopsis membranacea. Sand grass. A small, tussocky grass with slender stems from 6 to 12 inches long, leaves bright green. It is found in sandy soil and is a useful forage plant, being also valuable to the Indians for its abundant crop of edible seeds.

Panicum urvilleanum. A strong, coarse grass with rather stiff, pale green leaves a foot or more long. It grows in loose dry sand, and has little, if any, forage value.

Pleuraphis rigida. Blue-stem: Span., Galleta. A coarse-, almost woody-stemmed, stiff grass growing in large dense clumps to a height of from 2 to 4 feet, and in the driest of soils. The stems appear dry and dead except at the tips, which are pale bluish green. It is an excellent forage-plant and of the greatest value to desert travellers.

Sporobolus airoides. Span., Zacaton. A coarse, stiff bunch-grass 2 or 3 feet high, flowering in loose, spreading panicles. It grows usually in alkaline soil and makes fairly good forage.

Tridens pulchella. A low, tufted grass from 2 to 6 inches high, common on dry hills and mesas, often among rocks, and noticeable for its small dense panicles of blossom, in which the tips of the glumes (flower-bracts) are tinged with purple. It has practically no forage value.

Hesperocallis undulatus. Desert lily: Span., Ajo. A true lily, with narrow, ribbony, crinkle-edged leaves lying flat at the base of the straight flower-stem, which is about 2 feet high. Flowers 3 or 4 inches in diameter, fragrant, white with green veining on back of petals, several to a stem. Blooms in mid-spring.

Hibiscus denudatus. A shrub 1 or 2 feet high, with scanty gray-green leaves and large, handsome flowers, white with dark purple "eye." Blooms in late spring.

Hoffmanseggia microphylla. A tall, loosely growing plant found in dry desert cañons. Usually a number of the slender cane-like stems grow in a clump together. Leaves twice compound, of numerous minute leaflets: flowers yellow, in an open elongated cluster.

Hofmeisteria pluriseta. A small bushy plant growing in the crevices of rocky cliffs, the stems slender but woody, and the leaf-blades like a flattened tip on the leaf-stems. Flowers in small heads, abundant but not showy.

Hymenoclea salsola. Salt bush. A common, large, grayish bush with small, narrow leaves. Flowers very small, greenish, in profuse clusters at end of twigs. Blooms in late spring.

Hyptis emoryi. Lippia. A tall bush of the lower mountain slopes, up to 10 feet high, with rather straight stems usually branching from the ground. Leaves gray-green: flowers small, numerous, lavender colored, in loose spikes. The leaves and blossoms have a lavender-like smell. Blooms from mid-spring to autumn.

Isocoma acradenia. A small shrub with narrow, dark-green leaves and small, yellow flowers; common and widely distributed. Blooms in early spring.

Isomeris arborea. Bladder-pod. A vigorous, ill-smelling shrub 4 to 8 feet high, with light-green, triply-divided leaves and clusters of showy, yellow flowers. The seed-vessel is a large pale green pod. Blooms from earliest to late spring.

Krameria parvifolia. A common bush of the lower mountain slopes, 2 feet or so high, with few, inconspicuous leaves and purplish gray, much-interlaced stems and twigs. Flowers deep claret color: seed-vessels small, round, prickly. Blooms in mid- and late spring.

Larrea glandulosa. Creosote bush. Greasewood: Span., Hediondía. The commonest and most widely distributed shrub of the desert, growing up to 12 feet high, in strong, somewhat brittle stems diverging from the ground. The branches and twigs are regularly marked with rings. Leaves small, glossy, bright dark green, sticky, with strong tarry odor: flowers profuse, bright yellow, maturing to small, round, woolly seed-vessels. Blooms from mid-spring to midsummer.

Lycium andersonii. A strong bush usually 4 or 5 feet high, but in open desert a low patch of stiff intertangled stems. Leaves small, gray: flowers few and small, tubular, pale lilac: fruit a small, transparent, edible (but insipid) red berry. Blooms in mid-spring.

Malvastrum rotundifolium. Five-spot. A small, upstanding, hairy plant, often branching, with roundish leaves and handsome cup- or globe-shaped flowers of pale lilac with a carmine spot at base of each of the five petals. Blooms in late spring.

Martynia proboscidea. Elephant's trunk, Devil's claw. A rank, weedy plant, not common, with large, roundish leaves and a few handsome flowers, white with yellow and purple markings. The seed-vessels are disproportionately large, from 6 to 10 inches long, curved and tapering, splitting as they dry into two long, springy horns connected at base. Blooms in summer and into autumn.

Mentzelia involucrata. A plant of the open desert, a foot or more high, with thistly-looking, gray leaves and very handsome, large, satiny flowers, white or creamy with fine vermilion pencilling. Blooms in mid-spring.

Mirabilis aspera. A small, bushy plant with slender branching stems and grayish leaves, found near the base of mountains. Flowers white, primrose-like, opening at evening. Blooms in late spring.

Mohavea viscida. A small, hairy plant with straight, usually single stem and narrow leaves. Flowers large, deep cup-shaped, satiny, greenish-creamy with small purple dots: petals saw-edged. Blooms in mid-spring.

Nama demissum. A pretty little mat-like plant, sending out spoke-like arms at ends of which are small carmine flowers. Blooms in mid-spring.

Navarretia virgata. A small, dried-out-looking plant of the open desert. Leaves inconspicuous: flowers numerous, pale bright blue. The last of the noticeable spring flowers, continuing into early summer.

Nicotiana bigelovii. Coyote tobacco. A many-stemmed plant, 1 to 2 feet high, with dark-green leaves and white, narrow-tubular flowers. Blooms midsummer to autumn.

Nolina parryi. A yucca-like plant of dry mountain-sides, not common. Leaves long, narrow, spiky, bluish green: flowers whitish, in a compact elongated cluster 2 or 3 feet long, on a tall stem rising from the centre of the sheaf of leaves. Blooms in mid-spring.

Œnothera gauræflora. A small plant with straight, stiff, usually single stem bearing a cluster of small pinkish flowers. The bark is white and shreddy and the seed-vessels tongue-like and curved. Blooms in late spring.

Œnothera pallida. Sun-cups. A slender-stemmed plant with rather narrow, pointed and toothed leaves. Flowers bright yellow: seed-vessels curly with double twist. Blooms in mid- and late spring.

Œnothera scapoidea. A small plant with single stem 6 to 8 inches high, and a cluster of little pinkish flowers. One of the earliest spring flowers but blooms on into early summer.

Œnothera trichocalyx. Evening primrose: Span., Yerba salada. A low, strong, rather spreading plant with large, rather narrow, grayish green leaves and very large fragrant flowers, white (pink when faded) with sulphur-yellow centres, opening at night. Blooms in mid- and late spring.

Olneya tesota. Ironwood: Span., Palo fierro (or hierro). A trim tree, up to 20 feet high, with thorny twigs and grayish green leaves composed of many leaflets. Flowers dull blue, like small pea-blossoms: fruit a pod. Blooms in early summer.

Palafoxia linearis. A common, straggling plant of many slender stems up to 3 feet high. Leaves few, narrow, dark gray-green: flowers lavender or pinkish, tubular, with long calyx. Blooms almost all the year.

Parosela (formerly Dalea) californica. A stiff, woody bush, up to 3 feet high, with clear, yellowish bark. Leaves small, gray, narrowly divided: flowers plentiful, resembling pea-blossoms, dark bright blue. Blooms in mid-spring.

Parosela (formerly Dalea) emoryi. Dye-weed. A gray, weedy bush 2 or 3 feet high, easily identified by the orange satin which the flower-heads leave on hands or clothing. Leaves small, composed of several leaflets: flowers tiny, purple, in small close clusters. Blooms mid-spring to late summer.

Parosela (formerly Dalea) mollis. A small, grayish plant with much-divided leaves and tiny, rosy-purple flowers in woolly-looking clusters. Blooms in late spring and early summer.

Parosela (formerly Dalea) schottii. A large, rather thorny bush, up to 6 feet high. Leaves very narrow, dark bright green: flowers resembling pea-blossoms, dark brilliant blue. Blooms in mid-spring.

Parosela (formerly Dalea) spinosa. Smoke-tree, Indigo-bush. A small tree, up to 15 feet high, common in washes. Practically leafless, the tree is a mass of whitish spiny twigs. Flowers small but very abundant, resembling pea-blossoms, dark brilliant blue. Blooms in early summer.

Pectis papposa. Chinch weed. A low, small, rounded plant, vividly green, with bright yellow flowers. It has a strong, rather unpleasant smell. Blooms throughout summer.

Perityle emoryi. A small plant found growing among rocks. Flowers white, daisy-like. Blooms in mid-spring.

Petalonyx thurberi. Sandpaper plant. A low, rounded, whitish bush with a peculiar roughness to the touch. Leaves small, light-green, scaly: flowers profuse, light-yellowish green. Blooms in late spring.

Phacelia campanularia. Canterbury bell. A small, usually single-stemmed plant, with roundish, rather hairy leaves, and large, deep-purple, bell-shaped flowers. Found (on the desert) only in cañons or near water. Blooms in mid-spring.

Phacelia sp. Wild heliotrope: Span., Vervenía. A straggling, soft-stemmed, rather hairy plant, up to 4 feet high, with small, compound leaves and profuse, heliotrope-blue flowers in curling clusters. Blooms early to late spring.

Philibertia linearis. Twining milkweed. A strong creeper found on willows or other strong supporting plants, growing up to 6 or 8 feet high. Leaves few and grayish: flowers pale lavender, in a close rosette. Blooms in mid-spring.

Phoradendron californicum. Mistletoe. A parasite very common on the mesquit and other leguminous desert trees. It is leafless, but has numerous small pink or white berries.

Phragmites communis. Span., Carrizo. A reed-like grass or cane, up to 10 feet high, with long, narrow leaves, found in damp places on the open desert.

Pluchea sericea. Arrowweed: Span., Cachanilla. A straight-growing, cane-like plant, up to 10 feet high, abundant in damp places both in cañons and on open desert. Leaves gray, narrow, willow-shaped: flowers small, clustered, dull pinkish purple. Blooms in midsummer.

Prosopis glandulosa. Mesquit: Span., Mezquite. A wide-branching, thorny tree, up to 20 feet high, found singly or in thickets. Leaves of many leaflets, resembling small leaves of the pepper-tree: flowers yellowish "spikes" (like pussy-willows); fruit long, narrow pods, in clusters. Blooms in late spring.

Prosopis pubescens. Screwbean mesquit: Span., Tornillo. A smaller and slenderer tree than the foregoing, favoring alkaline soil. Leaves and flowers similar to the above, but somewhat smaller: fruit twisted pods, like screws, in clusters. Blooms in late spring.

Prunus eriogyna. Wild apricot. A large, branching, thorny bush, up to 8 feet high, found in some desert cañons. Leaves small, bright light green; flowers numerous, white, like small plum blossoms: fruit reddish yellow when ripe, with a small quantity of sweetish pulp. Blooms in early spring.

Psathyrotes ramosissima. A low, compact, rounded plant with light-gray leaves and small, yellow flowers. Blooms in late spring.

Purshia tridentata. Bitter-brush. A strong, woody bush 5 or 6 feet high, with a casual resemblance to the common creosote bush (Larrea) but rare. Flowers bright yellow. Blooms in late spring.

Rhus ovata. Sumac: Span., Mangla. A large, compact, roundish bush or small tree, native to coast regions, but sometimes found in or near desert cañons. Leaves dark bright green, glossy, suggesting those of the laurel: flowers white or pink, profuse, in very close clusters: fruit a reddish sticky berry. Blooms in late spring.

Salazaria mexicana. Bladder bush. A roundish bush, up to 3 feet high, rather rare. Leaves few and small, gray: flowers showy, white and purple; the calyces become inflated and look like little round bladders. Blooms in early summer.

Salvia carduacea. Thistle sage. A thistly-looking plant a foot or so high, with large prickly grayish leaves and handsome light purple flowers in round-headed clusters. Blooms in late spring.

Salvia columbaricæ. Span., Chia. A small plant a foot or so high, usually with a single stiff stem rising from a few deeply-cut leaves and bearing one or more clusters of small purple flowers closely grouped in rings. Blooms in mid-spring.

Sesbania macrocarpa. Wild hemp. A straight, slender, spindling plant, up to 8 feet high, found in damp ground in Imperial

Valley and near the Colorado River. Flowers yellow, pea-like. Blooms in mid- and late summer.

Simmondsia californica. Goat-nut, Quinine plant. A strong shrub, up to 6 feet high, with gray-green leaves somewhat like those of the manzanita. Flowers whitish, inconspicuous: fruit a small, brown, edible nut with smooth, pointed husk. Blooms in mid-spring.

Sphæralcea ambigua. Wild hollyhock. A loose-growing plant, up to 3 feet high, with grayish stems and leaves. Flowers numerous and striking, of a peculiar light vermilion color. Blooms in mid-spring and early summer.

Stephanomeria exigua. A low, slender-stemmed plant bearing a white starry flower something like that of the single pink. Blooms in mid-spring.

Stillingia annua. A very small but hardy-looking plant with stiff, saw-edged, light-green, upright leaves. Flowers inconspicuous.

Suæda ramosissima. A common, loose-growing bush of the open desert, 3 or 4 feet high, with very slender, bright-green, juicy stems that give a pink stain on being crushed. Leaves and flowers inconspicuous.

Trichoptilium incisum. A small, almost white plant, very woolly, with small, composite, yellow flowers. Blooms in early summer.

Washingtonia filifera. Fan-palm. The native palm of the desert, found in many cañons and occasionally in the open desert, though never in dry soil. Up to 70 feet high. Fronds light-green, with stringy filaments: flowers small, creamy, in long, drooping clusters: fruit a small hard berry, black and sweet when ripe. Blooms in early summer.

Yucca brevifolia. Joshua tree, Yucca palm. A tree-yucca, up to 30 feet high, with stiff, strong arms and tufts of blade-like leaves, found in certain mountain and high mesa localities. Flowers whitish, bell-shaped, in large clusters, rather ill-smelling: fruit a short, thick pod which remains closed when mature and dry. Blooms in early spring.

Yucca mohavensis. A small tree-yucca, somewhat branching, with tufts of very long, dagger-like leaves, found in similar localities to those inhabited by the foregoing. Flowers also similar: fruit a large blunt pod which becomes soft and edible when ripe. Blooms in late spring.

Yucca whipplei. Spanish bayonet: Span., Quijote. The common yucca of the coast mountains, with a very large spike of creamy, bell-shaped flowers on a tall, straight stalk rising from a sheaf of long, stiff, spiky leaves. Fruit becomes hard and splits open when ripe. Blooms in late spring.

UPDATED PLANT LIST

(Obsolete nomenclature appear alphabetically on left
followed by revisions consistent with
Munz's *Flora of Southern California*, 1974.)
By Robert L. Moon

Abronia aurita	*Abronia villosa* var. *aurita*
Amsinckia spectabilis	this species not common on desert, most likely *A. tessellata* or *A. vernicosa*
Aphyllon cooperi	*Orobanche cooperi*
Argemone hispida	*Argemone corymbosa*
Arrow-weed	*Pluchea sericea*
Aster orcuttii	*Machaeranthera orcuttii*
Astragalus coccineus	Scarlet locoweed
Bladder-pod	*Isomeris aborea*
Burro-weed	*Ambrosia dumosa*
Cercidium torreyanum	*Cercidium floridum*
Cerus giganteus	*Cerus gigantea*
Dithyren californica	Spectacle-pod
Echinocactus cylindraceus	*Echinocactus acanthodes* or *Ferocactus acanthodes*
Epicampes rigens	*Muhlenbergia rigens*
Eremiastrum bellioides	*Monoptilon bellioides*
Eremocarya micrantha	*Cryptantha micrantha*
Eriodictyon tomentosum	*Eriodictyon trichocalyx*
Eschscholtzia sp.	Desert poppies
Eulobus californicus	*Camissonia californica*
Fagonia californica	*Fagonia pachyacantha*
Hofmeisteria pluriseta	*Pleurocoronis pluriseta*
Isocoma acradenia	*Haplopappus acradenius*
Larrea glandulosa	*Larrea tridentata*
Lobelia splendens	*Lobelia cardinalis*
Malvastrum rotundifolium	*Eremalche rotundifolia*
Mamillaria tetrancistrus	*Mamillaria tetrancistra*
Martynia proboscidea	*Proboscidea althaeifolia*
Mesquite	*Prosopis glandulosa*
Mirabilis aspera	*Mirabilis begelovii* var. *aspera*
Mohavea viscida	*Mohavea confertifolia*
Navarretia virgata	*Eriastrum sapphirinum ssp. dasyanthum*
Notholaena cretacea	*Notholaena californica*
Ocotillo	*Fouquieria*
Oenothera gauraeflora	*Camissonia boothii spp. decorticans*
Oenethera pallida	*Camissonia pallida*
Oenothera scapoidea	*Camissonia claviformis ssp. aurantiaca*
Oenothera trichocalyx	*Oenothera deltoides*
Opuntia basilaris	Beavertail cactus
Opuntia echinocarpa	most likely *O. acanthocarpa*
Opuntia ramosissima	Pencil cactus

Oryzopis membranacea	*Oryzopis hymenoides*
Parosela sp.	may still be listed as *Dalea*
Philbertia linearis	*Sarcostemma cynanchoides*
Phragmites communis	*Phragmites australis*
Pleuraphis rigida	*Hilaria rigida*
Prunus eriogyna	*Prunus fremontii*
Purshia tridentata	*Purshia glandulosa*
Sesbania macrocarpa	*Sesbania exaltata*
Simmondsia californica	*Simmondsia chinensis*
Stillingia annua	*Stillingia spinulosa*
Sueda ramosissima	*Sueda torreyana* var. *ramosissima*
Tridens pulchella	*Erioneuron pulchellum*
Yucca mohavensis	*Yucca schidigera*

INDEX